The Inquiring Organization

The Inquiring Organization

Tacit Knowledge, Conversation, and Knowledge Creation: Skills for 21st-Century Organizations

CATHERINE KANO KIKOSKI AND
JOHN F. KIKOSKI

Westport, Connecticut
London

Library of Congress Cataloging-in-Publication Data

Kikoski, Catherine Kano.
  The inquiring organization : tacit knowledge, conversation, and knowledge creation : skills for 21st-century organizations / Catherine Kano Kikoski and John F. Kikoski.
    p. cm.
  Includes bibliographical references and index.
  ISBN 1–56720–490–2 (alk. paper)
  1. Knowledge management. 2. Organizational learning. 3. Communication in organizations. I. Kikoski, John F. II. Title.
HD30.2.K55 2004
658.4'038—dc22   2003058157

British Library Cataloguing in Publication Data is available.

Library of Congress Catalog Card Number: 2003058157
ISBN: 1–56720–490–2

First published in 2004

Praeger Publishers, 88 Post Road West, Westport, CT 06881
An imprint of Greenwood Publishing Group, Inc.
www.praeger.com

Printed in the United States of America

The paper used in this book complies with the Permanent Paper Standard issued by the National Information Standards Organization (Z39.48–1984).

10 9 8 7 6 5 4 3 2 1

We dedicate this book
to the memory of our parents,
who embodied the principles of faith,
family, work, and above all, love.

We think better together.

—Plautus (Titus Maccius Plautus)
Roman dramatist (254?–184 B.C.)

Contents

Acknowledgments

No one ever gets where they are alone. We are grateful for the support of colleagues, friends, and family who were important in the long process of researching and writing this book.

Our first debt of gratitude is to Erik Valentine, who shepherded us through our first book and had faith in us again with this book. It was due to his foresight and enthusiasm that the present book was launched. His successors, Hilary Claggett and Nick Philipson, quietly and professionally helped us through the later stages of the publishing process, as did the staff at Impressions Book and Journal Services, Inc.

Allen Ivey continues to inspire us. Once again, we wish to acknowledge our continuing personal as well as intellectual debt to the mentor who introduced us to the wonder, significance, and intellectual study of face-to-face communication. We stand among his legion of students who, in their humble way, continually seek to improve the interchanges and inquiry that make us human. We continue to find new dimensions and applications for his scholarly work that makes it relevant to this new era.

We also honor the memory of three other professors who mentored us and helped us find our path. Robert Thompson of Wesleyan University was an inspiring mentor who gave Catherine the opportunity to conduct research and publish in the field of Physiological Psychology. Historian William "Willie" Kerr, also of Wesleyan University, pointed John in the direction of teaching and research long before he was able to see that path for himself. In addition, polymath scholar of global politics, Ferenc Vali of the University of Massachusetts, Amherst, was caring and supportive, not just professionally but—more important—personally.

We also are grateful for the assistance of the staff at two libraries. The entire staff of the Pius XIIth Library at Saint Joseph College deserve our thanks. Ably led by Linda Geffner, they met our many requests with cheerfulness and dispatch. We are especially indebted to Kathleen Kelly for her unending kindness and perseverance. Kathleen consistently went to extraordinary lengths to find and secure material for this book, despite the difficulty and time involved in any particular request. At Sacred Heart University's Ryan-Matura Library, Kim Macomber, and especially Sachi Spohns, provided cheerful assistance and long-term help.

We also wish to thank Eric Zematis, Anthony Franceschi, and Marc Paradis of Saint Joseph College's Information Technology Department. A special thanks to Eric Zematis for his generous and expert help. Writing a book is a technologically different enterprise today, and we are grateful for their assistance and expertise. Three individuals were helpful in trying to track down some very specific pieces of information. We are indebted to: Carolyn Davis of the Special Collections Research Center, Syracuse University Library; Janet Godden, Deputy Publisher, Voltaire Foundation, Oxford University; and Gene Kim, Associated Press, Washington, DC.

We also would like to thank colleagues at Saint Joseph College and Sacred Heart University—Walter Myers, Mindy Miserendino, and Edward Papa—for their generous scholarly comments. Ed's insights are especially appreciated. Gary Rose's support as a colleague has always been appreciated. Matthew Uzinski was helpful as a student research assistant.

Our three children—John, Andre, and Nicole—were sources of inspiration as well as love during much of the time it took us to find our way through this long project. Our children enriched us with their business and professional perspectives. John was not only our reviewer but also our consultant on many aspects of this book. His business acumen as well as managerial skills were invaluable. Despite a hectic schedule, his interest in this project never flagged. Andre was enthusiastic and supportive about the writing of this book. Nicole's fresh outlook, subtle insights, and grace of expression contributed immensely to this work. In reviewing the book, she brought a novelist's elegance and facility of expression to our writing, in addition to her business savvy. Once again, in our second manuscript together, we express our dearest love to our three children.

Preface

At the birth of the Information Era, astute managers sensed there was a new question in the air. Knowledge had emerged as the chief resource for organizations, and this development posed a new challenge. Organizations quickly lived or died by their response to the question of how to incorporate knowledge into their organizations. Since then, managers and organizations have concentrated on learning knowledge. As the challenge was interpreted then, the objective of many firms was to become learning organizations.

Today, in the accelerating information economy of the early 21st century, there is another question in the air. As the velocity and complexity of the Information Era increased, the challenge shifted for managers and organizations—the challenge became to congruently align themselves with the realities of this new era. Organizations live or die faster than ever by their response. Today's question is: How can each organization *create new knowledge and innovate quickly enough* to remain competitive in the race to survive?

The individuals and organizations that will thrive in this 21st century may not be those that just learn, but those that inquire to create new knowledge—which, for their competitors, may still be unknown. The thrust of this book is that managers and firms today need to focus on *inquiring to create new knowledge*.

This book suggests that the days of the learning organization are drawing to a close. Organizations will still have to learn, but to survive, if not thrive, they will need to become more than learning organizations. Simple logic makes the case.

Today's reality is forcing a subtle but powerful shift that may not as yet have been recognized: when we learn, we can only learn knowledge that, *ipso facto,* is explicit or already known. Such knowledge is public and therefore confers no competitive advantage on organizations. Only tacit knowledge confers that competitive advantage for, *ipso facto,* it is the private, personal knowledge that is not yet known.

This book imputes a new meaning to one of the most widely acknowledged premises of the Information Era: *Knowledge is the "oil" of the information economy.* Just as oil fueled the industrial economy, knowledge fuels the information economy. But could it be that the true fuel of the information economy may not be the explicit knowledge that everyone knows? Rather, it is our tacit knowledge—the new knowledge that is not yet known—that will confer the competitive advantage on certain firms and propel the economy forward. *Tacit knowledge is the "oil" of the information economy.*

This book also focuses upon another, perhaps even more powerful, proposition: Those who know how to surface or create tacit knowledge will possess inexhaustible supplies of intellectual fuel for the information economy. The individuals and organizations that will thrive will be those that apply the conditions that foster continuous knowledge creation—the *sine qua non* of success in the 21st century. Those organizations that are congruent with these new challenges will be successful. They will be *Inquiring Organizations. This book is about how to surface tacit knowledge, and thereby continuously create new knowledge.* The future belongs to those organizations that inquire in order to surface tacit knowledge on a continuous basis.

Conversation between colleagues joins and multiplies their knowledge. While conversation may be how managers spend most of their time over the course of a day, it may be what management theorists least study. Therefore, this book proposes a set of communication competencies that comprise a process of stances, questions, and skills from which flow the new sorts of conversations that foster the continuous creation of new knowledge.

In his classic work, *The Fifth Discipline: The Art and Practice of the Learning Organization,* Peter Senge identified the challenge of what was to him the learning organization and what is to us the inquiring organization: "The discipline of team learning involves mastering the practices of dialogue and discussion. . . . Despite its importance, team learning remains poorly understood. Until we can describe the phenomenon better, it will remain mysterious. . . . Until there are reliable methods for building teams that can learn together, its occurrence will remain a product of happenstance."[1]

This book seeks to dispel some of that mystery and happenstance. It is a work about inquiry and knowledge creation in the 21st century. There can be no higher goal for individuals or organizations in an information economy. Contemporary organizations exist in a high-velocity, complex, and nonlinear environment. No single individual can possess the knowledge to make good decisions or to innovate quickly enough to assure survival. Today, whether we realize it or not, we all are interdependent. Leaders will still need to be decisive at times. However, leaders will depend more than ever on the collective sensing by their colleagues of new and ambiguous situations and their collective intelligence in navigating the new territory we all are in. For it could be that information era organizations rely and thrive more on inner consent than outward compliance. The question is whether this interdependence will be recognized, and so lead to the knowledge creation that competitive advantage, if not survival, require.

This book proposes a new direction for management in this new era. It may be the first, but is not the final word. In keeping with its spirit, the authors hope that mutually respectful and generative conversation as well as inquiry can improve the lot not just of organizations, but the human condition of those individuals—all of us—who work in and for them. The journey into new territory continues.

NOTE

1. Peter M. Senge (1990) *The Fifth Discipline: The Art and Practice of the Learning Organization* (New York: Currency Doubleday), pp. 237–238.

CHAPTER 1

The Era of the Inquiring Organization

No man is wise enough by himself.

—Plautus[1]

The information economy has had a profound impact on organizations. The first to sense it were those who worked in the high-technology companies of the last quarter of the 20th century. Woven together, each information technology they developed—mainframe and microprocessor computers, the Internet, and wireless systems—created the information economy that shifted from a centralized, closed-loop infrastructure to a decentralized, open-loop environment. This economy's defining characteristic is the creation and transmission of greater flows of information faster than ever before. Consequently, individuals and organizations today need to learn more information and create more knowledge faster than ever before.

The frenetic information economy first forced managers to answer two questions: "How do organizations learn?"; that is, "How do organizations stay ahead in the globally competitive race to maintain their only sustainable competitive advantage—knowledge?" Historically, the corporations that best responded to this question—companies such as Microsoft, General Electric, and Skandia—flourished in the late 20th century. A major management trend was born: *Organizational Learning*. A cottage industry of researchers and consultants sprouted to serve the needs of firms that recognized the challenge and sought to become *Learning Organizations*.

Economies, however, change over time. Today, an even higher-velocity bioinformation economy is forcing managers and their organizations to answer even more fundamental questions: "How do individuals and groups create knowledge?"; that is, "How do individuals and groups—the fundamental building blocks of organizations—create the new knowledge that enables them to innovate fast enough to stay ahead of competitors in the globally competitive race to survive?"

Astute managers have come to realize that knowledge is binary, and is composed of two interdependent components: (1) the transmission and learning of existing knowledge that *ipso facto* must already be known; and (2) the creation of new knowledge that *ipso facto* must be unknown. When the pace of change is slower, the first component—the learning of already existing knowledge—predominates. Stonemasons today learn and transmit much the same knowledge as did another stonemason, Socrates, who practiced this craft 2,500 years ago. Similarly, what railroad conductors do today is quite like what they did more than a century ago. However, when the pace of change accelerates, the second component—the continuous creation of new knowledge—comes to predominate. Today's airline transportation executives have real-time marketing, logistics, supply chain, and fuel-hedging financial information continuously available to them that revolutionizes their jobs.

The task of biotechnology researchers today epitomizes the soul of the information economy: to inquire into the new realities—the new knowledge that their inquiry and that of others has created—and then, because the very act of inquiry creates new knowledge, reflexively inquire again. It is possible that the task of managers in an inquiring organization is coming to be no less.

Organizations are approaching, if they have not already passed, a tipping point. It is not learning existing knowledge that is key to organizational success, but rather inquiring to continuously create new knowledge. The 21st century is the era of the *Inquiring Organization*—the organization that survives and thrives because it creates the conditions for creative inquiry by those it employs, and thus is always on the cutting edge of change.

WHAT THIS SHIFT MEANS TO BUSINESS

Business once was a relatively stable, predictable profession. During much of the post–World War II Industrial Era, its conduct could be described by the relatively stable word "administration." The very title of the discipline and the many "Schools of Business Administration" named after it, as well as its most valued degree, the Master's in Business Administration (MBA), all tacitly attest to the homeostatic past of "administering" business—but not to its turbulent future.

Homeostasis, or equilibrium, no longer describes what managers do or contend with—the shortening and merging of internal corporate business cycles is proof of this fact. The time period is shorter between getting an order and delivering it, receiving raw materials and producing the finished product, and selling the product off the shelf and replacing it. Once long-lasting, rigid hierarchies are merging into more fluid, process-focused ad hoc teams to get today's projects done today.

What is happening at the level of organizations also is occurring at the level of industries. To shift to that level, the shortening and merging of these corporate business cycles combined with the simultaneous shifts in the larger environment mean that sectors, if not entire industries, are dying, while others simultaneously are being transformed. In short, the business model life cycles of entire industries are accelerating and undergoing upheaval.

In such a situation, the organizations that have created the conditions for creative inquiry by their managers are likely to have an advantage over their competition in creating the successful business models of the future. Only those organizations that have configured themselves to inquire will be able to continuously create the new knowledge that such new business models will require. Some possible illustrations follow:

- Publishers thought that they were in the business of publishing books, and that they were different from television networks and movie studios. With the coming of the Information Era's Internet, book publishers discovered that they were not just in the business of publishing books, but of "providing content." Further, books and bookstores are just one of many retail endpoints in a broader consumption "delivery system." Over time, what we call a book could be transformed: the physical nature of books—whose covers, spines, static print, and paper pages provide the words of one author at a time—could be replaced by the bytes of e-books whose memories and screens enable the viewer to scroll through the content (some in motion, color, and sound) of many content originators at a time, or another undreamed of pay-per-work wireless, personal digital assistant (PDA), or cell phone delivery systems for authored works.

- Health insurance companies believed that they were in the business of paying policyholders' medical bills when these individuals were horizontal and sick in the hospital. Now they realize that their business also is to encourage policyholders to stay vertical, healthy, and out of the hospital altogether.

- Colleges are discovering that "going to college"—carving four years out of one's life to bring one's atoms to a "placed" campus to take courses according to fixed class schedules and lock-step syllabi—is becoming a dated practice. Today, colleges are "going to students." Students anywhere, via the Internet, are taking courses from placeless cybercampuses, at any time of the day or night, while flexibly weaving these courses into personal schedules that may include full-time careers. In addition to pursuing career interests and earning salaries, students will pay substantially lower tuition than they would in the current business model of "placed" colleges.

In every industry, executives should factor in the time period it takes for: (1) the new business models to be developed; (2) the new technological infrastructures to be put into place, and, most importantly; (3) for human practice to catch up with these capabilities. They also should factor in a historical fact: just as movie theaters survived the coming of both television transmissions and video stores, they also will survive digital video discs (DVDs) and video streaming over the Internet. However, today there are far fewer movie theaters than before, and they are in a different form. Only the nimbly innovative survived. We suggest that the same will happen in other areas.

In each of these cases, the business models of entire industries are being transformed. However, in each of these industries—publishing, health insurance, and education—some organizations in the future will be providing authored works, others will be insuring self-service wellness programs as well as sickness programs, and still others will be offering a more personalized higher education—but all according to new models.

There will be casualties along the way—many of them—for in every sector, each organization will have to find its own, unfamiliar way to deal with the new realities. The successful organizations will be those whose colleagues have acquired the skill to mutually inquire and continuously create the new knowledge from which new business models as well as daily operating innovations will emerge. As one insightful Silicon Valley executive put it: "How we got here, is not how we will get there."

WHAT THIS MEANS TO MANAGEMENT

In the new economy, high velocity, complex, and nonlinear information, as well as the conditions they create, reflexively fold back on themselves and thus never establish a state of stability or homeostasis. Such an environment engenders the need to continually peer into the future and to continually innovate, that is why management today has become an inquiry, a quest . . . to perceive, to cognize:

This shifts the entire emphasis in the new economy, from the managerial challenge—of making things, of getting things right . . . to the visionary challenge—of seeing through the fog, and of accommodating others' interpretations of what lies ahead. This gives a very, very different set up. The people who win in the new games are the people who have better cognition, the people who can figure out how these games are going to work. The people who lose are invariably those who wheel out the old frameworks. . . . So the whole game now, in the new economy, is a cognitive one. It's figuring out how each new industry is going to play. And we usually do that by wheeling out our old cognitive frameworks. And if those cognitive frameworks are too narrow, we misinterpret the market and totally blow it. That's why whole management teams are thrown out when things go wrong, you just don't throw out the CEO. The reason is that the whole team had an old way of looking at things, and what you need is a new way of looking at things.[2]

How can managers find a way to accommodate "others' interpretations of what lies ahead" in the new economy? Should they *re-cognize* the familiar but old cognitive frameworks that are "too narrow," or *cognize* anew the unfamiliar but new frameworks that open up new vistas? How do managers bring about "a new way of looking at things?" Through what general approach can this be brought about, and by what pragmatic steps can such an approach be applied?

These questions reverberate with the conclusions of a high-level meeting of academic researchers and practitioners of management at Massachusetts Institute of Technology (MIT) in the early 1990s. Reflecting on the radical changes already occurring, participants concluded:

Rational decision making, traditional design principles, power- and leadership-based models, shareholder- or financial market-driven change, organizational development, and the stakeholder view of the corporation all came in for criticism. None of these served as a comfortable metaphor for describing the challenges facing contemporary organizations for either academics or practitioners. . . . Instead, what emerged . . . was *an emphasis on change that challenges and reconfigures the tacit knowledge or deep assumptions* [italics added for emphasis] about how organizational boundaries, technologies, strategies, and human resources should be arranged.[3]

Perhaps it is time for a new metaphor—the Inquiring Organization—that provides firms with the capability to meet the high-velocity indeterminacy that confronts them. Perhaps it also is time for a new type of conversation that can foster the mutual inquiry that the era calls for, and to determine how managers can access the *"tacit knowledge or deep assumptions"* that contemporary organizations need to meet novel challenges.

The shift to Inquiring Organizations that create knowledge carries enormous implications. In one sense, it is about enabling every individual and every group that performs any function at any level of an organization to democratically become knowledge creators. In another sense, this shift is about the ultimate wellspring of knowledge—inquiry among individuals and groups—that is perhaps the most fundamental and significant, yet unheralded, component of organizational success in the 21st century's accelerating economy. It is important, however, to examine the following questions: "Where do we inquire?"; "How do we inquire?"; and "What does this process of inquiry entail?"

THE "BETWEEN": THE NEW FRONTIER FOR INTELLIGENCE

It is the conventional belief that intelligence lies within us as individuals. In the 21st century, however, intelligence must be accessed not just *within* but *between* individuals. Today's organizations exist in an environment that is complex, accelerating, and nonlinear; thus, no one individual can know enough to make the sound decisions that are necessary to ensure the survival of a firm. The group, with its collective interpersonal intelligence, has become central.

The 20th-century philosopher Martin Buber took the meaning of "inter" to a more personal level when he introduced the concept, the sphere "between" to describe a "still uncomprehended . . . (but) . . . primal category of humanity."[4] Buber taught that the sphere or distance "between" (for our purposes) individuals is crucial to the dialogues and relationships that help us to know one another's thinking and bring meaning to our lives.

The new frontier of the 21st century is the space "between" individuals—whether it is the physical space through which humans have interpersonally communicated through all of time, or the virtual cyberspace of technologically mediated communication that is opening up today. If the frontier of inquiry is the between, then what is the most valuable source of knowledge to bring forth?

TACIT KNOWLEDGE: THE GREATEST UNTAPPED SOURCE OF KNOWLEDGE

Managers are coming to appreciate the extraordinary importance of tacit knowledge. As one leading scholar put it: "creating new knowledge is not simply a matter of 'processing' objective information. Rather, it *depends on tapping the tacit and often highly subjective insights, intuitions, and hunches of individual employees and making those insights available for . . . the company as a whole*"[5] [italics added for emphasis].

Two propositions underlie the extraordinary importance of tacit knowledge: (1) *We know more than we can say*, and (2) *Perhaps the totality of our knowledge is first tacit before it can become explicit.*[6] Let us examine each proposition.

The first proposition is *we know more than we can say*. Much of the knowledge that enables us to carry out our "normal" or "everyday" activities is tacit. Is it possible to verbally describe how we play a musical instrument or ride a bicycle? Could scientific researchers convey how the ideas for a successful series of experiments emerge? Although books exist that explain how to accomplish each of these tasks, somehow they fall short of a "second kind of knowing" that requires a different kind of voice.

The second proposition is *perhaps the totality of our knowledge is first tacit before it can become explicit*. Much of the knowledge that enables us to do creative work—developing a new technology or a new product, or designing a building—is tacit. An architect's drawing of a building reflects his or her explicit knowledge; the drawing embodies the geometries, dimensions, materials, and techniques that create a finished object of quantifiable components. However, these constituent elements emerge from the architect's tacit knowledge—including the natural talent, formal education, experience, taste, preferences, judgment, skill, and other elements—that make this drawing possible. Which body of knowledge is greater? Which sort of knowledge comes first: explicit or tacit? If these two propositions are true, then what treasures might be stored in the minds of an organization's employees waiting to be tapped?

THE FOCUS OF THIS BOOK: TACIT KNOWLEDGE AND CONVERSATION

It is ironic that although corporate executives have spent billions of dollars on the hardware and software of information technology, the Internet, and intranets, perhaps the most effective means of transmitting and creating knowledge literally lies at their disposal, underappreciated and unrealized. Unfortunately, expenditures on human "conversational technology" have not kept pace with outlays for electronic information technology. Despite their importance, conversational skills—most importantly, the conversational skills that foster knowledge creation—are not adequately taught in our schools or addressed in management training. More specifically, neither are the conversational skills that foster knowledge creation.

Following an exhaustive scan of research, a team of leading scholars came to a conclusion about the amount of reliable research in this area. They wrote:

In scientific studies of management, the role of conversation has . . . received little attention . . . [and] *no studies specifically examine conversations in business settings as part of an enabling context . . . for knowledge creation*[7] [italics added for emphasis].

Conversation may be even more important in the information economy than it was in the industrial economy. Alan Webber, former managing editor of the *Harvard Business Review,* and cofounding editor of *Fast Company* magazine, points out that conversation is the only means by which managers can share and develop what they know. Webber stated that, "the most important work in the new economy is creating conversations."[8]

One celebrated study conducted in the "old" industrial economy of the 1970s concluded that managers spent 78 percent of their time on the job engaged in face-to-face conversation.[9] In the late 1990s, Phonak—a Swiss high-technology company that is among the world's leading researchers and manufacturers of cutting-edge personal hearing systems as well as hearing computers and is squarely located in the "new" information economy—made a similar discovery. In tracking its internal communication practices, Phonak executives were surprised to discover that only 20 percent of information exchange among their employees took place via computers and information technology, but that "up to 80 percent of the information exchange within it takes place through personal dialogue."[10] Face-to-face conversation remains the principal mode for internal business communication—whatever the economic era.

The Internet is the most pervasive and revolutionary component of the information economy, and, in a phrase, the Internet itself is nothing less than conversation. There is no other word to describe the e-mails, instant messaging, listservs, or chat rooms that comprise the core of the Internet. The millennial year 2000's underground best-seller, *The Cluetrain Manifesto: The End of Business as Usual*, examined the pervasive effect of the Internet on markets, organizations, and the people who work in them. It concluded that today:

Markets are conversations. . . . Markets consist of human beings, not demographic sectors. . . . The Internet is enabling conversations among human beings that were simply not possible in the era of mass media. . . . In both internetworked markets and among intranetworked employees, people are speaking to each other in a powerful new way.[11]

Conversation has been and will continue to be centrally important to transmit knowledge. *Conversation now is integral to discovering and creating knowledge among groups.* To date, there has been no clear articulation of how to bring about such conversations. It will be the endeavor of this book to address the unfolding process of a mutually generative conversation.

NOTES

1. Plautus (Titus Maccius Plautus) *Miles Gloriosus* (The Glorious Soldier), act III, scene 3.

2. W. Brian Arthur (1999) "New Economics for a Knowledge Economy: The Law of Increasing Returns," in *The Knowledge Advantage: 14 Visionaries Define Marketplace Success in the New Economy*, edited by Rudy Ruggles and Dan Holtshouse (Dover, N.H.: Capstone), pp. 195–212, see p. 209.

3. Rodrigo Magalhaes (1998) "Organizational Knowledge and Learning," in *Knowing in Firms: Understanding, Managing and Measuring Knowledge*, edited by Georg von Krogh, Johan Roos, and Dirk Kleine (London: Sage Publications), pp. 87–122, especially p. 87, quoting Michael Useem and Thomas A. Kochan (1992) "Creating the Learning Organization," in *Transforming Organizations*, edited by Thomas A. Kochan and Michael Useem (New York: Oxford University Press), pp. 391–406, especially p. 391.

4. Martin Buber (1965) "What Is Man?" in *Between Man and Man*, with an introduction by Maurice Friedman (New York: Macmillan Co.), pp. 118–205, especially p. 203. See the further treatment of Buber in chapter 9.

5. Ikujiro Nonaka (November–December 1991) "The Knowledge Creating Company," *Harvard Business Review* 69 (6), pp. 96–104, especially p. 97.

6. Michael Polanyi (October 1962) "Tacit Knowing: Its Bearing on Some Problems in Philosophy," *Review of Modern Physics* 34 (1), pp. 601–616. Also see Polanyi's other thoughts on tacit knowledge as found in (January 1966) "The Logic of Tacit Inference," *Philosophy: The Journal of the Royal Society of Philosophy* XLI (155), pp. 1–18, and his book (1966) *The Tacit Dimension* (Garden City, N.Y.: Doubleday & Company).

7. Ikujiro Nonaka, Georg Von Krogh, and Ichijo Kazuo (2000) *Enabling Knowledge Creation: How to Unlock the Mystery of Tacit Knowledge and Realize the Power of Innovation* (New York: Oxford University Press), p. 127. For two of the rare studies on conversation in the area of organizational change, see Jeffrey D. Ford and Laurie W. Ford (July 1995) "The Role of Conversations in Producing Intentional Change in Organizations," *Academy of Management Review* 20 (3), pp. 541–570; and Frank J. Barrett, Gail Fann Thomas, and Susan P. Hocevar (September 1995) "The Central Role of Discourse in Large-Scale Change: A Social Construction Perspective," *Journal of Applied Behavioral Science* 31 (3), pp. 352–372.

8. Alan M. Webber (January–February 1993) "What's So New about the New Economy?" *Harvard Business Review* 75 (1), pp. 24–30, 32, 41–42, especially p. 28.

9. Henry Mintzberg (1973) *The Nature of Managerial Work* (New York: Harper & Row), p. 38.

10. Nonaka et al., op. cit., p. 131.

11. Rick Levine, Christopher Locke, Doc Searles, and David Weinberger (2000) *The Cluetrain Manifesto: The End of Business as Usual* (Cambridge, Mass.: Perseus Publishing), p. xii.

CHAPTER 2

Two Management Traditions and Knowledge Creation: From Modern to Postmodern Management

We have built the industrial economy on nature—land, labor, and capital. We have learned how to mine below the surface of the earth, but we have not learned how to mine the riches of the human mind. We know how to transform the raw materials of nature into finished products. But, do we know how to transform raw ideas into finished products and services?

—Charles Savage[1]

The ideas presented in the above statement may well capture the trajectory of where the Information Era calls us to go. The trajectory of this age calls us forth to create knowledge, yet today, management remains enmeshed in practices from the past that inhibit knowledge creation. Current but obsolete management practices and organizational structures prevent us from mining "the riches" not just of the individual, but of collective human minds. Incongruities exist between the old "Modern Management Tradition" (as we term it) of the Industrial Era, and the new realities of the Information Era. To transcend this incongruence may require a new management tradition.

Managers are caught in a situation in which the skill set they possess is not producing the intended results that it once did. They are experiencing confusion and frustration in attempting to do their jobs. A late-20th-century survey of 200 high-level executives in major corporations around the world concluded: "The challenges managers face have escalated. Chaos, complexity, and contradiction are common in today's business environment."[2] There is good reason.

Managers have long dealt with change and challenge in the business environment, but this epoch of history is different. Executives and corporations know this, and experience the change in their daily activities differently. During the period between the 1970s and 1990s (which marked the twilight of the Industrial Era and the emergence of the Information Era), a major or paradigmatic shift occurred in how American corporations viewed the extent of change with which they had to contend. According to one seasoned management consultant, in the early 1970s:

- 60 percent of corporations saw no imminent change in their future; by the 1990s that figure plummeted to 1 percent.
- 35 percent saw sporadic incremental change ahead of them, the 1990s figure was 24 percent.
- only 5 percent of corporations envisioned continuous overlapping change in the future, while in the 1990s it skyrocketed to 75 percent.[3]

The environment for doing business had shifted over the decades. The post–World War II decades were an era of relative stability, continuity, linearity, and predictability. The same cannot be said of today's environment.

Peter Drucker captured this shift in the 1960s and again in the 1990s. In 1968, he wrote: "Measured by the yardsticks of the economist, the last half-century has been an Age of Continuity—the period of least change in three hundred years."[4] However, by 1999, a mere three decades later, Drucker described today's totally new world with these words: "We live in a period of PROFOUND TRANSITION—and the changes are radical. . . . READING this book will upset and disturb a good many people, as WRITING it disturbed me"[5] [emphases in original]. Compared with the past, the current era is one of instability, discontinuity, and abrupt revolutionary upheaval. Managers are constantly wheeling and tacking in this turbulence, seeking to guide their organizations to safe harbor.

During the Industrial Era, managers believed that the best way to manage was through a series of steps that emulated the modern scientific tradition of rational analysis: planning, decision making, and problem solving. This was exemplified in the startling array and number of quantitative and quantitatively based approaches—from statistical decision trees and linear programs to algorithms—that were introduced into every manager's toolkit in a faithful attempt to replicate the success of the scientific method in the field of management. As a leading management text of the Industrial Era put it:

In spite of their best efforts, managers often cannot pursue goals in a totally rational, maximizing mode. . . . [D]ecision-making tools . . . have been designed to foster this kind of rationality by taking the data manipulation process outside the human head and turning it over to mathematical formulas and, in most cases, processing by computers.[6]

The guiding principle here was that managers possessed the rational knowledge and process that were requisite to bring about the changes that their organizations required. However, this approach may not be congruent with the turbulence of this new era. In the late 1990s, after interviewing many senior-level executives in a variety of organizations, one management research team concluded:

The first difficulty for many managers is that mission-critical "solutions" today are not always available through traditional, rational analysis. The questions facing them do not conveniently yield to deterministic methods—and this denies the science of management as practiced for almost a century. Since Frederick Taylor first applied precise data-gathering techniques to the workplace, we have wanted management to be more science than art.[7]

A differing approach may be more fitting and useful to help managers cope with this new era's challenges. This approach would open new possibilities to mine the minds of workers—the true source of wealth in this era. The central task of management in today's environment may be to create knowledge. Such a task calls for a new capability to be embedded within organizations. Such a capability can range from innovating seemingly minor yet significant cost savings or processing modifications in daily operations, to developing totally new business models. It is possible that the Modern Management Tradition—by which many managers continue to manage today, and according to which most of today's organizations were designed—has created conditions that militate against the emergence of new ideas and domains of knowledge. The rationale here is that the Modern Management Tradition that prevailed during the Industrial Era does not offer the capabilities to create new knowledge (from business models to minor production line improvements), that is the only avenue by which managers will meet the new challenges posed by the Information Era. Many of today's managers, however, still rely on tools from the past to address the challenges of the present.

As the Industrial Era drew to an end, a variety of forces converged to create a set of new challenges with which the Modern Management Tradition was incongruent. What were the sources of these turbulent new challenges, and how did they come about?

SOURCES OF TURBULENCE IN THE NOVEL BUSINESS ENVIRONMENT

The most important thing I've learned since becoming CEO is context. It's how your company fits in with the world and how you respond to it.
—General Electric CEO Jeff Immelt[8]

A number of factors have contributed to the turbulence of this new environment, and may be summed up in the unfolding of two major late-

20th-century trends: (1) the globalization of business in the 1970s and 1980s, which rendered the locale of business transactions more numerous and placeless; and (2) the Information Revolution—the growth of communication technologies, and especially the Internet in the 1990s—that added to the volume, velocity, complexity, and disruptiveness of products, services, competition, and communication in the Information Era. In the 21st century, the intersection and synergy of these trends multiplied and transformed the practices and boundaries of organizations around the planet.

Globalization emerged in the 1970s, after America's World War II adversaries and allies—Germany and Japan, as well as England and France—rebuilt their war-devastated economies. At about that time, Pacific Rim entrepreneurial economies—like those of Taiwan, Korea, Hong Kong, and Singapore—also began to realize the fruits of their free-market economic policies.

From 1945 until the 1970s, America experienced the last flush of what Peter Drucker termed an "Age of Continuity,"[9] and the country prospered as never before. Workers assumed never-ending economic growth and job security. Managers assumed steady profits and corporate stability. The commanding heights of business in that era were dominated by industrial behemoths that uninterruptedly traced their roots to late-19th- and early-20th-century inventions—the electric light bulb for General Electric (GE), the automobile for General Motors (GM), and the telephone for AT&T. As futurist Alvin Toffler put it, "For many of these firms 1955–70 were years of almost uninterrupted, straight-line growth in an equilibrial environment. In such a period . . . (m)anagers look smart . . . if they simply do 'more of the same.' "[10] The nature of the business environment during that era indeed was relatively stable, linear, and predictable.

The globalization of business revolutionized and changed the rules for business competition. No market was safe from foreign competitors—here or abroad. Companies around the world were compelled to expand beyond their home borders, just as they faced foreign competition at home. The energy crisis of the early 1970s triggered and symbolized the emergence of globalization, as less-expensive, high-mileage, high-quality foreign imports captured so much of the American automobile market that Ford, and especially Chrysler, almost went bankrupt. Since then, foreign competition in cars, as well as every other product and service, has intensified. Managers had to confront a new reality: as globalization intensified in the 1970s and 1980s, no market and no product were safe from intense competition.

The second cause of turbulence was the Information Revolution that got under way in the 1970s and 1980s, intensified in the 1990s with the spread of the World Wide Web, and continues to accelerate in the new millennium. With the convergence of new and different communication technologies during the last few decades—such as the telephone, television, satellite, mainframe computer, facsimile machine, cell phone, personal computer, laptop computer, broadband, PDA, and wireless connectivity—the planet has become a common communication platform. However, new communication technologies and products are not the only source of this turbulence.

Two additional factors synergistically created even more turbulence: the *volume* and the *velocity* at which information moves through today's information economy. The amount of information transmitted during a 24-hour day is staggering. In 1997, for the first time, more e-mails were sent than were conventional letters via snail mail. At the turn of the millennium, almost two billion e-mails were sent daily.[11] The volume of digital information today has grown so much that it is common for managers to spend at least an hour each workday engaged in something unheard of before 1995—reading and responding to e-mail. In addition, no manager needs to be told that the new economy is fast—a random review of best-selling business books at the turn of the millennium conveyed managers' concern with speed: *Blur: The Speed of Change in the Connected Economy; Blown to Bits: How the New Economics of Information Transforms Strategy;* and Bill Gates's *Business @ the Speed of Thought: Using a Digital Nervous System.*[12]

The next source of turbulence for managers was the *complexity* (if not the hypercomplexity) *of information and competition.* Information today tends to be less patterned and more fragmented than in the past. The information economy's velocity does not allow the necessary time for information to become complete. More than ever, managers are compelled to act on smaller fragments of information. In addition, today's intensely competitive environment generates a level of complexity that rapidly creates and destroys competitive advantages. As the Wharton School's Peter Cappelli notes: "One consequence of the increasing competition . . . is that companies must work harder to find markets where they can enjoy some protection, no doubt temporary, from the grinding pressure of competitors."[13] There is no safe harbor.

In such a complex, diffuse environment, stability is impossible to realize because of constantly emerging and changing technologies and global competition, both of which constantly create disequilibria. New as well as newly merged competitors are constantly entering markets and gaining temporary and sometimes permanent advantage—permanent enough, that is, to weaken, if not eliminate, formerly dominant market leaders—until the newcomers themselves are challenged. It is not just high-technology companies that compete in such an environment, but rather organizations, suppliers, and customers in virtually every sector of the information economy. In short, the Information Era's globalized, connected hypercompetition itself breeds hypercomplexity: "Stable equilibria are impossible because constantly shifting technology, global competitors, and strategic positioning will result in frequent or almost constant disequilibrium in which new entrants and established competitors disrupt the balance of power and gain temporary superiority."[14]

The pace of disruptive technologies is a final source of turbulence. Disruptive technologies continually and unexpectedly introduce new factors and new realities for managers to deal with at a volume, velocity, and unprecedented level of complexity. Some readers may remember when the typewriter (Smith Corona) was disrupted by word processing on the mainframe computer (Wang), the mainframe computer by the desktop computer (Apple), the desktop computer by the personal computer with a Microsoft Operating System and Applications (Compaq), the personal computer by the Personal Digital Assistant or PDA (Palm Pilot), the Palm Pilot by the Integrated PDA (Blackberry), and the Blackberry by the handheld computer (HP). At each step of the way, disruptive technologies smashed the business models of not just firms, but entire industries. To take just two examples: the number of stockbrokers and travel agents has plummeted as their one-time customers have gone online to buy stock and make travel plans. In such a disruptive environment, who can forecast? Who can plan? How does one make sense of the environment and respond?

Harvard Business School's Clayton M. Christensen studied an array of companies—among them, Sears-Roebuck, Digital Equipment Corporation, the Harley-Davidson Motorcycle Company, and Apple Computers—and asked why each company, once supreme in its sector, stumbled and sometimes failed? He purposefully examined well-managed firms known for their ability to execute, listen to their customers, and innovate new technologies, "and yet still (lost) market dominance." The common explanation, Christensen concluded, was "disruptive technologies."[15]

The pattern we observed arises out of a key tenet of the concept of "disruptive technologies"—that the pace of technological progress generated by established players inevitably outstrips customers' ability to absorb it, creating opportunities for upstarts to displace incumbents.[16]

The disruptive technologies associated with telecom deregulation and wireless communications posed problems to wireline AT&T, while the disruptive shift from film-based photography to filmless digital cameras and cellular phone cameras posed similar problems to Eastman Kodak. In 2004, both exemplary companies of the Industrial Era were removed from the 30 core stocks that make up the Dow Jones Industrial average for poor performance and being unrepresentative of the Dow Jones basket of stocks—after approximately three-quarters of a century each on the list.[17]

HOW MANAGERS RESPONDED TO THIS TURBULENCE

Managers initially responded to the turbulence unleashed by globalization, the Information Revolution, and disruptive technologies in ways that were congruent with the then-conventional practices. On the surface, their responses might have seemed spontaneous and unconnected. Retrospectively, however, the dim shape of a pattern emerges, and we begin to apprehend that each approach at solving these problems no longer worked as effectively as it once had; or that the limits of that approach's effectiveness had been reached, while global and connected competition relentlessly intensified. Each shift imperceptibly moved managers further away from then-conventional management practices—the ways in which managers had managed during the industrial or modern era, or what we term the Modern Management Tradition of the Industrial Era. Indeed, it is now apparent that the steady stream of measures that managers took to meet the business crises of the late 20th and early 21st centuries were increasingly incongruent with the unfolding realities of a new epoch.

Management's first response to this new environment was orthodox— cutting "normal" costs for "normal" operations in response to "normal" market pressures and business cycles. According to the conventional "template" of Industrial-Era management, cost cutting to make operations more efficient involved a set of standard procedures—cut labor costs, as well as reduce material and energy expenses. During the 1990s, Dow Chemical cut its capital spending by 44 percent in just five years, only to discover that its competitors had done the same.[18]

In the 1990s, cost cutting was given a new dimension by the emergence of a second major management response: "reengineering." Introduced by Michael Hammer, who was educated as an electrical engineer, "reengineering" asked managers to carefully examine every position and process in their internal business operations. The purpose was to refine operating procedures, and thereby justify the elimination of factory workers as well as middle managers who were found to be redundant.[19] Reengineering eventually was responsible for the loss of millions of white-collar as well as blue-collar jobs. To accomplish this goal, Hammer applied his updated version of Frederick Winslow Taylor's early-20th-century "Principles of Scientific Management."[20] Taylor's "scientific management" approach originally applied time-motion study techniques to the physical work of early Industrial-Era factory laborers. Throughout the 20th century, Taylor's "Principles of Scientific Management" pervaded management thinking and practice. Using his "scientific management" approach, countless firms cut costs and increased production, thereby operating their Industrial-Era, "machine-model" organizations more efficiently. Taylor's approach was successful and widely adopted. In fact, Peter Drucker concluded that virtually all of the 20th century's productivity gains as well as capitalism's triumph over communism could be attributed to Taylor's application of the scientific method to physical work.[21] Similarly, Hammer applied his updated version of "scientific management" to the organizational processes, as well as to the intellectual work of late-industrial/early-Information Era managers. In so doing, reengineering became the biggest management fad of the fading Industrial Era.

After initial successes, however, problems emerged. As Alan Webber pointed out:

The problem started with the name itself, which forces a simple mechanical view of what is really a complex human system. Companies are flesh and blood, yet reengineering tries to treat them like machines. In doing so, it fundamentally misses the hidden issues that guide most companies. The heart of a company is its people, relationships, and values—but reengineering completely ignores these assets. Despite its "clean slate" rhetoric, reengineering most often addresses the structure that exists, rather than what needs to be invented to ensure future success. More deliberately, reengineering is done without the participation of the knowledge workers in a company. . . . All these realities of reengineering expose it as a status quo phenomenon wearing the clothing of change. It offers another technique to cut costs and increase quality when what we need is a strategy to cut costs and increase *knowledge*[22] [emphasis in original].

Using Hammer's concept of reengineering, corporations fired millions of middle managers. Although reengineering cut the costs of most firms that adopted it, it did not increase their revenues. Only about one-third of surveyed companies reported that reengineering had helped them in the vital area of generating new revenues by bringing new products or services to market or by growing existing markets.[23] It is widely recognized that these massive firings were disastrous for corporate morale. It is less widely recognized how disastrous they were for the reservoir of organizational knowledge that these workers represented. Reengineering cost companies their "institutional memories"—those managers who implicitly knew which initiatives had worked and which had failed in the past (and why), as well as who to definitely see (or not see) to get a new venture off the ground. Soon however, there wasn't much fat left to cut in corporations. Cost cutting would continue, but cost cutting alone has never been a recipe for organizational survival, let alone success.

During this twilight period of the Industrial Era, chief executive officers (CEOs), engaged in a second tactic congruent with the then-conventional approach to management. They temporarily increased earnings by altering the structure of their corporations. CEOs: (1) divested marginal units in businesses that were not related to their corporation's core competencies; (2) artificially propped up stock prices via buybacks of their own stock, or by paying out proceeds from the sale of divisional spin-offs to stockholders as dividends; (3) sought to improve Industrial-Era economies of scale by expanding remaining core businesses via mergers and acquisitions; and (4) even engaged in white-collar crime by falsifying financial records and company reports, sometimes in collusion with auditors (as the Enron–Arthur Andersen business debacle illustrates). The squeeze on profits continued, however, and competition intensified.

A final response to the unrelenting demands of the globalized Information Era—the *Learning Organization* and *Knowledge Management*—surfaced in the 1990s. In 1990, MIT's Peter Senge introduced the idea to mainstream management practice that an organization's best response in the Information Era was to learn.[24] Because other approaches had reached the limit of their effectiveness, Senge's new approach "caught fire." Soon, every executive wanted his or her organization to become a Learning Organization, and one of the major management trends of the 1990s was born.

In 1991, Ikujiro Nonaka extended this explicit recognition of knowledge's central role in organizations with his influential concepts—the Knowledge Organization and Knowledge Management.[25] Nonaka recognized that it was not land, labor, or capital that were the sources of wealth, but something central to this new era—knowledge itself. He further stated that only organizations that continually learned and managed knowledge would possess a sustainable advantage over their competitors. This eminently sensible response to the new environment was widely accepted as a valid approach by managers. Indeed, a 1998 survey of 300 CEOs of the world's largest corporations found that the greatest corporate challenge they saw for their firms (after globalization) was "knowledge management," and, more pragmatically, how their organizations could become more effective Learning Organizations.[26] However, the question arises: "Learning may be a necessary response for organizations in the 21st-century's information age, but is it sufficient?"

One major thesis of this book is that to focus on learning alone is an insufficient strategy in the Information Era. Learning is important, but the next stage for organizations is to realize that learning what is known is not sufficient for organizational survival in the fast-paced, turbulent environment of the Information Era. Rather, inquiring into and sharing what is not yet known, what has yet to come into being—creating new knowledge—becomes the necessary *sine qua non* for organizational survival. That is why creating new knowledge is the centerpiece of this book: because in the Information Era, the basic business models of all firms, how they operate on a daily basis, and the unconscious assumptions of how managers manage their daily operations are being questioned, reconceptualized, and inquired into.

There may be an iron "Law of Congruence" that was as true for cold-blooded dinosaurs that died out when the Ice Age occurred as it is for organizations today: *change with the environment, adapt, or become extinct.* As the business environment changes, so must the business models of firms, their overarching structures, their daily practices, and their basic assumptions about management. What progressively needs to emerge is a new approach that enables managers to better deal with these new realities, and to find new ways for organizations to redefine themselves, as well as to transcend the concept of management itself.

For example, Jack Welch, who took charge of an increasingly arthritic GE in the early 1980s, set out to redefine GE through the famous "workout" sessions that he initiated. This company-wide interactional process, based on small New England town meetings, ultimately involved hundreds of thousands of employees from every level who revolutionized the company through dialogue. Welch called these workouts a critical factor in GE's spectacular success during the last two decades of the 20th century.[27] Such a development was a precursor to what we term a new tradition, the Postmodern Management Tradition, for dealing with the new realities of a new era.

WHERE WE ARE TODAY: THE NATURE OF CHANGE HAS CHANGED

Today, the nature of change has changed. Business scholar Charles Handy may have put his finger on it when he wrote: "Change is not what it used to be."[28] Change no longer is the incremental, continual refinement of known business models and management practices that it once was. As one longtime consultant put it: "For the first time in my experience, I am hearing successful CEOs say they do not know what will become of their industries or how to plan for their companies' future."[29] Managers live and work in a much different milieu, a much different world than ever before.

The critical questions that managers need to ask in the Information Era are not the same as those they posed during the Industrial Era. Yesterday, managers had an implicitly internal focus when they asked, "How do I run my (existing) business more efficiently?" Today, they also must have an external focus as they scan the environment and ask: "What are the new (and as-yet implicit) business ideas and models for my organization?" Yesterday, they asked: "How can I locate (an existing) need for a new product in the marketplace?" Today, due to the speed at which markets change and competitors move, managers ask: "How do I discover the products and services that consumers want *before* consumers know that they want them?" Yesterday, managers asked: "What does the (stable, linear, finished) environment tell me?" Today, they ask: "How do I make sense of the (unstable, nonlinear, unfinished) environment that confronts me?" Managers have difficulty even apprehending the nature of change they must navigate if their organizations are to survive.

Today we are immersed in change that is so high velocity, nonlinear, and discontinuous that it "blows apart" the once-stable, "taken-for-granted" business models of firms and entire industries—banks and bro-kerage houses, newspapers and television networks, and schools and health care. This process of "deconstructing" or "blowing to bits" the very models by which businesses and industries are organized is just beginning.[30]

What is true of the firms we manage is also true of how we manage them. In 1999 Peter Drucker analyzed eight of management's most fun-damental assumptions, and concluded that, until the early 1980s, most of them:

were close enough to reality to be operational, whether for research, for writing, for teaching or for practicing management. By now all of them have outlived their usefulness. They are close to being caricatures. They are now so far removed from actual reality that they are becoming obstacles to the Theory and even more serious obstacles to the Practice of management. Indeed, reality is fast becoming the very opposite of what these assumptions claim it to be. It is high time therefore to think through these assumptions and to try to formulate the NEW ASSUMPTIONS that now have to inform both the study and the practice of management[31] [emphasis in original].

No wonder managers feel overwhelmed. Not only is the "what"—the organizational structures and procedures—they are managing changing, but so is the "how"—the theory of management itself. We are at a point where many managers feel locked into coping with the present, and be-wildered in their attempt to make sense of the future. Perhaps there is a clarifying insight, however.

A CLARIFYING INSIGHT: TRADITION

There may be a concept that provides a clarifying insight for managers in their predicament—tradition. At first glance, tradition may appear to be a paradoxical concept. Of what possible relevance could "tradition"—a term from the past—be to managers in the future-oriented turmoil of today? There is a very practical reason for the choice of this concept. We do not use "tradition" in the sense of dry ritual that is followed year after year, with seemingly little relation to everyday lives—like the tradition and ritual of some monarchies. Rather, we suggest the use of tradition in the sense of a shared basis for living that binds people together through common values, thoughts, and action over time. In addition, it may be a new, but clarifying thought for managers to realize that during the Industrial Era, they may have been unconsciously managing according to a particular "tradition of management."

We deliberately chose the concept of "tradition" for three reasons: (1) because a tradition can be associated with a particular era of time; (2) because different eras can have different traditions; and (3) because traditions unconsciously, but powerfully, bind people together with common values and behaviors.

Tradition is connected with the element of time. There was a "Greek Tradition" and a "Roman Tradition" into which the young were socialized, and which provided common values, common ways of looking at the world, and commonly shared bases for action. A classicist friend once remarked that the Greeks and Romans whom she studies were as different from humans today as someone from another culture might be different from an American. Tradition can make us as similar to or as different from each other in our responses, and have the same impact on us as does culture.

Anthropologists long have taught that tradition provides societies with the basis for a shared outlook, a "fabric for action." The surprise may be that this has been true for managers in industrial society. When we speak of tradition, we have in mind: "a 'way of being' . . . a way of understanding, a background, within which we interpret and act . . . [in] . . . our interactions with others who share the tradition . . . [and that] . . . invisibly gives shape to our thought."[32]

Within a tradition, members tend to approach situations from a common perspective and by remembering the common experiences of similar, previous situations; that is, "we always exist within a pre-understanding determined by the history of our interactions with others who share the tradition."[33] In most instances, such "pre-understandings" of a current situation (in light of similar previous situations one has experienced) provide a pattern into which the situation "fits." This "pre-understanding" or pattern then provides a proven set of responses for its solution. Such intellectual operations normally are unconscious and tacit, for a tradition (and its operations) is "concealed by its obviousness."[34] Managers normally are unaware of how they conduct such mental operations, and are unaware of the tradition that allows them to do so in unconsciously scripted collaboration with colleagues. Perhaps this explains why managers are so confused today—they have not yet "connected the dots"; they are unaware of the tradition that blinds them to the cause of their own confusion. Thus, managers today may not only feel confused, but also frustrated and disoriented because they are not just moving from one epoch of time, but from one tradition of management to another.

THE PARADIGM SHIFT OF MANAGEMENT TRADITIONS

There was a management tradition that was linked to the Industrial Era, and that organically grew out of and congruently "fit" those "old realities." We term this the Modern Management Tradition. There is another management tradition that is linked to the Information Era. This tradition also organically grew out of and congruently "fit" the changing "new realities." We term this the Postmodern Management Tradition. Whether or not they are aware of it, managers unconsciously have been caught in the bewildering transition from the Industrial to the Information Eras, as well as the transition from the Modern Management Tradition to the Postmodern Management Tradition.

Managers unconsciously think and act in professional situations according to a "tradition" of management, and thus unconsciously are part of that "tradition's" widely shared "pre-understandings" of what they should do, and even how they should think in organizational situations. Through such a tradition, managers share a collective "way of understanding, a background, within which (managers) interpret and act."[35] To date, managers have shared a common approach by which they have commonly managed. They were formally taught this management tradition in their undergraduate and MBA as well as MPA (Master's in Public Administration) classrooms. They also informally learned this management tradition during their socialization and experiences in the workplace with others.

This issue brings up the following question: Can a historically or experientially based tradition exist in business, and can it have a subtle but powerful influence? Review what Donald Valentine—founder and long-time head of Sequoia Capital, one of the best-known early Silicon Valley venture capital firms—had to say on this issue:

Every company, eventually, accumulates legacy customers and applications. They are run by silver-haired guys who are very protective of the past. They are historically-oriented. They just do not believe in the abandonment of the past. For a bunch of reasons, they are locked into it. Most recognize what's going on. They just can't decide what to do about it. Remember how late it was when Microsoft discovered the Internet? 1995. They must have been on a trip to Mars. When Gates finally discovered the Internet, he did something about it. But his case is extremely rare.[36]

There is a Modern Management Tradition that has been "concealed by its obviousness." Because each management tradition is congruent with its era, perhaps it is time to "unconceal" the Modern Management Tradition. If this is the era of new business models for firms, perhaps it is the era for new management models for managers.

WHAT IS THE MODERN MANAGEMENT TRADITION?

A 1990s global survey inquired into the toughest problems that senior-level executives faced in this chaotic environment. Their greatest difficulty was that the solutions they sought to their novel problems were "not always available through traditional, rational analysis," and that the questions they faced did not "conveniently yield to deterministic methods." The authors of the study concluded: "This denies the science of management as practiced for almost a century. Since Frederick Taylor first applied precise data-gathering techniques to the workplace, we have wanted management to be more science than art."[37] They continued:

Today as in decades past we are all Taylorists—and we are all something else that is just emerging. . . . We share a tradition, in place since the work of Frederick Taylor, of attacking management problems rationally. . . . Many managers simply expect the optimal solution to emerge from concentrated, quasi-algorithmic analysis. We tend to respond as Taylorists, *and then to doubt what we have done, often with good reason.*"[38] [italics added for emphasis]

This passage reflects the enduring influence of Frederick Winslow Taylor who first infused management with the objective rationality of the scientific method. It also conveys the influence of the Modern Management Tradition, and the frustration it is causing among managers who are seeking to manage according to its precepts today.

What has been the core of the Modern Management Tradition? In a powerfully unconscious way, it has been the scientific tradition. It was Francis Bacon who, through his formulation and articulation of the scientific method, wrested man's method of inquiry away from its fixation with theology and the eternal afterlife. Bacon equipped humankind with a method of empirical analysis for objective action—the scientific method—to address and improve humankind's present existence in this temporal world.[39]

He provided us with the power of a new way of seeing, thinking, and interpreting. Bacon's achievement should continue to be appreciated, because the scientific method provides a process to rationally and objectively gather data to determine the problem, formulate a hypothesis, and empirically test the hypothesis. The scientific method has immeasurably improved human existence, and—given the immensity of its success—has been a powerful model for other disciplines to emulate. Management, along with many other humanistic and social disciplines such as psychology and economics, has done its best to do so. Reflecting on human existence since that time, and the improvements that science has brought about—better health, longer life spans, material abundance, and everything from indoor plumbing and clean water to antibiotics and the

Internet—the scientific method has been a powerful force for the good in human existence.

How, however, has the scientific method impacted management, and especially the Modern Management Tradition? One respected scholar opened an influential article on management theory that he published at the height of the Industrial Era by stating: "until recent years, almost all of those who have attempted to analyze the management process . . . [looked] . . . for some scientific underpinnings."[40] He concluded by comparing advances in the older (and more exact) physical sciences with the younger (and less exact) social sciences of which he considered management to be one.

But it was particular sort of science that pervades the Modern Management Tradition. According to Reuben McDaniel, "Many understandings of organizations are based on Newtonian Physics."[41] In his 1687 *Mathematical Principles of Natural Philosophy* or *Principia Mathematica,* Newton believed he had discovered the eternal, universal and regular laws according to which all motion (then known) could be objectively measured, understood and predicted—from tides to the solar system. According to this epistemology, the eternal, universal, and regular laws of nature (and later of organizations) can be discovered with sufficient objective information and mathematical analysis. Once the eternal and universal laws that describe their operations are objectively discovered and applied, nature (and organizations) operate according to the metaphor of a machine—regularly, rationally, and predictably—and with symmetry and harmony. Thus: "Large effects have large causes," and "if a given tactic works once, it can be counted on to work again."[42] Such an approach leads to an objective cause-and-effect, linear kind of thinking and action. As with billiard balls, hitting billiard ball A with a specified force from a specified angle leads to a predictable outcome for balls B and C. Such a perspective fits a world or environment that is seen as orderly, regular, rational, and smoothly running—a world or environment that is linear and predictable. Linearity and predictability apparently adequately fit the 17th-century environment in which Isaac Newton lived, as well as much of the Modern era that his approach to science created. It is this Newtonian epistemology of science that still pervades the Modern Management Tradition today.

DRAWBACKS OF THE MODERN MANAGEMENT TRADITION

A practical way to determine the drawbacks of the Modern Management Tradition would be to ask managers the essence of what they do. Most managers would agree that the essence of what they do on a daily basis is to make decisions and solve problems. Management sought to adapt and infuse the power of the objective, rational, scientific tradition into these central operations of what managers do every day—decision making and problem solving. As Peter Drucker put it at the height of the Modern era in 1954: "Whatever a manager does he does through making decisions. . . . The importance of decision-making in management is generally recognized. But a good deal of the discussion tends to center on problem-solving."[43]

Economist Herbert Simon thought differently. He was a path-breaking student of decision making and problem solving in the managerial context. A Nobel Prize winner in 1978, it was Simon who pointed out that the model for management—rational decision making and problem solving—that was taught in business school classes and assigned in readings, although infused by and modeled after the scientific method, was wanting. However, it was the "scientific" decision-making model that was consciously held up as one example for executives to practice during the Industrial Era.

According to the Modern Management Tradition, managers who make decisions and solve problems believe that they should do so by gathering all objective data, explicitly identifying the problem, thoroughly listing alternative strategies, totally determining the consequences that flow from each strategy, completely and comparatively evaluating all consequences from every strategy, and selecting or synthesizing the one strategy that is optimal. Thus, they attempt to perform their central tasks by following as close to the model of scientific procedure as limited time and imprecise reality permit.

Simon himself stated the limitations of this "rational" or scientific approach as an idealized version of decision making in the "real world." As he wrote: "It is impossible for the behavior of a single, isolated individual to reach any high degree of rationality. The number of alternatives he must explore is so great, the information he would need to evaluate them so vast that even an approximation to objective rationality is hard to conceive."[44] Simon's explanation for how managers actually reach decisions introduced the concept of "bounded rationality" by which they "minimaxed" or "satisficed" (i.e., made the "best" decision possible, given the information and time available). Simon is famous for recognizing the limits of rationality in decision making. What may not have been adequately recognized is his appreciation for the limits of conscious rationality in decision making.

Here, Simon recognized the domain of tacit knowledge when he stated: *"The central concern of administrative theory is with the boundary between the rational and the nonrational aspects of human social behavior"*[45] [emphasis in original]. In other words, Simon identified the role of what we term intuition or tacit knowledge in the critical area of management and decision making. This insight may not have been sufficiently appreciated in management theory and practice to date. Later in his career, Simon concluded: "Every manager needs to be able to analyze problems systemically.... Every manager needs also to be able to respond to situations rapidly, a skill that requires the cultivation of intuition."[46]

Clayton M. Christensen, a leading scholar of Information Era organizations, concurs. He found that, in the current business environment of "fast history," the exercise of what we term "conventional management rationality" often leads to corporate failure, not success.[47] Christensen identified three reasons for the failure of "conventional management rationality" by disruptive technologies: (1) the initial products or services that result from disruptive technologies usually are inferior to existing products but are more convenient and/or cheaper, and therefore result in lower, not (rationally satisfying) higher, profits; (2) the (rationally satisfying) most profitable customers of successful firms usually don't want (because they usually can't use) the initial products of disruptive technologies; and (3) the initially simpler and/or inferior commercial applications of disruptive technologies usually are purchased by smaller, fringe customers, rather than (rationally satisfying) larger, mainstream customers. Instead, disruptive products generally are embraced and purchased by a market's least profitable (and rationally unsatisfying) customers. Hence, companies that follow the conventional wisdom of "listening to their best customers" and providing the new products they want (and that promise greater immediate profitability and growth), rarely see fit to invest in a truly new technology until it is too late.[48]

There are, perhaps, two philosophical as well as two pragmatic points in which the scientific method and its offspring, the Modern Management Tradition, are incongruent with the Postmodern Era.

The 20th-century German philosopher Hans-Georg Gadamer explored the relationship between the scientific method and human affairs in his magisterial work, *Truth and Method*.[49] The basic thesis of his book is that the "truth" about human beings can never be realized by using the scientific "method." According to Gadamer, the scientific method seeks "general laws" that are true in every situation, in every setting, and through all of time. However, Gadamer points out, disciplines like history (and professions like management) that deal with human beings simply do not possess the universal and eternal regularities of the physical world of science. Gadamer further asks whether the social world that man creates can be studied—as scientists study physics—using the standardized procedures of the scientific method.[50] Could it be that managers' attempts to understand the current, unstable business environment are hampered by their unconscious reliance on the scientific method that seeks stable regularities, that (in the case of science) are called "laws"?

The scientific method's "standardized procedures" of inquiry were comparable with the formal procedures that ostensibly governed managers' behavior during the Industrial Era. During that era, organizations encouraged employees to deal with situations, make decisions, and solve problems "by the book." Describing Industrial Era paragon AT&T at its height in 1972, futurist Alvin Toffler wrote: "Most Bell people . . . have been encouraged to look for standardized procedures, officially approved ways of dealing with their problems. *During the Industrial Era, the company that was most effective in prescribing rules for behavior—the company with the most carefully thought-out 'rule book'—frequently had the most efficient organization*"[51] [emphasis in original]. In short, managing "by the book" worked during the stable, linear Industrial Era, because the relatively stable business environment of the Industrial Era closely resembled the stable physical world of Newtonian science. Yet, as Toffler pointed out: "*As the novelty ratio rises, however, the utility of the rulebook declines, and the companies that have poured the most energy and skill into creating it are frequently the ones least able to deal with the new reality whose essence is the break-up of the old rules*"[52] [emphasis in original].

What happens to a manager's "book of standardized practices" in the disruptive, nonlinear Information Era of "batch production," "multiple-option," "niche" markets? Would it be advisable to rely on "pre-existing routines" and "standardized" practices in this new era, or innovation? Writing in a confidential report to senior executives in 1972, Toffler forecast that, in the future, more decisions would be individually made by employees at every level of AT&T:

A higher percentage of the decisions made by its managers, as well as its operators, lineman, installers, business representative and others, now require "non-programmed" thinking, evaluation and learning. More information about both the internal and external environment must be scooped up, assembled, analyzed and weighed before decisions can be made. More and more, the individual is faced with situations in which the implementation of an existing policy or procedure could lead to disaster. The individual is faced, in short, by situations in which he must *invent* a response. . . . The positive side of novelty is that it can elicit from employees and managers alike an enhanced level of creativity or imagination in their work—provided the structure encourages, rather than suppresses, this quality. Rising novelty ratios therefore demand both a new kind of management and a new kind of structure.[53] [emphasis in original]

What Toffler presciently foresaw in the 1970s is self-evident today. Managers need to reconceptualize many of their management practices. The objective is to seek a new approach to management that encourages a heightened level of imagination and creativity from every individual at every level in an organization. Moreover, it may be that managers should not even attempt to draw up comprehensive, thorough, and detailed "rational" plans for their organizations. As Jack Welch learned from 19th-century Prussian military strategist Johannes von Moltke, in battle, "circumstances inevitably change."[54] Perhaps endeavors like business that seek to understand, plan for, and deal with discontinuous events in very changeful circumstances are better explored via a back-and-forth fluid process in the between of individuals that surfaces unique inferences. Such an open approach lends itself to surfacing ideas that fit unique circumstances rather than a lock-step process whose aim is comprehensive generalization.

In today's current environment, it would be advantageous for managers to understand how each unique situation evolves. The 20th-century German philosopher Hans-Georg Gadamer suggests that situations evolve not according to the universality of the scientific method, but rather according to their own uniqueness, and should be understood as such. He writes: "However much general experience is involved, the aim is not to confirm and expand these general experiences in order to attain knowledge of a law, eg [*sic*] how men, peoples and states evolve, but to understand how this man, this people or this state is what it has become—more generally, *how has it happened that it is so*"[55] [italics added for emphasis].

How might a philosopher's insight apply to the challenges that today's managers confront? Consider the words of Clayton M. Christenson: "If history is any guide, the practices and business models that constitute advantages for today's most successful companies confer those advantages only because of particular factors at work under particular conditions at this particular time."[56] Perhaps managers too could better understand the situations they face in today's fragmented environment by simply asking: "How has it happened that this is so?"

Gadamer further asks whether humans can be "objective," as the scientific method demands, in their pursuit of understanding. Can we separate who we are from what we know? Gadamer's response was that it is not possible. He feels that the "personal knowledge" that each human possesses is a richer and more freely flowing wellspring of information than is "objective" knowledge, which is more impersonal and restrictive. Gadamer submits that each one of us, through our individual human experience, builds up personal "pre-understandings" or "fore-knowledge" of persons, problems, and situations; and that such "pre-understandings" are unconsciously triggered by every situation that humans encounter.[57] For example, should an individual be told that the president of a major construction company was outside the room, waiting to come in, most might have a certain "pre-understanding" of whom to expect. Imagine the surprise when a 30-year-old young woman steps through the door! Similarly, managers build up subjective experiences over their careers that tell them how to interpret certain situations, and then how to address them. What happens, however, when a manager's personal "pre-understanding" of how to interpret a situation or "fore-knowledge" of how to address it becomes incongruent with the realities of a turbulent, new environment?

Foreknowledge once allowed managers to "backward reference"—that is, "to project the past into the future" so as to successfully apply their prior experience and knowledge to the reality of a business problem.[58] Not so long ago, such "backward referencing" earned them high hierarchical positions and salaries. This, however, is no longer the case. Perhaps too many managers manage according to the certainties that they acquired as part of their formal education or business experience. Unconsciously influenced by the Modern Management Tradition, they tend to lump situations, people, and solutions into homogeneous categories that obscure nuances and ignore differences—a dangerous practice in this fast-paced world so full of variation and novelty. It may be that too many managers today "manage" according to the determined, fixed, backward-referencing truths of the "scientific-influenced" Modern Management Tradition. Perhaps, by its very nature, this Modern Management Tradition hampers the creation of knowledge that is necessitated by today's fast-changing environment.

The Modern Management Tradition implicitly led managers to manage according to the assumption of a stable, rational, objective approach in which problem solving and decision making were congruent with a stable, rational, objective world—much like the stable, rational, objective world of science. It may be, however, that these assumptions no longer fit with the nonlinear, disruptive, realties that confront managers today.

In the 21st century Information Era, it is not so much the smoothly running, linear, and predictable Newtonian paradigm that explains the operations of our world, or how we should act in accordance with it, but quantum theory and chaos theory. The 17th century Newtonian view of the world and the science that explained it was predicated on linearity and certainty. The 21st century's quantum theory and chaos theory view of the world and the science that explains it is predicated on non-linearity and uncertainty.[59] The conceptual or paradigmatic shift occurred with German physicist Werner Heisenberg's 1927 discovery of the principle of uncertainty.

According to this principle, the motion—the speed and position of a subatomic electron (whose existence was unknown in Newton's time)— could not be simultaneously ascertained, and therefore is indeterminate and unknowable. As Rueben McDaniel put it: "if we believe that the world is unknowable, then our approach to management and organizations will be fundamentally different. . . . The basic conclusion of quantum theory is that the future behavior of a system is not predictable, regardless of how accurately one knows its present state."[60] Thus, no matter how much data we collect or how long or with how many algorithms our computers analyze them, no matter how complete or accurate our data is, "our world is fundamentally unknowable."[61]

Chaos theory suggests that given their non-linearity, systems—including the largest one, our world—are inherently unstable, if not chaotic. Chaos theory also holds that not just large, but small changes in a system can produce major effects. James Gleick, author of *Chaos Theory*, is famous for his concept of the "Butterfly Effect," according to which the fluttering of a butterfly's wings in Asia might trigger a hurricane in the Caribbean.[62] Similarly, the actions of 19 men on three commercial aircraft on September 11, 2001, changed a nation and the world.

In the more stable Industrial Era, managers were able to successfully forecast the future with some success. However, the indeterminacy of our present era has dissipated the power of leaders to control situations through managerial actions. Kenneth Chenault, CEO of American Express, succinctly described the humbler yet still-crucial role of leaders in today's world: "The role of a leader is to define reality and to give hope."[63]

Physicists already have made the shift from Newtonian physics to quantum theory and chaos theory. Perhaps such a shift by management theorists and practioners could provide insights and understandings that are not just new but necessary in this new era. Perhaps it is time for managers to shift from the Newtonian-infused Modern Management Tradition to the quantum theory and chaos theory-infused Postmodern Management Tradition.

Clayton M. Christensen's insightful work illuminates the incongruence (and even folly) of the Modern Management Tradition in today's environment. According to Christensen, managers need to take a very different approach in an era of disruptive technology—and events. In the Industrial Era, managers had the time to plan carefully, and to check on the accuracy of forecasts as well as the reliability of customer or information inputs, before aggressive execution. In disruptive situations, however, "action must be taken before careful plans are made."[64] Christensen explains how this is so: "Markets that do not exist cannot be analyzed. . . . Not only are the market applications for disruptive technologies *unknown* at the time of their development, they are *unknowable*"[65] [emphasis in original].

In disruptive environments, managers know less than ever before about their markets, what consumers need, or how large markets can become. In such circumstances, plans serve a different purpose: "They must be plans for *learning* rather than plans for implementation."[66] Managers should approach disruptive business situations "with the mindset that they can't know where the market is."[67] Therefore, they must surface and discover the information about new markets that is most necessary and-critical, and must determine in what sequence it is needed. Project and business plans need to mirror those priorities: "so that key pieces of information would be created or important uncertainties resolved, before expensive commitments of capital, time, and money were required."[68] As is true of many situations involving transition, growth, and change, the shift from the Modern Management Tradition to the Postmodern Management Tradition took place before it was consciously realized.

The case of GE's success under the leadership of Jack Welch provides some concrete examples of how to successfully transition from the Modern Management Tradition. Early in his tenure at GE, Welch recognized that it was necessary for GE to become: "an organization that could systematically foster the creation of new ideas."[69] A constant flow of new ideas would be mandatory if GE were to stay competitive by increasing its revenues and productivity. To do so, Welch believed that GE would have to abandon many of its past practices and seek a new way. The "old way" was exemplified by Henry Ford's Industrial Era production line and approach to management. It called for managers to analyze the work to be done, and "then devise rules even an idiot [could] follow. Managers, divorced from their actual work, [became] bureaucrats,"[70] while their frustrated subordinates did the work. "Brilliantly though such methods worked during most of . . . [the 20th] . . . century, they won't help us much in the next."[71] Welch's goal at GE was no less than to *transcend the concept of management itself*"[72] [italics added for emphasis]. The methods that Jack Welch used to make GE one of the world's premier corporations were a "quantum change" and "fundamentally different, from the managerial techniques taught at most business schools and practiced at most corporations. Understanding the new methods, no less than creating them, require[d] a *new intellectual framework*"[73] [italics added for emphasis]. In essence, Jack Welch led GE to abandon the Modern Management Tradition and to seek the "new intellectual framework" that we have termed the Postmodern Management Tradition.

CONCLUSION

There may be a need for another approach to the essence of management—the process by which managers have made decisions and solved problems. It is possible that in seeking a new approach to management, we may discover that communication always has been the "essence" of management. A new process of communication is both the means and the goal of successful management in the information economy of the 21st century. This chapter makes the point that organizations need to shift from Learning Organizations to Inquiring Organizations. It is not enough for firms to learn what already is known; if they are to survive, let alone thrive, they also need to inquire, and thus bring into being new knowledge that is yet unknown.

Today, the basic business models of corporations and entire industries are being reconceptualized, because they have become incongruent with new, information era realities. Management may need a new tradition, a new way of inquiring and managing—one that is not just the creation of the top "brains" of an organization, but is the co-creation of all. It may not just be individual geniuses with a "vision" who successfully lead organizations in today's complex environment. Such individuals exist, and organizations will continue to need them; however, few organizations will be lucky enough to have two or three "Bill Gates" in a row to guide them. Perhaps organizations will be better served by adopting a process that allows them to tap into the collective intelligences of all employees throughout the organization, rather than the intelligence of just one or a few individuals at the top.

Above all, today's managers cannot effectively "solve problems" if they make decisions according to a Modern Management Tradition that implicitly assumes linearity in an increasingly nonlinear world; nor can managers assume continuity in a discontinuous world, or universal "laws" in an environment of increasingly fragmented and temporary market realities. Managers need to move beyond the problem solving and decision making that characterized the Modern Tradition of Management of the Industrial Era. Perhaps in the Postmodern Management Tradition of the Information Era, managers will become the collective generators of possibilities and creators of knowledge. Managers then can become inquirers in Inquiring Organizations and discover and create new knowledge in new ways. Today, we need a way to multiply intelligence by "parallel processing" humans in the same way that we parallel process computers; to create the conditions to help humans do what only humans can— mutually surface and create knowledge. With each passing day, it becomes clearer that managers and organizations require *"a new intellectual framework"*[74] that allows them to *"transcend the concept of management itself"*[75] [italics added for emphasis].

NOTES

1. Authors' paraphrase of Charles M. Savage (1996) *5th Generation Management*, rev. ed. (Newton, Mass.: Butterworth-Heineman), pp. xx–xxi.

2. The Price Waterhouse Change Integration Team (1996) *The Paradox Principles: How High-Performance Companies Manage Chaos, Complexity, and Contradiction to Achieve Superior Results* (Chicago: Irwin Professional Publishing), p. 7.

3. Daryl R. Conner (1992) *Managing at the Speed of Change: How Resilient Managers Succeed and Prosper Where Others Fail* (New York: Villard Books), p. 44.

4. Peter Drucker (1968) *The Age of Discontinuity: Guidelines to Our Changing Society* (New York: Harper & Row), p. 9. In this work, Drucker, with his usual prescience, forecast the discontinuous turbulence with which managers today are contending.

5. Peter F. Drucker (1999) *Management Challenges for the 21st Century* (New York: HarperBusiness), pp. ix–x.

6. John B. Miner (1978) *The Management Process: Theory, Research, and Practice,* 2nd ed. (New York: Macmillan), p. 117.

7. The Price Waterhouse Change Integration Team, op. cit., p. 7.

8. *Fast Company* (April 2004) "Top 10 Leadership Tips from Jeff Immelt" p. 96.

9. Drucker (1968), op. cit., p. 9.

10. Alvin Toffler (1985) *The Adaptive Corporation* (New York: McGraw-Hill), p. 1.

11. Thomas A. Stewart (2001) *The Wealth of Knowledge: Intellectual Capital and the Twenty-First Century Organization* (New York: Currency), p. 7. For an up-to-date estimate of the world's total yearly production of print, film, optical, and magnetic content, see Peter Lyman, Hal R. Varian et al. (2000), "How Much Information." Available at http://www.sims.berkeley.edu/how-much-info-on [date] cited in Ibid., p. 338.

12. Stan Davis and Christopher Meyer (1998) *Blur: The Speed of Change in the Connected Economy* (New York: Warner Books); Philip Evans and Thomas S. Wurster (2000) *Blown to Bits: How the New Economics of Information Transforms Strategy* (Boston: Harvard Business School Press); and Bill Gates (1999) *Business @ the Speed of Thought: Using a Digital Nervous System* (New York: Warner Books).

13. Peter Cappelli (1999) *The New Deal at Work: Managing the Market-Driven Workforce* (Boston: The Harvard Business School Press), p. 95.

14. Richard D'Aveni (1994) *Hypercompetition: Managing the Dynamics of Strategic Maneuvering* (New York: The Free Press), p. xviii.

15. Clayton M. Christensen (1997) *The Innovator's Dilemma: When New Technologies Cause Great Firms to Fail* (Boston: Harvard Business School Press), p. 1.

16. Clayton M. Christensen, Michael Raynor, and Matt Verlinden (November 2001) "Skate to Where the Money Will Be," *Harvard Business Review* 79 (10), p. 74.

17. Floyd Norris (April 2, 2004) "3 Substitutions Made in List of Dow 30," *New York Times,* pp. C1, C6. Perhaps Kodak should not be prematurely counted out; it holds almost 1,000 patents that are related to digital photography. Ironically, "Kodak invented the first digital camera in the mid-1970's." Claudia H. Deutsch (April 19, 2004) "Advice to Help Kodak Compete in the New World of Digital Photography," *New York Times,* p. C4.

18. Stewart, op. cit., p. 24.

19. Michael Hammer and James Champy (1993) *Reengineering the Corporation: A Manifesto for Business Revolution* (New York: HarperBusiness).

20. See Robert Kanigel (1997) *The One Best Way: Frederick Winslow Taylor and the Enigma of Efficiency* (New York: Viking).

21. Peter F. Drucker (1994) *Post-Capitalist Society* (New York: HarperBusiness), pp. 38–39.

22. Alan M. Webber (1999) "Knowledge Is Power! Welcome Democracy!," in *The Knowledge Advantage: 14 Visionaries Define Marketplace Success in the New Economy,* edited by Rudy Ruggles and Dan Holtshouse (Dover, N.H.: Capstone), pp. 41–47, especially pp. 43–44.

23. The Price Waterhouse Change Integration Team, op. cit., pp. 199–200.

24. Peter Senge (1990) *The Fifth Discipline: The Art and Practice of The Learning Organization* (New York: Currency/Doubleday). Senge's work builds on that of Chris Argyris and Donald Schön (1979) *Organizational Learning: A Theory of Action Perspective* (Reading, Mass.: Addison-Wesley Publishing Co.). Although there were

many contributing streams of thought, this book (which Senge calls a "landmark") gave birth to the organizational learning movement. See Peter Senge (May 2003) "Taking Personal Change Seriously: The Impact of Organizational Learning on Management Practice" *The Academy of Management Executive* 17 (2), pp. 47–50, especially p. 47.

25. Ikujiro Nonaka (November–December 1991) "The Knowledge-Creating Company," *Harvard Business Review* 69 (6), pp. 96–104. See also Georg von Krogh, Kazuo Ichijo, and Ikujiro Nonaka (2000) *Enabling Knowledge Creation: How to Unlock the Mystery of Tacit Knowledge and Release the Power of Innovation* (New York: Oxford University Press).

26. Rudy Ruggles and Dan Holtshouse (1999) "Gaining the Knowledge Advantage," in *The Knowledge Advantage: 14 Visionaries Define the Marketplace Success in the New Economy*, edited by Rudy Ruggles and Dan Holtshouse (Dover, N.H.: Capstone), pp. 1–23, especially pp. 7–11.

27. Noel M. Tichy and Stratford Sherman (1993) *Control Your Destiny or Someone Else Will: Lessons in Mastering Change—from the Principles Jack Welch Is Using to Revolutionize GE* (New York: HarperBusiness), pp. 237–259.

28. Charles Handy (1990) *The Age of Unreason* (Boston: Harvard Business School Press), p. 4.

29. William Fulmer (2000) *Shaping the Adaptive Organization: Landscapes, Learning and Leadership in Volatile Times* (N.Y.: AMACOM), p. 78.

30. Evans and Wurster, op. cit., especially pp. 39–67.

31. Drucker (1999), op. cit., p. 5.

32. Terry Winograd and Fernando Flores (1986) *Understanding Computers and Cognition: A New Foundation for Design* (Norwood, N.J.: Ablex Publishing Corp.), pp. 7–8. We are indebted to these authors for the application of tradition to organizations.

33. Ibid., p. 7.

34. Ibid., pp. 7–8.

35. Ibid., p. 7.

36. Fulmer, op. cit., p. 26.

37. The Price Waterhouse Change Integration Team, op. cit., p. 7.

38. Ibid., p. 14.

39. See Perez Zagorin (1998) *Francis Bacon* (Princeton, N.J.: Princeton University Press), pp. 25–128.

40. Harold Koontz (July–August 1962) "Making Sense of Management Theory," *Harvard Business Review* 40 (4), pp. 24–26, especially p. 24.

41. Reuben R. McDaniel, Jr. (1997) "Strategic Leadership: A View from Quantum and Chaos Theories," *Health Care Management Review* 22 (1), pp. 21–37, especially p. 22.

42. Ibid., p. 23.

43. Peter F. Drucker (1954) *The Practice of Management* (New York: Harper & Row), p. 351.

44. Herbert Simon ([1945]/1976) *Administrative Behavior: A Study of Decision-Making Processes in Administrative Organization,* 3rd ed. (Reprint, New York: Free Press), p. 79.

45. Ibid., p. xxviii.

46. Herbert A. Simon (February 1987) "Making Management Decisions: The

Role of Intuition and Emotion," *The Academy of Management Executive*. Vol. 1, pp. 57–64, especially p. 63.

47. The term "fast history" was attributed to Harvard Business School Dean, Kim B. Clark, by Clayton M. Christensen (1997) op. cit., p. xiv.

48. Ibid. See especially Christensen's "Introduction," pp. ix–xxxiv, for a concise introduction to his work.

49. Hans-Georg Gadamer (1975) *Truth and Method,* ed. and trans. from the 2nd ed. (1965) by Garrett Barden and John Cumming. (New York: Seabury Press).

50. Ibid., pp. 5–10.

51. Toffler (1985) op. cit., p. 89.

52. Ibid., p. 89.

53. Ibid., pp. 88–89.

54. Tichy and Sherman, op. cit., p. 63.

55. Gadamer, op. cit., p. 6.

56. Clayton M. Christenson (Winter 2001) "The Past and Future of Competitive Advantage," *MIT Sloan Management Review* 42 (20), pp. 105–109, especially p. 105.

57. Gadamer, op. cit., pp. 235–240. For further discussion, please see chapter 3, note 39.

58. Amadeo Giorgi (1990) "Phenomenology, Psychological Science and Common Sense," in *Everyday Understanding: Social and Scientific Implications,* edited by Gun R. Semin and Keneth J. Gergen (London: Sage Publications), pp. 64–82, especially p. 76.

59. James W. Begun (December 1994) "Chaos and Complexity: Frontiers of Organization Science," *Journal of Management Inquiry* 3 (4), pp. 329–335; William Bergquist (1993) *The Postmodern Organization: Mastering the Art of Irreversible Change* (San Francisco: Jossey-Bass); James Gleick (1987) *Chaos: Making a New Science* (New York: Viking); L. Douglas Kiel (1994) *Managing Chaos and Complexity in Government: A New Paradigm for Managing Change, Innovation, and Organizational Renewal* (San Francisco: Jossey-Bass); I. Nonaka (Spring 1988) "Creating Organizational Order Out of Chaos: Self-Renewal in Japanese Firms," *California Management Review* 30 (3), pp. 57–73; Reuben R. McDaniel, Jr. (1997) "Strategic Leadership: A View from Quantum and Chaos Theories," *Health Care Management Review* 22 (1), pp. 21–37; Richard Priesmeyer (1992) *Organizations and Chaos: Defining the Methods of Nonlinear Management* (Westport, Conn.: Quorum); Ralph D. Stacey (1992) *Managing the Unknowable: Strategic Boundaries between Order and Chaos in Organizations* (San Francisco: Jossey-Bass); Ralph D. Stacey (1995) "The Science of Complexity: An Alternative Perspective for Strategic Change Processes," *Strategic Management Journal* 16, pp. 477–495; R. A. Thietart and B. Forgues (January–February 1995) "Chaos Theory and Organization," *Organizational Science* 6 (1), pp. 19–31.

60. McDaniel, op. cit., p. 24.

61. McDaniel, op. cit., p. 24.

62. Gleick, op. cit., pp. 20–23.

63. John A. Byrne and Heather Timmons (October 29, 2001) "Tough Times for a New CEO," *Business Week,* p. 70.

64. Christensen (1997), op. cit., p. 160.

65. Ibid., p. 147.

66. Ibid., p. 147.

67. Ibid., p. 160.

68. Ibid., pp. 160–161
69. Tichy and Sherman, op. cit., p. 8.
70. Ibid., p. 19.
71. Ibid., p. 19.
72. Ibid., p. 19.
73. Ibid., p. 21.
74. Ibid., p. 21.
75. Ibid., p. 19.

CHAPTER 3

Theories of Communication in Management: Modern to Postmodern

Clearly things are out of balance. . . . Instead of applying particular techniques or theories across the board and to excess, managers in the best organizations focus on the paradoxes in their markets, organization, and business model. Each is trying to make sense out of organizational and competitive situations that seem plainly illogical or vastly inconsistent with the past and with expectation. Each is trying to come to grips with the inherent contradictions and tensions of their organization. Each is attempting to achieve enduringly superior performance by managing paradox. . . . Increasingly, managers are realizing that there is often a gap between even the most attractive general theory or technique and their specific problems. They identify what seems to be the right formula, input their particular variables—and hope that the output will be a smashingly elegant, effective answer. Unfortunately, management techniques are not universally true mathematical formulae. They can yield answers, but these "answers" may spawn more chaos, complexity, and contradiction.[1]

—The Price Waterhouse Change Integration Team

The conclusion reached by the Price Waterhouse Change Integration Team captures the quandary of managers today who still practice from within the Modern Management Tradition. This team interviewed over 200 senior-level executives in a diverse array of service and manufacturing organizations around the world. Their conclusion captures the tension and paradoxes involved in the realization that managing according to the conventional paradigm or tradition has reached its limitations. This research is emblematic of the search to discover a new way to manage in this new territory that managers find themselves. The old map that guided managers in the familiar territory of the Industrial or Modern Era is obsolete. There is no new map yet for this new territory of the Information or Postmodern Era. In such circumstances of bewilderment and disorientation, one often is forced back upon fundamental principles. This chapter suggests that the fundamental principle of management that heretofore has been unconsciously assumed—but now must take center stage—is communication. Winston S. Churchill is famous for having said: "Courage is rightly esteemed the first of human qualities because . . . it is the quality which guarantees all others."[2] It could be that communication plays the same important role for management.

In a classic 1973 study, McGill University's Henry Mintzberg examined a vital area of management.[3] Rather than look into an abstruse area of management theory, Mintzberg chose a practical, but overlooked question: "Just what *do* managers do every day?" Much had been written about the many facets of management, but no one had asked how managers actually spend their time on the job. The results were, but perhaps should not have been, surprising. There was absolutely no question what managers did on the job. By a wide margin, they talked. Mintzberg's chief finding was that the typical manager spent an astounding 78 percent of each and every day on the job engaged in face-to-face communication. More than any other activity, management involved communication.

It may have been insufficiently recognized that management and communication are intertwined. Face-to-face communication was by far the most predominant management activity in the slower moving, more predictable Industrial Era. Face-to-face communication could be even more important in the higher velocity, less predictable Information Era.[4] Perhaps communication always has been the vital, but overlooked, core of management. Two of Joe Welch's closest observers understood this when, examining his tenure as CEO of GE, they concluded, "Reduced to its essence, his main challenge has been communication."[5]

Just as there was a tradition of management during the Industrial Era, so there was a tradition of discourse. We have been as unaware of these traditions as we have been unaware of managing and speaking. The modern tradition (and practice) of management was greatly impacted by the scientific method. The scientific method defined the Modern Era. As discussed in the previous chapter, the business environment of the Modern Era was relatively slow moving, stable, linear, certain, and predictable. As one acute observer of CEOs found: "Up until the 1980s . . . American companies basked in domestic prosperity, faced no threats from abroad and were under no pressure to change their fundamental business models."[6] Similarly, the relatively structured scientific method was useful in creating and interpreting the Modern Era. However, we are now in a different era that is faster moving as well as more unstructured and unpredictable. The dilemma for managers is how to meet the demands of today's environment. Some managers are beginning to realize that the old tools of yes-teryear do not serve the present needs. It is as if we are using the tools of blacksmiths or automobile mechanics to fix biotech problems.

The task of the manager has changed. The central question may be: "What is the new task of managers in an increasingly random and non-linear environment?" The suggested response is to pay more attention to and transform what managers do most every day—communicate. This chapter delineates important assumptions that undergird the role of com-munication in management during the Modern and Postmodern Eras. The following are assumptions and practices that undergird the role of com-munication in management in both the modern and postmodern tradi-tions. These assumptions and practices will be amplified in the remainder of this chapter.

Modern Tradition	Postmodern Tradition
Learning	Inquiry
Linear language	Systemic and collaborative language
Focus on the physical world	Focus on the social world
The "within"	The "between"
The expert "knower"	The "not-knower"
Managers as problem solvers and decision makers	Managers as collaborators and co-creators of possibilities
One reality, one story	Many stories, many realities

COMMUNICATION IN MANAGEMENT: THE MODERN TRADITION

According to the still-prevailing Modern Management Tradition, there is an established approach with established tenets, modeled after the sci-entific method, for making decisions and solving problems. This approach is congruent with a relatively orderly, unchanging world of tried and proven rules. According to its first tenet, managers get their information to accomplish their tasks from an objective world. A second tenet of the modern tradition is that there is one reality, and that the universal laws of science as well as management explain it. A third tenet of modern management is that the world is relatively stable, predictable, and there-fore linear. One can fruitfully plan, administer, and be a mender of proven organizational processes when they break down. Intelligence and knowl-edge reside within the individual, whose task it is to respect the organi-zational hierarchy and its processes. Similarly, managers "manage" according to the predetermined and unchanging rules or laws of management itself, if not their own organization's "rulebook." Thus, in the Modern Era, managers tended to be denied "self-agency"—the ability to freely be self-determined, and to think and act for themselves based on their own beliefs and viewpoints.[7] The modern view posits that the world exists external to the person, can be observed and known through rational analysis, is rooted in absolute truth, and can be objectively apprehended through objective analysis. In keeping with this perspective, knowledge can be known only by individuals. These unchanging conditions and universal laws paradigmatically dominated every aspect of management in that era. Thus, it is fitting to say that the Modern Management Tradition unconsciously provided the template for managers to manage during the Modern or Industrial Era.

Learning

According to the Industrial Era's modern view, inquiry should be conducted according to the structure of the scientific method. This method relies on an explicit, rational, objective, and impersonal process. The purpose is to derive answers that emanate from "hard data" in order to explain and solve problems created by an unchanging world. Typically, managers view themselves as pragmatic, sensible *doers* who practically limit their inquiry to the quantifiable "hard facts" that their scientific approach to management demands. For example, the performance appraisal process that is so central to the development of human resources embodies the scientific method: "facts" are gathered according to a prescribed method and prioritized according to an objective, a priori standard; and the final evaluation of an employee's qualitative performance is assessed in quantified numbers. This illustration demonstrates the inherent difficulties in applying the "scientific method" to a very human situation in which we attempt to evaluate human endeavor with numbers.[8]

The scientific method itself is reductionistic: it breaks down a whole into parts in order to "scientifically" examine them. It develops and tries to prove one thing—a hypothesis. Derived by reason, it is an explicit process that deals with explicit knowledge and tends to be categorical. One relies on reason, and excludes intuition. Although useful in validating a hypothesis, the use of the scientific process alone can be limiting in terms of knowledge creation. It is these overlooked aspects of the scientific method that continue to unconsciously infuse the theory of management as well as the practice of managers today. Perhaps, in this new era managers can benefit from exploring new approaches beyond the scientific method.

Linear Language

According to the modern view, language represents objects, persons, and events in the objective, physical world "out there"; that is, separate from humans. Language is held to be most effective when it accurately and objectively describes those objects, persons, or events.

Language also may be seen as a linear conduit that impersonally conveys and describes information. It should be detached, empirical, and devoid of human content (i.e., devoid of values, emotions, and so forth). In fact, one's personal emotions (if not hunches) should be minimized, if not eliminated, in the interest of dispassionate objectivity. Such language, according to the scientific method, facilitates the step-by-step deductive method of logical reasoning, and is the linear or digital (i.e., precise and explicit) language for the "sharing of information about objects."[9]

Similarly, the language of business is clear, specific, factual, terse, and direct. "Let's lay our cards on the table," or "Let's stop beating around the bush and get to the point" are common business expressions. In the modern tradition, language is considered to be a pragmatic tool toward a results-oriented end. Managers, who generally have been white males, do not tend to place a high value on indirection or ambiguity in their speech. Business conversations tend to be impersonal and brief. In making decisions, a general rule would be: "The more factual, the more hard data, the better."[10] In addition, the expression of emotion is frowned on, as are statements of tentativeness or uncertainty.[11]

Focus on the Physical World

The modern view also posits that there is a real, physical world that exists, and that it can best be known through objective analysis. This physical world is relatively unchanging and timeless. The relatively inflexible and objective scientific method is congruent with studying this unchanging and timeless natural world. From the 1940s until the 1970s, the environment in which business operated also was relatively slow moving and stable. According to the prevailing paradigm, the field of management was moving toward establishing a comprehensive science of organization, and it was believed that managers would make much use of scientific knowledge in their activities. As the "Guidelines for Management Practice" in a standard, industrial-era business textbook stated: " 'Seat-of-the-pants' and 'shoot from-the-hip' styles of decision-making simply will not be good enough. Intuition will give way to up-to-date scientific knowledge and problem-centered research. It follows that a manager should make all the use possible of existing scientific knowledge that is relevant to his activities . . . managerial decision-making and scientific decision-making have certain common features which should facilitate transforming scientific knowledge to management practice."[12] Few management theorists or practitioners would make such a statement today. Perhaps this late 1970s perspective marks the height of the modern approach to management—an approach whose influence endures to the present.

The "Within"

The widely held conventional view is that learning, understanding, interpretation, and discovery occur "within" individuals. The potential and capability for discovery lie only within the person alone. The great achievements of science as well as business are popularly perceived to be the work of individuals—for example, Copernicus, Newton, Edison, Einstein, J. P. Morgan, Andrew Carnegie, Henry Ford, and Bill Gates. The individual is the discoverer of knowledge as well as the creator of successful enterprises.

The "Expert Knower"

According to the prevailing modern tradition, it is individual leaders who have visions for their organizations, and their task then becomes to align their followers with these visions. The "expert knower" is supposed to understand where to take the organization, and people are expected to follow.[13] Possession of "expert" knowledge by the "knower" elevates the manager, thereby creating a hierarchy, which is the backbone of command and control organizations. The expert leader's experience with situations that are repetitive enables "backward referencing," and therefore justifies "telling" others (particularly those who "don't know" or "know less") what to do and how to do it. In the event of resistance to the leader's command, the "knower" is justified in persuading or using his/her hierarchical position power to leverage the desired outcome. One persuades others to adopt one's own singular "vision" for the sake of the organization, and has no need of others' "inexpert" or less-expert knowledge of a reality that one already has successfully interpreted and understands on the basis of one's past career experience.

Managers as Problem Solvers and Decision Makers

According to the Modern Management Tradition, the essence of management is decision making and problem solving. As Nobel Prize winner Herbert Simon stated: "What part does decision play in managing? I shall find it convenient to take mild liberties with the English language by using 'decision-making' as though it were synonymous with 'managing.'"[14] Today, many managers may unconsciously see the core of their activities in the same light. This modern approach is implicitly (but in a very real sense) linked to the scientific method of gathering sufficient objective information about a problem that is pathological to the homeostatic internal processes of the organization's system. Thus, the decision maker can expertly intervene to restore the system to its normal, healthy, or desired level of homeostatic efficiency.

British management scholar John Sparrow calls this "management by exception." As he describes it: "Management by exception is a system where managers design systems which are considered to be running adequately until a problem occurs. This exception is then reported to management in *their* terms, that is, using reports which describe the problem in the language of the system which management has developed"[15] [emphasis in original]. Managers are repairers of today's problems that are internal to the organization.

One Reality, One Story

In mathematics, there can be only one correct answer to a problem. Similarly, in the modern tradition that is so steeped in the scientific method, there is only one unchanging reality, and one story about it. It may be the story of the so-called eternal and universal laws of science, the story of the chief executive's vision, or the story—as Peter Drucker put it—that "[t]here is—or there must be—ONE right *organization structure*," or that "[t]here is—or there must be ONE right way to *manage people*"[16] [emphasis in original]. Here, Peter Drucker echoes the fading words of Frederick Winslow Taylor, the founder of "scientific" management, who held that in management (as in science), there was only "one best way"[17] to manage in the Modern Era.

Drucker goes on to state that such assumptions, grounded in another time

have outlived their usefulness. They are close to being caricatures. They are now so far removed from actual reality that they are becoming obstacles to the Theory and even more serious obstacles to the Practice of management. Indeed, reality is fast becoming the very opposite of what these assumptions claim it to be. It is high time therefore to think through these assumptions and to try to formulate the NEW ASSUMPTIONS that now have to inform both the study and the practice of management.[18] [emphasis in original]

Perhaps what Drucker is saying is that it is high time to espouse a new tradition of management, whose assumptions are more congruent with the reality of a new era.

THE EMERGENCE OF THE POSTMODERN MANAGEMENT TRADITION

Instead of pouring knowledge into people's heads, we need to help them grind a new set of glasses, so they can see the world in a new way. That involves challenging the implicit assumptions that have shaped the way people have historically looked at things.
                    —John Seeley Brown, Xerox, Palo Alto Research Center[19]

Toward the end of the 20th century, a new perspective emerged in the Western world that began to challenge the prevailing modern tradition. Intellectually, postmodernism surfaced first in industrialized states— Europe, and then in the United States—in an array of disciplines ranging from architecture, art, literature, philosophy, and others. These disciplines were reactions to the science and industrialization of the Modern Era that were characterized by uniformity, hierarchy, unity, continuity, singularity, order, and purpose. Postmodernism also had economic roots. The indus- trialized economy was a "massified" economy. It was a "mass" economy characterized by "mass" production, "mass" market, and a "mass" me- dia.[20] This late Industrial Era mass economy involved:

- centralization (for instance, of newspaper printing plants or television trans- mission stations);
- everyone reading or seeing the same information (a local newspaper, or one of only three network TV shows) at any given time;
- long runs of the same thing (whether black Model T Fords early in the Industrial Era, or uniformly white kitchen appliances later on);
- standardized, similar products (for one huge, uniform market); and
- a proclivity to bigness, whether in office buildings (the Pentagon), industrial plants (Ford's huge River Rouge plant where coal and iron came in one end and cars went out the other), shopping malls, regional schools, or massive pub- lic housing projects, that were presided over by behemothic, slow-moving, command-and-control organizations—whether corporate or governmental— governed by steep hierarchies and the formal power of one's rank.

In contrast, although it has no single definition, postmodernism is char- acterized by multiplicity, fragmentation, discontinuity, and complexity, if not chaos.[21] The postmodern economy is one of:

- decentralization, with everyone accessing different information sources—radio, network TV, cable TV, and the Internet;
- short runs of customized different things (batch production) for multiple, some- times tiny (niche), markets; and
- a proclivity toward smallness, whether in—schools, distributed office parks, factories—that are served by flatter, faster-moving, less-hierarchic, and more- informal organizations led in different situations by different individuals who are informally recognized as much by the relevant knowledge they possess as by the formal role they occupy.

If we add to the foregoing the impact of a globalized economy, as well as the velocity injected by new communication technologies and the dis- continuities of events, we can apprehend the etchings of the Postmodern Era not just for architects or literary critics, but for managers and execu- tives everywhere.

The stable, linear, modern world of the mature Industrial Era—which could be perceived through the single lens of science and understood by an individual observer—drew to an end with the close of the 20th century. In its place emerged the unstable, nonlinear world of the new Information Era—which could not be seen through a single lens or understood by a single observer.[22] Postmodernism means different things in different contexts, but in this particular context it is the attempt to bring together the multiple views of many participants in order to chart a new course for knowledge creation that is congruent with the new era. Practically, the old paradigm may have outlived its usefulness.

THEORETICAL UNDERPINNINGS OF POSTMODERNISM: HERMENEUTICS AND SOCIAL CONSTRUCTIONISM

Postmodernism holds that knowledge is communally or "socially constructed."[23] What this means is that although there undeniably is a physical world "out there" that exists and is separate from human beings, the moment we begin to talk about it, describe it, understand it, analyze it, interpret it—in any way begin to engage in conversation about how we know it—we begin to socially construct that world.

This is not an unfamiliar concept to managers. In the 1990s, Jean Lave and Etienne Wenger popularized what alternately have been called "communities of learning," "situated learning" or "communities of practice." Communities of practice are ancient, self-organizing groups that enable voluntary participants to informally exchange thoughts and ideas about common work issues. They socially generate knowledge on informal face-to-face and even virtual bases. This movement recognized that learning is social; that it "is a process that takes place in a participation network, not in an individual mind"[24]; and that it "is an integral and inseparable aspect of social practice."[25] In such communities of learning, the social process of interaction generates a higher level of learning. Lave and Wenger found that such social learning involves "the whole person"[26] in relation to their work activities, as well as their relationships to other members of the group. Such relationships enable participants to reach not only new and higher levels of work performance, but "to master new understandings."[27] It is now being recognized that learning new tasks and reaching new understandings can best occur in social interactions in which strong and meaningful relationships exist among participants. However, within such groups, multiple perspectives and interpretations of the same experience are likely to exist. To better understand this process, it may be useful to examine the role that hermeneutics and social constructionism play in one's perception of the world.

Hermeneutics

The theoretical underpinnings of postmodern communication theory are rooted in hermeneutics and social constructionism. The origin of the word "hermeneutics" is derived from Hermes, a mythical Greek God. Hermes was responsible for transmitting the Olympian Gods' often-ambiguous messages to man.[28] Because these messages were allusive, their multiple possible meanings required Hermes' interpretation. Hermes exemplified the possibility of dealing with the multiple meanings of the spoken word. Centuries later, hermeneutics became associated with the written word—first theologically, and then literary. During the Reformation, Martin Luther challenged Rome's singular interpretation of the Holy Word with the first of many versions of the Bible and other written Holy Texts. Later, hermeneutics became associated with the interpretation of secular literary texts. Today, we are returning to the original application of hermeneutics, the spoken word. Perhaps a true understanding of the spoken word asks that we not just speak, but that we give room to listen. Perhaps true hermeneutic interpretation asks not just for expression, but also for listening, for a process of back and forth—for creating a situation to speak and hear each other—that lends richness to understanding.

The hermeneutic process has contemporary application to organizations in general and to business in particular. One scholar wrote that in today's knowledge organizations that depend on intellectual capital: "Managers need to work with 'softer' information than in the past."[29] In the workplace, conventional conversations may not be sufficient to provide the kind of insights and information that this era requires. In fact, the demands of the era may be overwhelming managers' abilities to acquire the skills that are requisite to accessing keener insights into each others' perspectives, and bases for action. Rather, "[t]here needs to be a recognition that insights into each other's perceptions are necessary in . . . organizations. . . . There is overwhelming evidence to show that employees in different cultures, industries, organizations and departments come to think differently. There are discernable differences in the basic ways that they view problems/issues."[30] In order to bring new understandings to such perceptions, the hermeneutic process suggests that managers not just speak, but deliberately allocate time for attentive listening and careful reflection. Such a reflective, interactive process is likely to surface the varying interpretations and meanings that individuals can give to the same situation or problem.

Social Constructionism

Social constructionism stresses the importance of language.[31] It begins with the premise that language creates our social world. As 20th-century

German philosopher, Hans-Georg Gadamer put it: "Language is not just one of man's possessions in the world, but on it depends the fact that man has a world at all."[32] This insight sensitizes us to the notion that the only way the world can come to us and we can come to the world is through language. Language is the only way we can know, communicate about, understand, describe, and interpret the world. Language "is the vehicle through which we ascribe meaning, make sense of our lives, give order to our world, and relate our stories."[33]

This philosophical assertion has gained evolutionary credence with the discovery of a "language gene." This gene is responsible for the muscular coordination of the mouth, lungs, tongue, and throat required for speech, as well as for higher cognitive functions. Already existent in rudimentary form, genetic mutations that occurred approximately 50,000 years ago enabled the rapid articulation of speech, a capability that quickly spread through the human population. It was at this time when modern humans also began to engage in new activities such as ornamentation, art, and long-distance trade—which are among the foundations of human civilization. Because the remains of humans that are 100,000 years old are indistinguishable from those of 50,000 years ago, the most likely cause of such new behaviors was "some genetically based cognitive change . . . acquisition of language."[34] It is not just philosophical assertion, hermeneutics, or common sense, but evolutionary evidence that underscores the fact that humans not only possess language, but that the very world they have created depends on it.

Social constructionism recognizes that, for centuries, language was seen as *representing* each of the single realities—whether physical objects (rocks or water), living creatures (birds or humans), or events in the lifeworld—that were believed to constitute the world. However, social constructionism holds that humans socially construct—via conversation or communication with one another—their world through language. Social constructionists accept the world as it is, but they highlight that there may be multiple views, perspectives, and meanings that we can make of that world. Constructionists hold that individuals, through language, author their own truths from their own social or hierarchical position, as well as their own personal experiences. Such an awareness sensitizes us to the centrality and power of language that enables each one of us to perceive and create our own realities.

Social constructionist theory is congruent with the business context. From one perspective, "a corporation looks very successful. Its short-term profits and investments look impressive; morale is great among the executive staff; competitors look weak and disorganized."[35] From another perspective, however, "the corporation looks like a disaster waiting to happen: longer-term financial projections forecast major losses, personnel reports suggest slowly brewing labor problems, marketing analyses predict drops in consumer demand, and the entry of new competitors into the marketplace—along with technological breakthroughs—will change all the rules of the game. Which . . . [perspective] . . . should we believe? They are both correct. However, one report is likely to be sent to the corporate board of directors and stockholders and another to the executive officers of the corporation. Which report, if any, will the union leaders receive?"[36]

As the preceding example illustrates, a social constructionist stance acknowledges and induces an explicit awareness by which to perceive the multiple views or realities that other managers may develop of a problem or situation. Furthermore, the hermeneutic approach constructs the bridge that connects these different perspectives and creates the overlapping junctures that bring them together. Hence, a healthier organization is more likely to develop from a process that is the common creation of all. Hermeneutics and social constructionism open the door for different assumptions that are likely to produce different and more fitting solutions to the specific task at hand.

A postmodern stance enables us to identify the conditions through which a new sensitivity to language and a new kind of conversation can surface, and thereby trigger the collaborative inquiry, conception, and creation of richer forms of new knowledge.

Postmodernism presents a set of very new assumptions, as well as a new approach to knowledge creation in the history of mankind. Hitherto, the prevailing view was that individuals created and were the source of knowledge about an unchanging and certain world. This view was both characteristic of and congruent with management during the slower-moving Industrial Era. Today's tidal waves of technological change and information have overwhelmed the environment and static structure of Industrial Era organizations. The postmodern view is that individuals, through conversation, create and are a richer source of knowledge about a changing and uncertain world. Conversation in groups is more congruent with apt management in the faster-moving Information Era. The postmodern approach is more likely to help managers make sense out of the fluid realities that they face in their everyday tasks of the Information Era.

Postmodernism, hermeneutics, and social constructionism provide a different position from which to interpret and understand the world; they offer new ways to create knowledge. Metaphorically speaking, postmodernism makes the difference between the power of a stand-alone, single computer, and that of a group of networked computers that are parallel processed.

COMMUNICATION IN MANAGEMENT: THE POSTMODERN TRADITION

The postmodern approach to management and communication helps managers make better sense of the rapidly changing realities that confront them daily. Postmodernism's *a priori* concept is that human knowledge of the world is constructed via constantly unfolding conversations. This new approach highlights the importance of organizational theory less and the importance of human conversation more. This section suggests concepts that characterize postmodernism, and that lay the foundation for managerial communication in the Postmodern Era.

The postmodernist pragmatic framework takes familiar, everyday conversations and gives them new meanings. The emphasis here is on a new process of communication in groups. This sort of communication differs from the usual rhetoric of politics in organizations by which speakers try to persuade others to their point of view. Rather, postmodern communication begins with the common, ordinary daily conversations about situations that occur between individuals or among groups in work settings. It suggests the steadily unfolding conditions, practices, and techniques by which such a discourse can create new perspectives with new possibilities. We suggest that through all of time, communication has played a crucial, but underrecognized, role in joint human action in organizations. We also suggest that conversation today plays an especially critical role as the wellspring for the creation of knowledge. The intent is to make the heretofore-implicit awareness of conversation explicit. The intent also is to make these heretofore-random occurrences part of our continuous communication process. There follow the central precepts of communication in Postmodern Management.

Inquiry

If, in the modern tradition, managers inquired into quantitative "hard facts"; in the postmodern tradition, they inquire into qualitative "soft data." In the Industrial Era, their inquiry was into knowledge that was explicit, objective, and impersonal. However, in the Information Era, manager's inquiry may best be into knowledge that is implicit, subjective, and—as philosopher of science Michael Polanyi terms it—"personal."[37] In the past, the purpose of inquiry was to learn answers and solve problems that emanated from the hard facts of an unchanging reality. In this 21st century, the purpose of inquiry may be to surface yet-to-be known possibilities from each individual's intuition or tacit knowledge. Managers were pragmatic *doers* in one tradition and are *explorers* of a turbulent environment in the other. Postmodernism proposes that knowledge of a changing, unfinished world is collaboratively or "socially constructed" in conversation by humans.

As stated earlier, it is imperative to keep in mind that there exists a physical world "out there" that is objective and separate from humans. However, when we share our individual perceptions of the world, we begin to socially construct it. Moreover, *how* we converse about the world or our interpretation of it can literally create or construct different realities.

This is a very new assumption, a very new approach to knowledge creation—but then, this is a very new era.

Postmodernism holds that a new and different process of inquiry and knowledge creation may be more appropriate to this era of unfolding possibilities. This complementary process of inquiry is more flexible and fluid, and thereby more actively liberates the imagination. It also embodies more of the subjective emotion, as well as personal experience, that are inherent in human knowledge. In addition, rather than seeking universal, timeless "laws," this type of inquiry tends to generate specific "local knowledge" about "this situation," in "this place," at "this time."

According to the postmodernist approach, as soon as we begin to describe, discuss, explain, interpret, or forecast that physical world through communication with one another, we begin to not only create knowledge, but also to construct social realities, which, if we act on them, can create not just new knowledge but new realities.

Systemic and Collaborative Language

One of the difficulties that managers face in this Postmodern era is that they deal with a complex and turbulent environment using language that is incommensurate, for it is rooted in a linear, cause-and-effect perspective. Today's environment is one of increasing complexity, yet the perspective and language used to deal with it is, in large part, linear and therefore ineffective. From a systemic perspective, events are perceived to be in mutual interaction and influence. Hence, language is concerned with the way in which these different elements interact with one another. With this approach, a new epistemology, a novel way of thinking, emerges. This new epistemology is concerned with information that is recursive that is to say circular, rather than linear.

From a systemic perspective, each and every member of a system has equal power and responsibility for the operation of that system; each individual or element is a participant in creating that unique reality. According to Gregory Bateson, one of the major figures in the development of the systemic perspective: "Any person or agency that influences a complex interactive system thereby becomes a part of that system, and no part can ever control the whole."[38]

To the postmodernist, language generates knowledge. As Gadamer put it, language envelops and embodies all of our "fore-knowledge," and "pre-understanding" of situations.[39] By foreknowledge, he meant all of our personal experience that we bring to a situation; and by pre-understanding, he meant that by virtue of growing up and living in any tradition, humans inescapably acquire prejudices or points of view. The point, for Gadamer, is not to narrow our ability to understand a situation by denying any bias or point of view that we naturally possess, but rather to acknowledge and fuse it with what we hear another say in order to create a context for greater understanding through our own associations. As Gadamer expressed it: "To stand within a tradition does not limit the freedom of knowledge but makes it possible."[40] In urging that we acknowledge and incorporate our "fore-knowledge" and our "pre-understandings" into our communication with others, "Gadamer's emphasis is on insight" (or the hunches) that we humans incontrovertibly bring to and influence how we interpret or "know" something.[41] Thus, the interpretations, understandings, and knowledge we generate in conversation are supremely human, rather than being more objectively machinelike.

In addition, in actual conversation there also are communicative stances, word usages, collaborative language forms, and differing forms of questions that we can utilize. Such practices not only create the conditions for the generation of new knowledge, but help to surface the most important but least accessible knowledge—tacit knowledge.

Focus on the Social World

In the postmodern view, a real world exists, but it is increasingly one of "fast history" that is nonlinear, turbulent, increasingly complex, and even chaotic. As one management scholar put it: "A fundamental insight from chaos theory is that the unfolding world over time is unknowable."[42] This may be even truer in our world after the totally unexpected terrorist attacks on the World Trade Center and the Pentagon on September 11, 2001. On a lesser scale, the fall from grace of Enron, the sixth largest corporation on the planet in 2002, was also totally unforeseen. Equally unexpected was the destruction of 175 billion dollars of shareholder wealth in the WORLDCOM scandal, and any number of other episodic events emanating from terrorist, economic, or ecological causation in the 21st century.[43]

Business people face multiple realities that are unfinished and changing. Confronting such nonlinear, discontinuous realities, the postmodern communication approach of generating knowledge about "this person," in "this situation," in "this place," at "this time" may be more helpful and congruent with making sense and creating possibilities in "this new era." Such an approach may be more useful to managers in the current, unpredictable environment than are past practices. Furthermore, in such impermanent, fluid situations, individual "knowing" may be less valuable than is group or collective "sensing."

The "Between"

Postmodernists see interpretation, understanding, and knowledge as co-created and generated in the "between" of conversation with one another. A postmodernist would point out that Thomas Edison was not a "lone genius," but created a literal "knowledge factory" of researchers working in teams to produce the knowledge that resulted in light bulbs, phonographs, and motion pictures.[44] A fabled entrepreneur of this era, Andrew Carnegie also appreciated and gave public credit to what happens between the "most wonderful organization of young geniuses the world has to show or ever had to show."[45] Carnegie said of them: "Take from me all the ore mines, railroads, manufacturing plants . . . and leave me my organization, and in a few years I promise to duplicate the Carnegie company."[46]

Mapmakers and navigators need multiple points of reference rather than just one point of reference to interpret or make sense of where they are. Similarly, successful executives trying to chart their organizations' courses are better served by many voices vocalizing multiple points of view and multiple perspectives of the changing realities with which they must contend, rather than the monovocal voice of the individual "knower" or executive.

The "Not-Knower"

The postmodern tradition in management encourages the not-knowing stance while in communication with others.[47] This stance involves taking the nonexpert position of not-knowing. In so doing, one creates a nonhierarchical context that makes it possible for others to express themselves more freely. Socrates is acknowledged as the originator of the "not-knowing" stance. He took that stance in an effort to encourage unimpeded dialogue with his students. As one of the great Greek classicists describes it: "To be a Socratic is not to follow any system of philosophic doctrine. It implies first and foremost an attitude of mind, an intellectual humility easily mistaken for arrogance, since the true Socratic is convinced of the ignorance not only of himself but of all mankind."[48] What was a deliberate stance by Socrates may be a requirement for executives today.

The University of Michigan's Karl Weick echoes Socrates when he describes leadership today as the "Legitimation of Doubt." Weick suggests that, in this era of unpredictability and unknowability, it may be wise to acknowledge that the group possesses greater capabilities for sensing the environment than does any individual, because by admitting that one does not know, one invites others to participate: "People who act this way help others make sense of what they are facing. Sensemaking is not about rules and options and decisions. Sensemaking does not presume that there are generic right answers about things like taking risks or following rules. Instead, sensemaking is about how to stay in touch with context."[49]

Other management theorists suggest that today's organizations are in danger of being overrun by complexity. In the slower-paced Modern Era, management was seen as "80 percent action and 20 percent thought."[50] However, today it may be advisable to place "emphasis on getting 80 percent of the idea right first" via proactive communication, new forms of questioning, and reflection by managers.[51]

British management scholar John Sparrow makes an incisive point in suggesting that it is more important than ever for managers in contemporary organizations to secure insight into one another's thinking and perceptions. One wonders if the process of communication in the open and nonhierarchical context created by a not-knowing stance would be conducive to the new and proactive forms of communication that the Postmodern Era requires. To this end, Sparrow suggests a new model of management that he terms "Management by Perception." As he describes it:

Management by perception involves management in building models of situations as they are perceived by different stakeholders. The process of making these different perspectives explicit within organizations leads to an increase in shared understanding. Organizations then have more powerful predictive models of people (including employees, customers and competitors) and situations. They can also develop greater mutual insight among participants, and create greater flexibility in workgroups and the organization as a whole. The result of this is genuine continuous improvement in organizational systems. Managers can have effective models of situations as they are experienced by others.[52]

Perhaps Sparrow foreshadows the need to shift from a modern and hierarchical tradition in management to a postmodern, egalitarian, and collaborative tradition. Such thinking taps the resources of every participant of the work group, and brings forth a variety of perspectives that are likely to culminate in a potpourri of new ideas and approaches. The above passage precisely describes an applied group communication innovation, *the reflecting team process*, which will be developed in chapter 9.

Postmodern managers recognize that knowledge and meanings about situations that are co-created are more likely to be richer and thicker. The not-knowing stance draws forth new thoughts and possibilities that otherwise would not be expressed. It is also more likely to create a shared understanding that is the basis for effective joint action for implementation.

Managers as Collaborators and Co-Creators of Possibilities

Postmodern organizations could create a new context that would supplant: (1) crippling negative problems with empowering positive possibilities; (2) command and control direction from the top-down with a more egalitarian, horizontal distribution of sense making and knowledge creation throughout the entire organization—and especially from the margins to the center; (3) an internal focus on running organizations more efficiently with a broad scanning of the fast-changing external realities that threaten its viability if not its business model; and (4) final "certainty" by one superior with the exercise of curiosity by all colleagues.

Many "Stories," Many Realities

To postmodern managers, there are always many stories for any single problem or situation. The focus is to draw out the many perspectives. The key, however, is to do so within a process that also surfaces each situation's unique differences. The outcome is likely to generate many possibilities for that situation's resolution.

Knowledge Is Socially Created

Interpretations and understandings are hermeneutic; that is, they are conditioned by each individual's foreknowledge, pre-understandings, and experiences. In addition, such personal knowledge is continually shaped and reshaped by our individual experiences, interpretations, and understandings of them. In addition, because knowledge is socially or communally created, the crisscrossing of multiple views and perspectives in conversation further creates and re-creates new knowledge, new interpretations, and new understandings. Thus, in its reflexivity, knowledge continually evolves, mushrooms, and broadens.

The world and our reality are changing so quickly that they demand a new process of how to sense and interpret the ways in which we understand the world, and to provide bases for our actions. The Modern Management Tradition may lack the capability to evoke the complexities of these challenges and their continual folding over. Perhaps the Postmodern Management Tradition offers new and valuable alternatives.

CONCLUSION

This is a new era. It is time for a new tradition for managing organizations. Communication remains the *sine qua non* of management, yet how we communicate and manage in this era is, of necessity, fast becoming different. A new Postmodern Management Tradition is emerging that maximizes everyone's contributions. Indeed, the essence of the Information Era itself demands the emergence and confluence of every participant's knowledge. This may be the way for managers to find their way out of today's dilemmas and paradoxes.

This chapter treats the assumptions and practices that undergird the still-prevailing Modern Management Tradition as well as propels the emergence of the still-nascent Postmodern Management Tradition. It also highlights some of the many shifts required to transition into this new era: from learning to inquiry; from the "within" to the "between"; from individual knowing to collective knowing; from the leader as expert knower to the not-knower; and, finally, from managers as problem solvers and decision makers, to collaborators and co-creators of possibilities. The common denominator among each and every one of these shifts is how we communicate. Indeed, in this new era of information, in which communication has become so vital, the realization is growing among managers that the old tools of yesteryear do not serve the tasks of the present. What may be needed today are new tools to create the new maps to traverse the new territories.

NOTES

1. The Price Waterhouse Change Integration Team (1996) *The Paradox Principles: How High-Performance Companies Manage Chaos, Complexity, and Contradiction to Achieve Superior Results* (Chicago: Irwin Professional Publishers), pp. 6–8.

2. Winston S. Churchill (1937) *Great Contemporaries* (New York: G.P. Putnam's Sons), p. 185.

3. Henry Mintzberg (1973) *The Nature of Managerial Work* (New York: Harper & Row), p. 38.

4. See for example, Rosabeth Moss Kanter (2001) *Evolve: Succeeding in the Digital Culture of Tomorrow* (Boston: Harvard Business School Press), p. 274.

5. Noel M. Tichy and Stratford Sherman (1993) *Control Your Own Destiny or Someone Else Will: Lessons in Mastering Change from the Principles Jack Welch Is Using to Revolutionize GE* (New York: HarperBusiness), p. 12.

6. Jeffrey E. Garten (2001) *The Mind of the CEO* (New York: Basic Books), pp. 21–22.

7. "Self-agency" is a term introduced by Harlene Anderson (1997) *Conversation, Language, and Possibilities: A Postmodern Approach to Therapy* (New York: Basic Books), pp. 230–234.

8. John F. Kikoski (Summer 1999) "Effective Communication in the Performance Interview: Face-to-Face Communication for Public Managers in the Culturally Diverse Workplace," *Public Personnel Management* 28 (2), pp. 301–322.

9. Paul Watzlawick, Janet Beavin Bevelas, and Don D. Jackson (1967) *Pragmatics of Human Communication: A Study of Interactional Patterns, Pathologies, and Paradoxes* (New York: W.W. Norton), pp. 60–67, especially p. 63.

10. John F. Kikoski and Catherine K. Kikoski (1999) *Reflexive Communication in the Culturally Diverse Workplace* (Westport, Conn.: Praeger Publishers), pp. 55–108, especially p. 67.

11. Michelle Conlin (July 22, 2002) "She's Gotta Have 'It'." *Business Week*, p. 88.

12. John B. Miner (1978) *The Management Process: Theory, Research, and Practice*, 2nd ed. (New York: Macmillan Publishing Co.), p. 72.

13. Noel M. Tichy and Mary Anne Devanna (1986) *The Transformational Leader: The Key to Global Competitiveness* (New York: John Wiley & Sons), pp. 89–182.

14. Herbert A. Simon (1960) *The New Science of Management Decision* (New York: Harper & Row), p. 1.

15. John Sparrow (1998) *Knowledge in Organizations: Access to Thinking at Work* (London: Sage Publications), p. 12.

16. Peter Drucker (1999) *Management Challenges for the 21st Century* (New York: HarperBusiness), p. 5, see also pp. 9–22.

17. See Robert Kanigel (1997) *The One Best Way: Frederick Winslow Taylor and the Enigma of Efficiency* (New York: Viking).

18. Drucker, op. cit., p. 5.

19. Juanita Brown and David Isaacs (December 1996/January 1997) "Conversation as a Core Business Process," in *The Systems Thinker* newsletter (Cambridge, Mass.: Pegasus Communications), 7 (10), pp. 1–6, especially p. 1.

20. Paul Hawken (1983) *The Next Economy* (New York: Holt, Rinehart and Winston). See also Peter Drucker (1993) *Post-Capitalist Society* (New York: HarperBusiness), especially "Introduction: The Transformation," pp. 1–16, and chapter 1, "From Capitalism to Knowledge Society," pp. 19–47; William Knoke (1996) *Bold New World: The Essential Roadmap to the Twenty-First Century* (New York: Kodansha International); and any work by futurists Alvin and Heidi Toffler. For their briefest (and possibly best) treatment, see (1995) *Creating a New Civilization: The Politics of the Third Wave* (Atlanta: Turner Publishing Co.).

21. Ralph D. Stacey (1992), *Managing the Unknowable: Strategic Boundaries between Order and Chaos in Organizations* (San Francisco: Jossey-Bass); William Bergquist (1993) *The Postmodern Organization: Mastering the Art of Irreversible Change* (San Francisco: Jossey-Bass); A. Fuat Firat and Alladi Venkatesh (1993) "Postmodernity: The Age of Marketing," *International Journal of Research in Marketing* 10 (3), pp. 227–249; and R.A. Thietart and B. Forgues (1995) "Chaos Theory and Organization," *Organization Science* 6 (1), pp. 19–31.

22. Peter Drucker (1968) *The Age of Discontinuity: Guidelines to Our Changing Society* (New York: Harper & Row) and Peter Drucker (1993) *Post-Capitalist Society* (New York: HarperBusiness). See also Charles Handy (1990) *The Age of Unreason* (Boston: Harvard Business School Press) and Charles Handy (1995) *Beyond Certainty: The Changing World of Organizations* (Boston: Harvard Business School Press).

23. Peter L. Berger and Thomas Luckman (1966) *The Social Construction of Reality: A Treatise in the Sociology of Knowledge* (New York: Anchor Books/Doubleday); Kenneth J. Gergen (March 1985) "The Social Constructionist Movement in Modern Psychology," *American Psychologist* 40 (3), pp. 266–275; Kenneth J. Gergen (1994) *Realities and Relationships: Soundings in Social Construction* (Cambridge, Mass.: Harvard University Press); Lynn Hoffman (March 1990) "Constructing Realities: An Art of Lenses," *Family Process* 29 (1), pp. 1–12; Wendy Leeds-Hurwitz, ed. (1995) *Social Approaches to Communication* (New York: Guilford Press), especially the chapter by W. Barnett Pearce "A Sailing Guide for Social Constructionists," pp. 88–113; and John Shotter (1989) "Social Accountability and the Social Construction of 'You'," in *Texts of Identity,* edited by John Shotter and Kenneth J. Gergen (London: Sage Publications), pp. 133–151.

24. William F. Hanks "Foreword" in Jean Lave and Etienne Wenger (1991) *Situated Learning: Legitimate Peripheral Participation* (New York: Cambridge University Press), p. 15.

25. Jean Lave and Etienne Wenger (1991) *Situated Learning: Legitimate Peripheral Participation* (New York: Cambridge University Press), p. 31.

26. Ibid., p. 53.

27. Ibid., p. 53. See also William F. Hanks's "Foreword," p. 15. For more recent treatments, see Etienne C. Wenger and William M. Snyder (January–February 2000) "Communities of Practice: The Organizational Frontier," *Harvard Business Review* 78 (1), pp. 139–145, as well as Silvia Gherardi, Davide Nicolini, and Francesca Odella (1998) "Toward a Social Understanding of How People Learn in Organizations," *Management Learning* 29 (3), pp. 273–297.

28. See Paul Ricoeur (1981) *Hermeneutics and the Human Sciences: Essays on Language, Action and Interpretation*, edited, trans., and with an introduction by John B. Thompson (New York: Cambridge University Press) and Bruce R. Wachterhauser, ed. (1986) "Introduction: History and Language in Understanding," in *Hermeneutics and Modern Philosophy*, edited by Bruce R. Wachterhauser (Albany: State University of New York Press), pp. 5–61.

29. Sparrow, op. cit., p. 1.

30. Sparrow, op. cit., pp. 1–4.

31. Gergen (March 1985) op. cit., pp. 266–275; *Gergen (1994) op. cit.; Anderson, op. cit.*

32. Hans-Georg Gadamer (1975) *Truth and Method*, ed. and trans. from the 2nd ed. by Garrett Barden and John Cumming (New York: Seabury Press), p. 401.

33. Anderson (1997) op. cit., p. 204.

34. Nicholas Wade (August 15, 2002) "Language Gene Is Traced to Emergence of Humans," *New York Times*, p. A18. See also John Whitfield (October 4, 2001) "Language Gene Found," *Nature*, pp. 1–3 [science update]. Available at: http://www.nature.com.

35. Bergquist, op. cit., p. 59.

36. Ibid., p. 59.

37. Michael Polanyi (1962) *Personal Knowledge: Towards a Post-Critical Philosophy* (Chicago: University of Chicago Press).

38. Gregory Bateson (1970). "An Open Letter to Anatole Rapapport," *ETC: A Review of General Semantics* XXVII (3), pp. 359–363, especially p. 362.

39. Gadamer, op. cit., pp. 235–240, building on the work of Martin Heidegger's *Being and Time*, explores the "way in which integration through understanding is achieved" (p. 236). Gadamer holds that what he terms our "fore-structures," "fore-conceptions," or "fore-meanings," strongly influence what may be termed our fore-knowledge of a situation. "Pre-understanding" is a term drawn from Terry Winograd and Fernando Flores (1986) *Understanding Computers and Cognition: A New Foundation for Design* (Norwood, N.J.: Ablex Publishing Corp.), p. 7. Winograd and Flores were strongly influenced by Heidegger and Godamer.

40. Gadamer, op. cit., p. 324.

41. John Angus Campbell (1978) "Hans-Georg Gadamer's Truth and Method," *Quarterly Journal of Speech* 64, pp. 101–110, especially p. 108.

42. Reuben R. McDaniel, Jr. (1997) "Strategic Leadership: A View from Quantum and Chaos Theories," *Health Care Management Review* 22 (1), pp. 21–37, especially p. 25.

43. "Global 500: The World's Largest Corporations," *Fortune* (July 22, 2002), p. F-1; see also "Speedmeter," *Fast Company* (September 2002), p. 144. Please note

that according to "Speedmeter," the Enron scandal destroyed 60 billion dollars of shareholder wealth.

44. See Paul Israel (1998) *Edison: A Life of Invention* (New York: John Wiley & Sons), pp. 119–207.

45. Burton J. Hendrick (1932) *The Life of Andrew Carnegie,* vol. II (Garden City, N.Y.: Doubleday, Doran & Company), p. 5.

46. Ibid., p. 5.

47. Harlene Anderson and Harold Goolishian (1992) "The Client Is the Expert: A Not-Knowing Approach to Therapy," in *Therapy as Social Construction,* edited by Sheila McNamee and Kenneth J. Gergen (London: Sage Publications), pp. 25–39.

48. W.K.C. Guthrie (1969) *A History of Greek Philosophy: Volume III, the Fifth-Century Enlightenment* (Cambridge: Cambridge University Press), p. 449.

49. Karl Weick (2001) "Leadership as the Legitimation of Doubt," in *The Future of Leadership,* edited by Warren Bennis, Gretchen M. Spreitzer, and Thomas G. Cummings (San Francisco: Jossey-Bass), pp. 91–102, especially p. 94.

50. Sparrow, op. cit., p. 9.

51. Sparrow, op. cit., p. 9, citing a study by Helga Drummond (1992) "Another Fine Mess: Time for Quality in Decision-Making," *Journal of General Management* 18 (1), pp. 1–14, especially p. 4.

52. Sparrow, op. cit., p. 12.

CHAPTER 4

Tacit Knowledge

The thinking of a genius does not proceed logically. It leaps with great ellipses. It pulls knowledge from God knows where.

—Dorothy Thompson[1]

The supreme task of the physicist is to arrive at those universal elementary laws from which the cosmos can be built up by pure deduction. There is no logical path to those laws; only intuition.

—Albert Einstein[2]

In this new era, many managers need to reframe how they look at knowledge. This task is more pressing today, as a new, disruptive environment—social and political as well as economic and ecological—calls on us to bring forth a different sort of knowledge. The organizations that succeed in the 21st century will be those that best access and generate this critical resource. By knowledge, however, we do not mean what is conventionally called knowledge—explicit knowledge. This new knowledge—concurrent with the process by which we acquire it—is unique. The organization that thrives in the hypercompetition of the Informational Era will require this different kind of knowledge—tacit knowledge.

This chapter explores the nature and domains of explicit knowledge as well as tacit knowledge. Our primary focus is tacit knowledge, because it provides such a decided advantage for any organization that is able to tap its powers according to a systematic process. Organizations and their workers may be rich in tacit knowledge, but they may not yet possess a sufficient understanding of the nature—or even an awareness of the existence—of this knowledge, nor may they have yet discovered a process by which to consistently articulate and share it with others. It is the responsibility of each manager, and in the best interest of every organization, to find a way to access each worker's rich store of this new knowledge—tacit knowledge—that currently is unharvested.

Organizations constantly call on their knowledge workers (those who deal with knowledge in organizations) to creatively think "outside of the box," and generate creative ideas. However, most of those doing the urging do not yet recognize that it is the "known" knowledge that is "inside the box." If we seek to "think outside of the box," perhaps we need to recognize that there are two kinds of knowledge: the first kind is explicit, the second is tacit. This chapter begins by exploring explicit knowledge; the remainder of the chapter focuses on tacit knowledge, for to consistently surface it or bring it to our explicit consciousness, we first must grasp its nature and dimensions.

EXPLICIT KNOWLEDGE

Explicit knowledge is the most widely known and conventional form of knowledge. It is the type of knowledge with which we are most familiar. It also is the only sort of knowledge we are aware of using. In a word, explicit knowledge is the public and transmittable knowledge we speak, hear, read, and write. Explicit knowledge is the only kind of knowledge whose existence we recognize. It is the knowledge of which we are conscious, the knowledge that we can verbalize.

Cumulatively, explicit knowledge has had an enormous impact on civilization. Explicit knowledge is the public knowledge that can be communicated and shared. Through its spoken form, human thoughts are spread to others. In its written form, such thoughts can be permanently recorded, and so live beyond mortal life spans. Explicit knowledge has been key to mankind's advance from ancient hunting and gathering societies through the Agricultural and Industrial Eras. Language has been one of the key vehicles for mankind's progress and evolution. It is through language that humans, unique among life forms, have been able to build on the cumulative, recorded achievements of past generations. The complexity of oral expression and the permanence of written language have enabled humanity to reach unimaginable heights.

We are immersed in explicit knowledge. Our daily conversations convey messages of explicit information. At school, the lessons we read, the lectures we hear, the textbooks we study, and the formulae we memorize are replete with explicit knowledge. At work, we deal in the explicit knowledge of conversations, organizational memos, and written procedures, as well as consultants' reports and industry publications. In our leisure time, we deal with the explicit knowledge that is found in books and in the mass media—newspapers, magazines, television, and radio.

Explicit knowledge is the only sort of knowledge that is found on computer screens, hard drives, and on the Internet. Today, the Internet instantly provides anyone, anywhere with access to virtual universes of explicit cyber information. Explicit knowledge bathes our existence, and is the only type of knowledge of which we are conventionally aware. By virtue of its very nature, explicit knowledge is public and known.

Patents are an ideal example of explicit knowledge in a business context. Patents comprise a firm's intellectual capital that enables it to generate profits. However, were it not for the legal protection afforded them, the explicit, public knowledge found in patents would provide absolutely no competitive advantage to the organization that possesses it.

Today's managers are bombarded with information in this era, but few realize that it is all explicit information—information that other competitors possess or to which they can gain access. Although there is an abundance, if not an excess, of explicit knowledge, what may be needed today is a different sort of knowledge—one that is not public, but rather is private and unique to each organization.

Explicit knowledge served managers well in the modern or industrial business environment that was stable, knowable, linear, and predictable. Conscious and rational explicit knowledge was sufficient when managers could "take for granted" the slower pace and more predictable environment of the Modern or Industrial Era, which permitted managers to focus their conscious thoughts and energies inward, on "running" and improving the machinelike internal operations of firms. Explicit knowledge remains necessary if managers are to effectively deal with the known and ongoing conventional problems that continue to characterize every organization's day-to-day operations. Explicit knowledge was also adequate for the "long-range" planning that met the conventional and known needs of firms in the stable business environment of the Industrial Era. However, today's turbulent, nonlinear environment compels managers to pay more attention to evolving conditions and changing competitive landscapes that are external to the firm, and, for that reason, "less knowable" than was yesterday's explicit knowledge. Explicit knowledge alone may no longer be sufficient for the day-to-day internal operations of a firm, or for its guidance through the volatile and sometimes chaotic external environment of the Postmodern Era.[3] Explicit knowledge has long been recognized as important to managers and firms, but today it is of diminishing importance.

Columbia University Business School's Michael Tushman begins his courses by asking students what the following products share in common: cameras, color televisions, microwave ovens, and radial tires. Tushman's answer: each of these products was introduced by a company that dominated its new niche or industry because of its specialized knowledge. However, every company (Kodak, RCA, Raytheon, and Michelin, respectively) lost its dominant position as other firms learned and profited from the public, explicit knowledge that they initially had developed.[4] The lesson: in today's disruptive environment, organizations can no longer rely on explicit knowledge alone to provide a competitive edge.

In such an environment, the source of competitive advantage can no longer be *knowledge that is known*; rather, it must be *knowledge that is not yet known*, because this is the only knowledge that is novel. This new knowledge could be vital for the survival and success of organizations of every type. Thus, knowing how to create a context in which new knowledge can be accessed may make possible undreamed advances in the Information Era.

Americans tend to see achievement in individual terms. In popular myth if not in practice, pathbreakers in science as well as in business have been seen as individuals—Thomas Edison and Jonas Salk, Andrew Carnegie and Bill Gates. Indeed, inquiry no less than achievement is seen as individual. Increasingly, however, scientists have approached the epistemology of science—the way in which scientists come to know the world they deal with—less from an individual perspective and more from a collective perspective. Scientists no less than managers lead and coordinate teams, who collectively work together and inquire to generate new ideas and improve organizational processes, as well as new business models. In research and in business, the collective enterprise of teams is replacing the authoritative or expert individual knower, because what we know of the world, we know via language and communication with one another. Our knowledge of the world—scientific, business, and personal—is not an individual but rather a social achievement.

In this new Postmodern Era that we are in the midst of, we all need to recognize that our knowledge is rooted in socially interactive processes with one another—conversation in groups. Such a position provides the impetus and encourages a new way of knowing—not just individual, but an emergent epistemology of *collective knowing*. Scientists and managers alike who are concerned with discovery might benefit from recognizing the value of collective knowing and inquiry.

Solomon Asch, one of the 20th century's great psychologists, recognized the power that a social and cooperative approach to inquiry can provide. Asch's approach demarcates the divide between the old, modern paradigm and the new, postmodern paradigm. It is the difference between an individual knower who derives meaning (or who seeks to understand and make sense of the world) from his singular, individual experience, and the richness of team or collective knowing. According to the new, postmodern paradigm, the knower is not an isolated individual, but is deeply invested with others in the collective pursuit of knowledge, as well as the sharing of personal perspectives, ideas, and thoughts in the quest to understand the world.[5] Asch pointed out that perceptive individuals are among the first to appreciate the perspectives of others about the world, in order to improve their own understanding of it. He further recognized that the majority of what we know about the world depends on the perceptions of others. Therefore, what an individual "knows" is the outcome of the integration of the beliefs and perspectives of others with one's own. In Asch's work, "rational persons are intelligently using the information about the beliefs of others that is provided in order to improve their own knowledge of the world. It is the human predicament that the overwhelming bulk of our knowledge of the world is dependent upon the reports of others."[6] Such collaborations have the potential to generate new ideas and discoveries that are beyond the capability of any single individual.

More than a half a century ago, Solomon Asch recognized the power of social knowing—appreciating every individual's knowing, as well as respecting the collective enterprise of judgment and understanding.[7] In so doing, Asch gave us a new, collective perspective on knowledge that heretofore had been seen as individual. In so doing, Asch opened a new pathway to access both explicit and tacit knowledge.

In addition to the public knowledge that is commonly known as explicit knowledge, Asch provided an approach to access tacit knowledge. The domain of knowledge embodies two kinds of knowledge: explicit knowledge that is public, and a new knowledge that is private—tacit knowledge.

Explicit Knowledge: *Knowing That;* Tacit Knowledge: *Knowing How*

One way of distinguishing between explicit knowledge and tacit knowledge is to distinguish between *knowing that* and *knowing how,* between theoretical knowledge and embodied knowledge.[8]

Knowing that involves the conscious, regular reference to, and use of, explicit knowledge or rules that are common when an individual is initially learning a physical activity or an intellectual operation. Examples range from a more physical task such as learning to ride a bicycle, to the more intellectual task of a novice MBA's writing of a business proposal for the first time. Riding a bicycle involves much conscious attention to movement, as well as trial-and-error learning. Similarly, mastering the proposal-writing format involves much conscious reference to printed guidelines and their use—in other words, relying on explicit knowledge.

In comparison, *knowing how,* or *tacit knowledge,* is exhibited by experienced professionals who assess situations, make judgments, and take action without explicitly considering the guidelines and principles that are involved. Such professionals possess the "know-how" to function without conscious reference to the explicit theory undergirding their performance. Rather, they execute their skill without conscious deliberation or focused thought.

"Knowing that" may mean an individual has learned "that" Columbus discovered America in 1492, or "that" the appendix is found on the lower left side of a human's abdomen. "Knowing how" may mean that a teacher "knows how" to teach that fact so that a student remembers it, or a surgeon "knows how" to safely remove an inflamed appendix.[9] Thus individuals are said to possess know-how if they can perform a function unconsciously and seamlessly—or tacitly.

TACIT KNOWLEDGE: SOURCE AND CONTEXT

It is possible that each one of us knows more than we can say—that each individual possesses a vast reservoir of personal knowledge—what is yet "unsaid." The "unsaid" includes the entire background of one's experiences, unarticulated assumptions, and unconscious thoughts, as well as the inferences drawn from them. The 20th-century German philosopher Hans-Georg Gadamer termed this domain the "infinity of the unsaid."[10] Another 20th-century German thinker, Hans Lipps, stated that any thought carries with it a "circle of the unexpressed."[11] Both thinkers refer to the personal knowledge that each individual possesses that is unique and, once unlocked, can be a creative contribution to any collective inquiry. What is "unsaid" and "unexpressed" could be the reservoirs of tacit knowledge.

Tacit knowledge is the less familiar, unconventional form of knowledge. It is the knowledge of which we are not conscious, the knowledge that we cannot say. Tacit knowledge is the knowledge of which we are unaware, and unaware of using. This knowledge increasingly is being recognized as important to managers. This personal knowledge—concurrent with the process by which it is brought forth—differs from explicit knowledge. Tacit knowledge is the emergent knowledge that springs from the recesses of the human mind; it is novel and creates the learning curve for others to follow. Tacit knowledge could become the *sine qua non* that provides the competitive advantage for any successful 21st-century endeavor.

Tacit Knowledge: Origin and Meanings

The word "tacit" originates from the past participle *tacitus* of the Latin verb *tacere*, which means "to be silent" or "to pass over in silence." Some synonyms for tacit include implicit, inarticulate, unexpressed, and wordless. Tacit knowledge is the knowledge that we know, but cannot say. It is the kind of knowledge that is "understood," but difficult to verbalize. Tacit knowledge is wordless knowledge. It is the personal, private knowledge that all individuals possess—yet often remains untapped.

The word "tacit" also means intuitive and experiential. Tacit knowledge often involves deep emotional and physical, as well as intellectual, experiences. It is not uncommon to sense one's unconscious, tacit knowledge as physical or bodily "gut feelings" or "hunches" that provide a powerful impetus to actions in a situation, yet be unable to verbalize it.

The terms intuition and tacit knowledge are used somewhat interchangeably in everyday life as well as in this book. However, tacit knowledge differs from intuition. Every human being possesses intuition—a generalized awareness or sense of the situations around them. Thus, we may have an intuition or intuitively sense danger in a dark area of a city street at night. In contrast, tacit knowledge embodies an individual's education, natural talent, experience, and judgment that, for the purposes of this book, is occupationally or professionally focused. Hence, an experienced mechanic may have a tacit sense about what is wrong with a car from the sound of its engine, while another sort of tacit knowledge tells an experienced venture capitalist which of two business plans is superior for investment. Thus, tacit knowledge is unique to each individual.

Tacit Knowledge in the New Era

Tacit knowledge is widely distributed—every individual in every organization possesses it. One of the major tasks of Information Era organizations that seek to be successful is to create the conditions whereby everyone can verbalize their tacit knowledge. The idea is for every employee to maximize their contributions to the pool of ideas that provide a competitive edge for the firm. It is logical to surmise that tacit knowledge or intuition exist in the same sphere of unconscious operation. In fact, the human mind constantly processes information on an ongoing basis without the individual's conscious awareness of it. The "Eureka Moment!" occurs when our conscious mind learns what the subconscious mind already knows. As one researcher put it after reviewing thousands of responses to a management survey: "one of the skills that top managers rely on most frequently is their intuitive ability to make the right decisions."[12] Indeed, a 2002 study found that "fully 45% of corporate executives now rely more on instinct than on facts and figures in running their businesses."[13]

Furthermore, tacit knowledge will become even more important to managers who guide their organizations through the 21st-century environment. Today's business climate is unique. Unlike any other organizational environment, it is one of increasing velocity. Simultaneously, this intense environment is one of technological, economic, political, and social turmoil, if not disruptive change. Companies increasingly find themselves in turbulent and unforeseen "whitewater" environments.[14] Due to rapid advances in technology (the Internet is a prime example), old business models become obsolete and new ones emerge almost overnight. Increasingly, new competitors seemingly spring from nowhere. According to one

Fortune 500 CEO: "Often there is absolutely no way that you could have the time to thoroughly analyze every one of the options or alternatives available to you. . . . So you have to rely on your *business judgment*"[15] [italics added for emphasis]. In this context could judgment be another word for the "sensing" that is inherent in tacit knowledge?

Some managers are uncomfortable about revealing their reliance on tacit knowledge. More than half of the executives in one survey kept their use of tacit knowledge a secret. Women managers, in particular, felt that making public their use of intuition (or tacit knowledge) might undermine their credibility with male colleagues. However, male and female managers alike felt that their inability to explain just how they arrived at their "intuitive" decisions made it difficult to publicly disclose that they used intuition in making decisions. " 'I've even gotten to the point of telling others I'm just a good guesser,' reported one male manager."[16] A successful venture capitalist told us how he downplays his use of tacit knowledge. He tells those who ask where his original ideas come from: "I like to think about things in my spare time, and sometimes ideas just pop into my mind."

The suspicion of tacit knowledge is not new. In 1936, Chester Barnard— one of the earliest and most influential theorists of management— addressed this issue. He wrote of the uneasiness that successful professionals felt about the "bias" and "distrust" for what he called the "non-logical" (or tacit) mental processes. However, Barnard viewed these "non-logical" mental processes as crucial to success in such fields as stock and bond trading, politics, sales, and specifically, "in much of the work of business men or executives."[17] Almost three-quarters of a century ago, Barnard recognized the significance of tacit knowledge.

"Tacit knowledge," "intuition," "sensing," "hunches," "judgment" are increasingly being recognized as important resources by managers and firms seeking to establish preeminent positions in a turbulent environment. For many, tacit knowledge is a new domain about which little is known. For that reason, many managers still are not comfortable with it. However, many are also beginning to realize that tacit knowledge, or intuition, is critical to the key organizational tasks of creating new knowledge, generating new business models, improving business procedures, and successfully "sensing" their way through an increasingly unpredictable environment.

Life in a Tacit World

Without realizing it, we live in a tacit world. We unconsciously depend on tacit knowledge to perform most of the tasks in our daily lives. Our everyday "automatic" or "out-of-consciousness" actions—for example, walking, talking, bicycling, skiing, or working at a computer keyboard—

depend on this knowledge. It is tacit knowledge that makes it possible to walk without conscious thought. A skier, racing down a steep slope at high speed, is explicitly aware of only a few of the movements she is making, and when asked, would be unable to verbalize just how she makes the many, coordinated adjustments and movements that keep her from falling. Moreover, she is unaware of constantly referencing the various laws of gravity or physics by which she maintains balance while avoiding rocks and trees at high velocity down steep slopes. It is via tacit knowledge that we "know how" to walk, talk, bicycle, ski, or use the computer.

Tacit knowledge also is central to fields as disparate as business and science. Executives relate how their intuition led them to: (1) recommend *against* going ahead with a half-billion dollar capital project on the basis of their "feel for the future," despite overwhelming factual evidence to the contrary; (2) *refuse* to pull a new drug off the market, despite late-breaking Food and Drug Administration information about adverse animal reactions; and (3) *further investigate* the background of a seemingly conscientious new employee who did not "seem quite right," only to have deeper background checks reveal a criminal record.[18] In every case, later events proved these executives correct in their intuitive judgments. Albert Einstein acknowledged the importance of a non-fully conscious intelligence in scientific inquiry when he said: "The supreme task of the physicist is to arrive at those universal elementary laws from which the cosmos can be built up by pure deduction. There is no logical path to those laws; only intuition." Einstein acknowledged that discovery in the area of basic research comes not through the explicit intentionality of the scientific method, but the sudden epiphany or awareness of intuition.[19] Tacit knowledge also reverberates in Dorothy Thompson's insight, which opens this chapter: "The thinking of a genius does not proceed logically. It leaps with great ellipses. It pulls knowledge from God knows where."[20]

Expression of Tacit Knowledge as Decisions or Actions

Much of knowledge creation rests on the assumption that tacit knowledge is communicated verbally. However, tacit knowledge also can be communicated nonverbally. Managers frequently express their tacit knowledge in decisions or actions that are not necessarily verbal.

The history of business is replete with stories of success triggered by crucial decisions taken by executives who had no adequate words to explain them. One such decision, which saved Chrysler in the early 1990s, was taken by CEO Bob Lutz, who confessed that "he had no market research to support him, just his *gut instincts*"[21] [italics added for emphasis]. Lutz's decision resulted in the introduction of the Dodge Viper, an outstanding success that provided the momentum for Chrysler's turnaround in the 1990s. And, as some close observers wrote of General Electric's legendary Jack Welch: "When he became CEO, many of his most powerful ideas were little more than gut instincts."[22] Many CEOs attribute their success to their ability to make decisions based on their intuition.

The conventional description of tacit knowledge emphasizes its "wordless" nature. However, tacit knowledge also is something we physically or bodily know "without knowing how or why." Stated another way: "our intuition is telling us *what our body already knows to be true*"[23] [italics added for emphasis]. In 1938, Chester Barnard, a successful manager in his own right, called such operations: "non-logical processes." In his own words: "By 'non-logical processes' I mean those not capable of being expressed in words or as reasoning, *which are only made known by a judgment, decision, or action*"[24] [italics added for emphasis].

The history of successful business organizations substantiates the point that, very often, crucial decisions are made on the basis of intuitive or tacit knowledge. Managers often express their tacit or intuitive knowledge that they physically "feel" or bodily "sense" via their *judgments, decisions,* or *actions.* This explains how managers make the right judgment or decision without being able to explain their rationale.

The question may arise in the reader's mind: "Is tacit knowledge infallible and does the operation of intuition always lead to success?" The short answer is "no." Tacit knowledge is and will be fallible as long as human beings are fallible. More specifically, it has been pointed out that when it comes to intuition: "We naturally give more weight to information that confirms our assumptions . . . while dismissing information that would call them into question."[25] Furthermore, "we're irrationally influenced by the first information we receive on a particular subject . . . [and it] . . . determines and distorts how we process all subsequent data."[26] Finally, "Impatient with ambiguity, the . . . [intuitive] . . . mind naturally seeks closure . . . but an intelligent decision-making process often requires the sustained exploration of many alternatives."[27] However, each of these flaws seems to assume the use of *individual* intuition. The process of reflecting conversation will be discussed later in this book proposes a group process whose very nature erodes the statements made above. In fact, the process of reflecting conversation evokes not individual intuition, but collective intuitions. Furthermore, decisions are becoming more complex in our turbulent environment, and although the output of computer programs to support decision making is becoming more sophisticated: "You can't just run the numbers; you have to incorporate the expertise, judgment, and yes, intuition of seasoned professionals. You have to bring people into the evaluation stage of the decision-making process . . . a person or a group of people, rather than a computer."[28] The collective intuitions generated by a reflecting process could render intuition less fallible.

Tacit Knowledge Is Unique and Individual

Each individual's tacit knowledge is unique, for each one of us experiences, assimilates, and learns information from the environment in a different way and at a different pace. Each experience reflexively triggers different ideas within each one of us. We draw different lessons from the same experience. We develop diverse solutions to the same problem. Everyone sees differing possibilities for the same venture. Personal or tacit knowledge is at the core of the unique perspective that every person possesses. More than ever, organizations are thirsting for new ideas and new possibilities. It is especially important for leaders and managers in any setting to create a context in which tacit knowledge can be expressed and built on. However, only certain contexts trigger the emergence of new perspectives. This process makes it possible for fragments of ideas held by different individuals that appear unrelated to gradually cohere and create new possibilities.

Based on one's personal experience, each individual has an unlimited store of impressions and intuitions about situations that are unconscious. They are fluid but latent. We all have had the experience of such "intuitions" or "senses" unexpectedly springing into our minds. Sharing such impressions in conversation with other individuals activates them. Once activated, these fragments begin to take shape. The outcome of this process creates a gestalt or a structure. This is when a pool of ideas can become a "wellspring" of discoveries.[29]

Until recently, we have been largely unaware of the power that tacit knowledge exercises in a team setting. Tacit knowledge represents a staggering potential for organizations that has yet to be realized. *The crucial responsibility of managers and organizations that wish to succeed in the 21st century is to create the conditions for the expression of each worker's rich store of tacit knowledge that currently lies latent.* To date, our limited efforts have focused on tapping the tacit knowledge of individuals, yet together—in teams—we can be more intelligent, more insightful, and more creative than we can be as individuals.[30] Surfacing each individual's tacit knowledge creates a new milieu in which new ideas can trigger a sustained domino effect among a team of conversants. Such a process opens up new levels of creative vistas and undreamed-of horizons. If accessing tacit knowledge is the most crucial sustainable advantage for organizations in the 21st century, it is important to encourage every individual's expression of ideas, notions, and perspectives. *Shifting this phenomenon from happenstance to process could be the ultimate challenge of the Inquiring Organization in the 21st century.*

This new knowledge is inexhaustible and grows, rather than diminishes, with use. More importantly, this new knowledge is more likely to surface within a context that embodies certain characteristics. We speak here of the tacit knowledge whose enormous power we apprehend, but to date is locked up in the unarguable phrase and premise: "We know more than we can say." The remainder of this chapter is dedicated to exploring the characteristics and dimensions of tacit knowledge, this new kind of knowing.

CHARACTERISTICS OF EXPLICIT AND TACIT KNOWLEDGE

Explicit knowledge and tacit knowledge may seem to represent two ends of the same continuum. However, they are not separate or distinct from one another, but rather are differing domains of our unified, human intelligence, which—at some indistinguishable juncture—shifts from tacit to explicit knowledge and back again.[31] Nevertheless, for explanatory purposes, there follow some characteristics that distinguish explicit knowledge from tacit knowledge.

Explicit (Known)	Tacit (Not yet known)
Public	Private
Conscious/aware	Unconscious/unaware
Logical	Alogical
Certain, sure	Uncertain, tentative
Strong	Fragile
Hard	Soft
Structured	Unstructured
Goal oriented	Indeterminate
Stable	Unstable
Direct	Indirect
Perception	Subception
Rules/methods/facts/proof	Intuition/sensing

GENERAL DIMENSIONS OF TACIT KNOWLEDGE

It may be easier to describe tacit knowledge than to define it. Tacit knowledge is amorphous and paradoxical. Despite its importance, we know very little about it. Given its nature, it may be more fruitful to indirectly (rather than directly) address tacit knowledge, for when we directly focus on tacit knowledge, given its elusive nature, it is likely to escape us.[32] The main dimensions of tacit knowledge follow.

Tacit Knowledge Is Vast and Limitless

Tacit knowledge constitutes a vast and limitless part of our mind.[33] Axiomatically, if we tacitly know more than we can say, then that body of tacit knowledge that *we cannot say* is greater than the explicit knowledge that *we can say.*

A college student's effort to solve a quadratic equation could provide a useful illustration. To accomplish this task, the student draws on all of the mathematical knowledge that he has learned over the years from the time he learned how to count, through the arithmetic and algebra that he was taught in grade school and high school. Solving this quadratic equation requires that he apply all of this acquired knowledge in both a discriminating fashion and in a short time period. In such an instance, the student would be aware of and employ only a fraction of all the mathematical knowledge he possesses to perform this operation. Our lives are full of such instances.

Furthermore, the statement that is so common in the field of management—"Knowledge is the inexhaustible resource of the Information Era"—is not entirely accurate. Perhaps this statement only applies to tacit knowledge. By definition, explicit knowledge is already known, for it can be verbalized and, therefore, is limited knowledge. Only unverbalized knowledge—what is not yet known—is limitless. Only tacit knowledge can be the source of the inexhaustible range of possibilities, anticipations, and potentialities that constitute discovery and creativity. Explicit knowledge, by its nature, is limited; tacit knowledge is vast and limitless.[34] It is tacit knowledge that is the inexhaustible resource of the Information Era.

All Knowledge Is Tacit Knowledge, or Is Rooted in Tacit Knowledge

All knowledge either is tacit knowledge, or is rooted in tacit knowledge; that is, explicit knowledge depends on and is encompassed by tacit knowledge, whereas tacit knowledge "possesses" itself.[35] Scientists have identified implicit or tacit knowledge as a "deep" knowledge whose operations are dependent on cognitive processes of which we are unconscious. In evolution, it predates the development of other mental functionings among species. According to evolutionary theory, explicit knowledge or *consciousness* is a more recent development in humans.[36] Recent research suggests that language in human evolution may be only 50,000 years old.[37] Language is a clear example of explicit knowledge. The following examples from written and oral communication illustrate the heretofore unrecognized, but preponderant, role of tacit knowledge over explicit knowledge.

The process by which we learn to write a foreign language provides us with an example. In learning to write in a foreign language, we consciously engage in a back-and-forth process of checking and making reference to the explicit rules that govern the use of grammar in writing—rules that have to do with capitalization, spelling, conventions of style, and so forth. Later, when we become proficient in writing French, for example, we become unaware of and cannot exactly explain the tacit process by which we automatically and without reference apply these rules to the act of writing.

Oral communication in our native language provides us with another example that all knowledge has its origin in tacit knowledge. Oral communication is explicit knowledge *par excellence*. However, our choice of words—which word follows which and which word is the one that represents our intention—is entirely tacit, automatic, and beyond our capability to describe. The same is true of the performance of speaking: the simultaneous, unconscious, complex coordination of mental as well as physical capabilities is entirely beyond our consciousness while speaking, as well as beyond our ability to explain thereafter.

All knowledge either is tacit knowledge, or is rooted in tacit knowledge. All human understanding is tacit understanding. Explicit knowledge depends on and is enveloped by tacit knowledge, whereas *tacit knowledge possesses itself*.

Tacit Knowledge Runs the Spectrum from the Physical, to the Intellectual, to the Level of Discovery

Scholar Donald Schön recognizes the pervasiveness of tacit knowledge in everyday life. He terms the behaviors that embody tacit knowledge "knowing-in-action," and places these behaviors into two categories: (1) the more "publicly observable, physical performances" like skillfully riding a bicycle or hitting a tennis ball; and (2) the more "private operations"—with more intellectual content—like a physician's instant diagnosis of a patient's illness, or an accountant's deft analysis of a balance sheet. In both instances, according to Schön, the "knowing is *in* the action"[38]; we are able to express what we tacitly know via physical performance or private intellectual operations whose outcomes we can verbalize.

It may be that learning any task or craft follows a similar trajectory. Initially, we make frequent, explicit reference to the rules of performance. As we become more proficient and more professional, knowledge of "what to do next" becomes automatic or "second nature"—that is, tacit. As one scholar of tacit knowledge put it: "virtually all interesting complex human skills are acquired in a characteristic fashion. They begin with the labored, conscious, and overtly controlled . . . processes of the novice that gradually give way to the smooth, unconscious, and covertly controlled . . . processes of the expert."[39]

One might say that tacit knowledge moves across a spectrum—from publicly observable physical action at one end, to private intellectual operations, and to discovery at the other end. As table 4.1 indicates, at any point along the spectrum, the ratio of physical and/or intellectual behaviors rooted in tacit knowledge may vary.

Tacit Knowledge: Physical Performance

Tacit knowledge is first (but not exclusively) physical. It manifests itself in the seamless and out-of-consciousness public performance of physical tasks. Some examples of the physical manifestations of tacit knowledge would include walking, skiing, shooting a basketball, hitting a baseball, or even dancing.

Moving farther across the spectrum, tacit knowledge becomes crucial to behaviors that are partly physical and partly intellectual. Consider how we learn to drive a car. We first consciously read and learn the explicit knowledge that is found in the driver's manual, but then, as we practice, the print of the manual's text is shifted to the back (or to the unconscious part) of our minds, to be transformed into the tacit but complex operations of driving. The very act of driving itself is an out-of-consciousness, "automatic" experience in which we dynamically interact with, make judgments in relation to, and act in accordance with an environment that continually changes as we drive the car.[40]

Could it be that the knowledge that is necessary for the performance of physical behaviors—riding a bicycle or driving a car, for example—must be firmly rooted in tacit knowledge, if the skillful, automatic, high-level, out-of-consciousness performance of that task is to occur? Tacit knowledge appears to integrate the mind–body, conscious–unconscious, rational–arational interface of our physical–intellectual activities.

Table 4.1
The Spectrum of Tacit Knowledge

Physical	Physical/Intellectual	Intellectual	Discovery
Walking, skiing, shooting a basketball, riding a bicycle	Conversing, writing in a foreign language	Analyzing a balance sheet, diagnosing an illness	Surfacing a new thought, insight for a new idea

Tacit Knowledge: Physical Performance Combined with Intellectual Operation

Let us return to an example mentioned earlier—learning to write a second (or foreign) language—an act that increases the ratio of intellectual operations to physical behavior. When we are first learning (and haltingly writing) a foreign language, we consciously learn and continually make reference to the explicit rules that govern the use of grammar in writing— the rules of capitalization, spelling, conventions of style, and so forth. However, as time passes, and the explicit knowledge of the language textbook "sinks" into the back of our minds, we become unaware of and cannot exactly specify the tacit process by which we apply these rules in the act of more proficiently writing that foreign language.[41]

Moving farther along the spectrum, the act of speaking or oral communication in our native language provides another example of a physical performance that is combined with an even higher level of private, intellectual operation. Oral communication is explicit knowledge par excellence—it is knowledge we can say. However, it is conveyed via the "automatic," out-of-consciousness—or tacit—operation of speaking. When we speak, the physical, muscular, and glotular performances of our lungs, lips, tongue, and throat are unconsciously and simultaneously coordinated with our intellectual capabilities that are related to language. Further, as linguist Noam Chomsky points out:

> The system of language is only one of a number of cognitive systems that interact in the most intimate way in the actual use of language. When we speak or interpret what we hear, we bring to bear a vast set of background assumptions about the participants in the discourse, the subject matter under discussion, laws of nature, human institutions, and the like.[42]

The synchronized performance of such complex capabilities is entirely beyond our ability to explain and is without conscious reference to the shared "rules" of communication, as is tacit knowledge.[43]

Tacit Knowledge: Intellectual Operations

Tacit knowledge is a key element in the intellectual operations that go into the skillful performance of our professions. Tacit knowledge, for example, is integral to the unconscious and complex mental operations from which emerge the renderings of an architect, the economist's analysis of economic trends, the marketing executive's identification of a new market niche, and the physician's diagnosis of a patient. How do architects transform their private, aesthetic "senses" into the schematics of a pleasing new building? From whence might the "judgment" emerge that allows economists to intuitively anticipate moves in the economy before the "facts" are in? How do marketing specialists "know" when the timing is "right" to "position" a product for a market niche? How might we explain an experienced physician's "hunch" about the diagnosis of a patient's illness before all of the explicit "facts" of the tests are complete? All of these are demonstrations of the exercise of skillful intellectual or professional judgment that is rooted in tacit knowledge. In every case, the "out-of-awareness" learning that accompanies the years of experience in the practice of a craft surfaces the wordless "senses," "judgments," and "hunches" that so often "feel right."

In summary, there appears to be a progression or a spectrum of tacit knowledge. At one end of the spectrum are the more physical performances (or manifestations) of tacit knowledge—walking, skiing, or riding a bicycle. Next are the still physical but more intellectual manifestations of tacit knowledge—speaking our own native language, or learning to write in a foreign language. Moving across the spectrum are the less physical, but even more intellectual manifestations—the knowing-in-action—that experienced professionals (e.g., architects, economists, accountants, marketing executives, and physicians) "know but cannot say" as they skillfully and with judgment exercise the "know-how" by which they do their jobs unconsciously well. Finally, there is the tacit seat of wonder, creativity, and discovery.

Discovery

Tacit powers predominate in the very making of discoveries
—Michael Polanyi[44]

At the farthest end of the spectrum we posit that there is found the deepest and most profound level of the tacit mind—the limitless, internal universe from whence wonder, creativity, and discovery themselves spontaneously spring. It could be that in the vast reaches of tacit, inner space—like the gases of outer space that gather, circulate, coalesce, and then bring forth stars and planets—is an unstructured, indeterminate, unstable place where matter and forms are coming into being, and where creation surfaces and unfolds. According to quantum theory and chaos theory, planets and stars coalesce and form in outer space according to the same gestalt-like process whereby fragments become ideas in the inner space of tacit knowledge. It is here where meaning is found; where emotions reside; where we, like our creature ancestors, "sense" things at a level that is older and deeper than any language capability that our brain possesses. See figure 4.1 for ascending levels of development and performance of physical and/or intellectual behaviors rooted in tacit knowledge.

Evolutionary Bases of Explicit Knowledge and Tacit Knowledge

In the timeless expanse of evolution, tacit knowledge preceded and is older than explicit knowledge. As evolution unfolded, the operations of

Figure 4.1
The S Curve of Tacit Knowledge

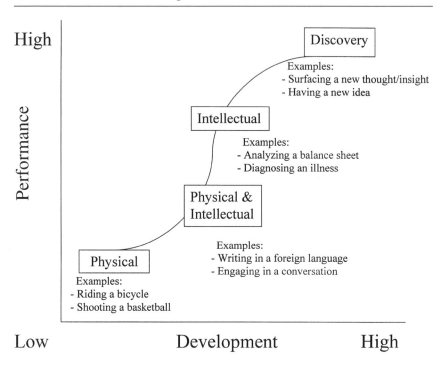

explicit knowledge and tacit knowledge emerged at different times in the human brain. The development of tacit knowledge, and then explicit knowledge, parallels the emergence of a primitive to a complex brain. It also parallels the unfolding of evolution itself.

There is a management application to this dimension of tacit knowledge. Understanding the evolution and physiological basis of tacit knowledge could be of immense importance to decision makers. It is via tacit knowledge that we *subceive* (or implicitly detect) the subtle but powerful covariances (changes or differences) in our environment that could signal danger—whether it be the stripes of a tiger barely visible through a bush, or a subtle change in the outcome of a marketing survey.[45] Such a capability to tacitly sense threatening (or promising) changes in an organization's environment—could be a crucial ability to today's successful decision makers. The contemporary environment for organizations is turbulent and unpredictable. Leaders no longer can "plan" their organizations' path into the future on the basis of "facts," but must "sense" their way on the basis of clues or cues. Thus, the ability to not just perceive, but—even more sensitively—to *subceive* subtle changes in the environment could be a powerful, new tool in this endeavor. Let us first examine the evolution of explicit knowledge.

Evolutionary Basis of Explicit Knowledge

Explicit knowledge differs from tacit knowledge. In terms of evolution, explicit knowledge is a newcomer to the evolutionary scene.[46] Physiologically, the operations of explicit knowledge generally take place in the newest and most developed parts of the human brain—the left and right cerebral hemispheres.[47] These corrugated hemispheres are the largest parts of the human brain. Their functions are most advanced in humans. For most people, the functions of the left hemisphere, especially the frontal cortex, are uniquely human. While specific functions occur throughout many parts of the brain, the left frontal cortex is where the higher-order functions of reasoning and planning are centered. Damage to another area of the left frontal cortex—Broca's Area—interrupts the ability to speak. This may help explain why explicit knowledge is verbal and why it is the knowledge we know and can say. The assumption here is that explicit processes largely occur in the newest and most developed cortical parts of the brain, and thus embody the higher-order capability of symbolic communication, or speech.

Explicit knowledge involves a level of *consciousness*—of our environment, others, and ourselves. Such a consciousness is uniquely human. The functioning occurs in two parts: a conscious cognition (or perception) of our external environment, and a consciousness of our "capacity to play a causal role in the inner workings of oneself."[48] Influential 20th-century French psychologist Jean Piaget called this capacity conscious functioning or "cognizing."[49] Earlier life forms that may be lower in evolutionary development certainly possess varying levels of awareness, but only humans appear to possess this unique, explicit level of "cognizing" or consciousness.

This explicit human consciousness is characterized by intentionality. We "perceive"; that is to say, we consciously and intentionally cognize aspects of our environment. As a Zen insight put it: "As for the outer world, you will be confronted by what you see. And what you see is primarily what you look for." When we perceive, *we engage the environment by intention.*[50] In comparison to tacit knowledge, those operations of explicit knowledge of which we are in conscious control tend to be cumbersome and labored. It is to this uniquely human level of consciousness to which we pay the most attention in education and organizations. The developments that flowed from explicit knowledge have carried mankind to undreamed-of levels. However, to think creatively, perhaps we need to transcend our explicit knowledge.

Evolutionary Basis of Tacit Knowledge

This section highlights three points about tacit knowledge: (1) it is evolutionarily older than explicit knowledge; (2) for that reason it may be the "knowledge we know, but cannot say"; and (3) there are at least two types of tacit knowledge—"fast" tacit knowledge and "slow" tacit knowledge. It is posited here as well that the operations that result in tacit knowledge have their origins in evolution.

The seat of tacit knowledge is older than that of explicit knowledge. Evolutionarily, it predates explicit knowledge.[51] The more physical varieties of tacit knowledge—or implicit cognitions that trigger reflexes—are older than the more intellectual forms of explicit knowledge. Tacit knowledge involves a generalized, "out-of-consciousness" awareness of the world around us (as well as of our inner intellectual workings) of which we are unaware. Humans share such physically tacit awareness with more primitive creatures. The processes of tacit knowledge generally seem to be located in the more primitive part of the brain that humans share with other creatures. Although much remains to be definitively established about the brain's operations, some scholars suspect that tacit learning goes on in the deeper circuitry of the brain—the basal ganglia and amygdala that are found near the tip of the spinal cord. This might explain why tacit knowledge is preverbal or unverbalizable.[52] The tacit processes occur at a neurological level that predates the capability to speak, as the discovery of a "language gene" only 50,000 years old seems to support.

Humans share reflexes (that depend on implicit cognition) with evolutionarily earlier life forms. Snakes and mice—whose brains are evolutionarily more primitive—possess "sensing" capabilities according to which they spontaneously react to changes in the environment around them. Although seemingly at rest, they reflexively dart away from a falling net or a pouncing cat.

Proceeding up the evolutionary scale to human beings, the following excerpt of a mountain climber in a dangerous situation relates how spontaneous and automatic "fast" tacit knowledge or intuition saved his life:

Having climbed down on a rope he found himself hanging in the air and several metres to the left of the chimney, with no more rope for a further descent which would have landed him on a ledge by which he hoped to reach the chimney. He determined to reach the opening by swinging on the rope. In doing this, the rope slipped from his feet, and his hands were not able to support his weight. . . . The next moment he realized that he had taken hold of the rope with his teeth. . . . In the next moment his feet waving in the air had caught hold of a projecting slab . . . this action, not belonging to the technique of mountain climbing, never previously considered, and, of course, never previously practiced, the only one which could save . . . [him] . . . arose spontaneously without any conscious deliberation.[53]

Humans share with other life forms this evolutionarily older and more physical "fast" tacit knowledge, which operates according to implicit cognition and quick reflexes.[54] Such "fast" tacit knowledge involves implicit cognition of often-subtle changes in the external world or environment, rather than any internal intentionality. "Fast" tacit knowledge triggers automatic, rapid, reflexive physical action that helps to ensure the survival of the individual creature as well as the species. Thus, humans and life forms that are lower on the evolutionary scale commonly possess an awareness of the world around them and of their own inner brain processing that are unintentional and of which they are unaware.

Humans retain this evolutionarily older and more physical "fast" tacit knowledge. However, they also possess a "slow" tacit knowledge capability. For example, "slow" tacit knowledge comes into use as managers examine and then mull over a balance sheet, concerned with an anomaly that they "know," but cannot say. Then, after a period of time, a solution suddenly "pops" from some unknown depth within them to their more surface consciousness, and they "know" (and can verbalize) what they heretofore could only "feel" was the problem. The differing natures of these two forms of tacit knowledge—"fast" and "slow"—are reflected in the practices of "snap judgments," as well as that of "taking the time to carefully think things over." Successful executives long have reported that they give themselves the opportunity to "think things over" before making important decisions; that is, they allow their "slow" tacit processes the opportunity to operate.[55]

Managers and firms might begin to trust and explore the potentialities of both "fast" and more physical tacit knowledge, as well as the "slower" more intellectual tacit knowledge. Perhaps we, like our most ancient ancestors, need to value the embodied, unverbalizable way of knowing by which we, like our primeval ancestors, can "sense" changes in an increasingly turbulent and chaotic environment before we can "say" them. Perhaps managers and firms also need to find a way to explore the "slower" form of tacit knowledge, in which they give longer consideration to problems and discoveries that lead to the epiphanies that create knowledge.

Finally, let us examine an expression—"gut feeling"—with which everyone is familiar because it describes an intuitive experience that most of us have had. A gut feeling occurs in the intestinal or stomach area that is triggered by a strong sense about a situation for which we have no explicit reasons or words. Daniel Goleman and his colleagues, in researching the neurobiological aspects of organizational leadership, addressed this topic:

Every day that a leader spends in a given business or career, his brain automatically extracts the decision rules that underlie one turn of events or another. . . . Whenever we face a moment in which these decision rules pertain, the brain applies them silently, coming to its wisest conclusion. Accordingly, the brain won't inform us of these judgments with words; instead, the emotional brain activates circuitry that runs from the limbic centers into the gut, giving us the compelling sense that *this feels right*. The amygdala, then, lets us know its conclusions primarily through circuitry extending into the gastrointestinal tract, that literally, creates a gut feeling.[56] [italics in original]

Tacit knowledge does not embody the sophisticated human level of consciousness, but rather involves a *generalized awareness* of our environment, of others, and of ourselves. Of the varied types of awareness that exist, tacit awareness is one that humans share with other, older, and more primitive life forms. Tacit knowledge is unique and possesses its own domain.

The Automaticity of Tacit Knowledge

Tacit knowledge is characterized by *automaticity*. The tacit level of the mind integrates impressions and processes information with an instantaneity and at a velocity that far exceeds that of explicit knowledge.[57] Tacit learning also is automatic. Information that we learn or acquire from the external environment tends to be rapidly and unconsciously registered.

The automaticity of the tacit mind echoed in the experience of Chester Barnard. He asked how some accountants and executives could merely look at complex financial statements, and, within seconds, see both problems and possibilities that "do not leap from the paper and strike the eye."[58] He asked how these executives could so rapidly make "out of a set of figures something to which then reason [could] usefully be applied."[59] Barnard again found his answer in what he termed the "nonlogical processes" that mysteriously operate in those "many circumstances . . . [in which] . . . mental efforts must be accomplished with such rapidity that the word 'thinking' does not apply."[60]

It is here, at the tacit level of the mind, where certain relevant elements of the external environment are first and unconsciously apprehended. It is here where the "fragments" of a problem or its solution first appear—become more and more distinct, and then draw closer and closer to form a gestalt, or begin to "make sense." Then, in a flash, they coalesce and suddenly surface to our awareness. It is at such moments that we are compelled to say "Aha!" or "Eureka!" It is at the tacit level of knowledge where the effortless integration of explicit knowledge, physical experience, and intellectual operations occur.[61] There is instantaneousness or automaticity to tacit knowledge.

Tacit Subception

Michael Polanyi associated the phenomenon of *perception* with explicit knowledge, but the phenomenon of *subception* with tacit knowledge.[62] Perception, Polanyi wrote, tends to involve more of a conscious act of intentionality. However, subception is more a process of *unconscious inference* of information from our external environment. It entails the ability to discriminate a complex pattern without being able to specify the clues by which we have done so. This generalized awareness appears to be unintentional, and is unlike perception, which is conscious and purposeful in its focus. We subceive—that is, we implicitly cognize—aspects of our environment. When we subceive, we unconsciously, indirectly, and inferentially *engage the environment not by intention, but rather by events.*[63]

How can the operation of subception help managers? How is it that Barnard's accountants and executives (mentioned earlier) can somehow "pick up on" information that does not "leap from the paper and strike the eye?" We suggest that the answer lies in differences. One answer is that we, like other life forms, *inferentially subceive covariances*—relevant differences, discrepancies, or changes in the environment—at the indirect, generalized, or tacit level of awareness.

Initially, such discrepancies or changes often are too subtle for explicit recognition and response. In fact, unconscious subception occurs at the tacit level of the brain's operations. To illustrate, in sudden, unpredicted situations of danger, subception makes possible the survival of the organism. As stated earlier, consider the spontaneous darting away of a resting snake or mouse from a sudden covariance or difference in their environment—the falling net of a herpetologist, or the rapid shadow of a pouncing cat in midflight. Their tacit subception was automatic and swift, and thus, they survived.

Similarly, at the human level, Ralph S. Larsen, chairman and CEO of Johnson & Johnson, relates how he approaches key management decisions:

[By the time] someone presents an acquisition proposal to me, the numbers always look terrific: the hurdle rates have been met; the return on investment is wonderful; the growth rate is just terrific. And I get all the reasons why this would be a good acquisition. But it's at that point—when I have a tremendous amount of quantitative information that's already been analyzed by very smart people—that I earn what I get paid. Because I will look at that information and I will know, intuitively, whether it's a good or bad deal.[64]

Subception may be even more critical to contemporary leaders who are caught in the turbulence of our era's unpredictable, disruptive "fast history." Such leaders (and their organizations) might be advantaged if they better understood and trusted the subception by which they inferred covariances or subtle differences in their firm's environments before others. They might be even more advantaged if they had at their disposal a process for better surfacing and verbalizing such subceptions to their colleagues in their organizations for collective action.

It is not surprising for CEOs who read this account to ask the question: "How can we duplicate the 'Ralph Larsens' in our organizations in order to maintain a competitive advantage?" This is the overriding objective in seeking to understand the dimensions of tacit knowledge—to develop the context whereby the Larsens in every organization can rise to the occasion by expressing their intuitions.

Tacit Knowledge Is Free, Nonintentional, Nonlinear, and Nonvolitional

No rules can account for the way a good idea is found for starting an inquiry.
—Michael Polanyi[65]

Because it is free and subject to no rules, tacit knowledge cannot be "managed," directed, or even attended to directly. Tacit knowledge also is nonintentional, nonlinear, and nonvolitional, and thus is best attended to indirectly. When it is attended to indirectly, the chances are increased that the "fragments" of a covariant in the environment, a troubling problem, or an incipient solution—unverbalized, and without intentional direction or consciousness—will progress from "fragment" to "form," and then suddenly enter our consciousness. This process is more likely to occur in an accepting and supportive environment; one cannot "make" an idea or emotion occur. If love is tacit, 19th-century French author George Sand was insightful when she wrote, "No human creature can command another to love"—Similarly, no human can command another to create knowledge.[66]

One cannot coerce, "produce," or oxymoronically "manage" tacit knowledge. It is quintessentially free, and is averse to rules, methods, or procedures, and thus is not subject to rational dominion. This dimension provides one reason why the scientific method is coming to be recognized as having limitations. Since the days of Francis Bacon, the scientific approach to inquiry has been the source of much improvement in humanity's condition. The unique power of the scientific method should continue to be utilized and valued in certain types of inquiry. However, the scientific method's explicit rules and explicit process—that produce and are congruent with explicit knowledge—are inimical to the "freeness" by which tacit knowledge coalesces and surfaces. In addition, the scientific method does not explain where the "good ideas" come from. Perhaps the nonlinear nature of the tacit level of our mind is most congruent with the nonlinear nature of the world and environment in which we find ourselves. It may be that the "sensing" dimension of tacit knowledge can help managers anticipate and make meaning of the current semichaotic environment. Such indirection, freedom, or nonintentionality is more congruent with, opens up, and enables our tacit powers to operate more fully.

Tacit Knowledge Is Fragile, Indirect, and Unconscious

A new idea is delicate. It can be killed by a sneer or a yawn; it can be stabbed to death by a quip and worried to death by a frown on the right man's brow.
—Charles M. Brower[67]

Tacit knowledge is fragile. As it is first coalescing in our minds, as we begin to find the words for it, we are tentative and often still unsure of what we ourselves are saying. Tacit knowledge is unlike explicit knowledge. Explicit knowledge is strong, sturdy, and the *lingua franca* of the agonistic, conflictual, "hand-to-hand combat" of the verbal interchanges called debate. There may be outcomes from the conflict that frequently characterizes business meetings, but the surfacing of tacit knowledge is not usually one of them. Tacit knowledge tends to be indirect, nonintentional, and unconscious. We all have had our moments, when things seem to effortlessly "come together," usually when we are not consciously or intentionally concentrating on the situation or problem that suddenly has been resolved. Usually, we are thinking about another matter, or are physically engaged in a task. Often, we have placed our mind "in neutral"— for example, as we are driving a car or gardening—when the idea or insight or integration "pops" into our consciousness.

Tacit knowledge tends to operate only when the limelight is not focused on it. In other words, it is more easily accessible and expressed in an environment in which not much is asked of it, and it is entirely free of constraints and tension. It roams freely in our minds. Tacit knowledge is like the shy child who, when attention is focused on her, has a problem reciting the nursery rhyme that she flowingly sang just a few minutes earlier alone in her room to her dolls. Sometimes the line between a child and an adult can be very thin. Advertising executive Charles Brower's insight is relevant, particularly in the organizational context. Expressing ideas can be unleashed or suppressed by the seemingly slightest of nonverbal responses. It may behoove us to attend with care and respect when new ideas are springing forth.

TACIT KNOWLEDGE, CHAOS THEORY, AND QUANTUM THEORY

There may be a congruence between the operations of the tacit mind and the dynamics of chaos and quantum theories that so much describe the contemporary environment of organizations.

According to these theories, the world we live in is fundamentally unknowable and unpredictable. Regardless of how much we understand and know about the state of the present environment, it is not possible to predict the future behavior of a system. Tacit knowledge may be congruent with the environment that confronts us today. As one management theorist put it:

Because the nature of the world is unknowable (chaos theory and quantum theory) we are left with only sensemaking. Even if we had the capacity to do more, doing more would not help. Quantum theory helps us to understand that the present state of the world is at best a probability distribution. As we learn from chaos theory, the next state of the world is unknowable. And so we must pay attention to the world as it unfolds.[68]

The complexity and unpredictability of the environment raises to unprecedented levels managers' needs to sense and anticipate changes in the environment. Given the nature of this era, it may be that linear and logical explicit knowledge may be of diminishing importance, and that nonlinear and alogical tacit knowledge may be of ascending importance. Both types of knowledge will continue to be valuable; and perhaps it is time for managers to make more room for a different kind of knowing—tacit knowledge.

A survey of more than 3,000 managers concluded that intuition is *"most helpful"* [emphasis in original] in making decisions in situations in which there is: "a high level of uncertainty . . . [and] . . . little previous precedent. . . . [when] Variables are often not scientifically predictable . . . facts are limited. . . . [and] do not clearly point the way to go. . . . [when] Time is limited and there is pressure to be right . . . [and there are] . . . several plausible alternative solutions to choose from, with good arguments for each."[69] These constraints typically describe managerial decision making in this era of uncertainty.

After a lifetime in high-ranking positions, Chester Barnard reached a similar conclusion. Barnard insightfully suggested that executives should utilize "nonlogical" mental processes when facing situations characterized by "impressions and probabilities not susceptible of mathematical expression and purely contingent uncertainties, including the possibility or the probability of the existence of unknown factors and their possible effect." He continued: "We know, however, that the mind must deal with just this kind of material in a very large part of personal and general affairs . . . 'intuition' is the only mental process that can apply to it."[70] The anticipatory or "sensing" characteristic of tacit knowledge is congruent with the environment that confronts managers today. Being able to access our tacit knowledge can help to anticipate what might come next.

CONCLUSION

Unverbalized tacit knowledge undergirds every physical action, just as there is a "tacit coefficient" to every one of our mental operations, judgments, decisions, and explicit statements. If we know more than we can say, then tacit knowledge constitutes a vast and fundamental part of our mind that has yet to be explored or tapped. Tacit knowledge appears to play a predominant, if not mysterious role in how we make discoveries. To enter this tacit dimension could open up new paths to creativity. If Dorothy Thompson is right—that the "thinking of a genius does not proceed logically [but] leaps with great ellipses [and] pulls knowledge from God knows where"[71]—where might that "where" be but tacit knowledge? There are no rules to account for the way a good idea emerges or an insight triggers an inquiry. The explicit rules of the scientific method may account for the replication or the validation of discoveries, but it is from the tacit dimensions of the mind that the initial idea for the discovery emerges. Tacit knowledge could be like the drivers that enable a computer's software to work—hidden and in the background, but indispensable.

Everyone possesses tacit knowledge. Insightful organizations will democratize knowledge from being closely held by an elite at the top, to being found within everyone at all layers of an organization's hierarchy. Thus, surfacing everyone's tacit knowledge is more important than ever before. It is difficult to overestimate the significance of this shift from explicit knowledge to tacit knowledge. This is an era of a growing World Wide Web and hyperfast computers. However, the power of discovery, innovation, and creativity still resides in individuals who wonder, develop ideas, solve problems, and encourage one another to go on. As one astute e-learning consultant put it,

[the explicit knowledge of] text alone is simply not enough for capturing the tips, the secrets, the thoughts on strategy, the candid asides, and the bigger overview of confusing primary materials and discrete disciplines. For professional firms, there is a huge gulf between "tacit" and "explicit" knowledge. . . . It is the tacit knowledge that is key and this is what the corporate client pays for.[72]

Humankind can only mine the material wealth of the Earth's crust for minerals or energy, or journey to the outer reaches of distant space by first learning how to tap the inner reaches of the human mind for the riches of its tacit creativity.

NOTES

1. Dorothy Thompson (1894–1961), influential foreign correspondent and foreign affairs commentator who had been married to and was writing about Sinclair Lewis in (December 1956) "Keep Away from Genius!" *Ladies Home Journal*, pp. 11, 14, 16, 18, especially p. 14.

2. Banesh Hoffmann, with the collaboration of Helen Dukas (1972) *Albert Einstein: Creator and Rebel* (New York: Viking Press), p. 222.

3. Georg von Krogh, Kazuo Ichijo, and Ikujiro Nonaka (2000) *Enabling Knowledge Creation: How to Unlock the Mystery of Tacit Knowledge and Release the Power of Innovation* (New York: Oxford University Press), pp. 71–82.

4. Roy Lubit (Winter 2001) "Tacit Knowledge and Knowledge Management:

The Keys to Sustainable Competitive Advantage," *Organizational Dynamics* 29 (4), pp. 164–178, especially pp. 165–165.

5. Donald T. Campbell (1990) "Asch's Moral Epistemology for Socially Shared Knowledge" in *The Legacy of Solomon Asch: Essays in Cognition and Social Psychology,* edited by Irvin Rock (Hillside, N.J.: Lawrence Erlbaum Associates), pp. 39–52.

6. Ibid., p. 41.

7. See, for example, some of his seminal work in Solomon E. Asch (1940) "Studies in the Principles of Judgments and Attitudes: II. Determination of Judgments by Group and by Ego Standards," *Journal of Social Psychology* 12, pp. 433–465; (1948) "The Doctrine of Suggestion, Prestige and Imitation in Social Psychology," *Psychological Review* 55, pp. 250–276; and his classic and most famous (1956) "Studies of Independence and Conformity: I. A Minority of One against a Unanimous Majority," *Psychological Monographs* 70 (9), pp. 1–70.

8. Gilbert Ryle (1949) *The Concept of Mind* (New York: Barnes & Noble), pp. 25–61.

9. See the discussion of Donald Schön's ideas in chapter IX of this book, "Reflecting Conversations." The static procedures, theories, or rules that Schön sums up as the "espoused theory" of technical, rational knowledge of the type taught in graduate schools seems to correspond to explicit knowledge. His term for truly professional performance—the more fluid, back-and-forth "reflection-in-action" that results in "knowing-in-action"—correspond with tacit knowledge.

10. Hans-Georg Gadamer (1975) *Truth and Method,* trans. by Garrett Burden and John Cumming (New York: Seabury Press), pp. 426–427.

11. See Brice R. Wachterhauser (1986) "Introduction: History and Language in Understanding," in *Hermeneutics and Modern Philosophy,* edited by Brice R. Wachterhauser (Albany: State University of New York Press), pp. 33–34, for reference to both Gadamer and Lipps quotations.

12. Weston Agor (1986) *The Logic of Intuitive Decision Making: A Research-Based Approach for Top Management* (Westport, Conn.: Quorum Press), p. 15.

13. The May 2002 study by executive search firm Christian & Timbers was cited in Eric Bonabeau (May 2003) "Don't Trust Your Gut," *Harvard Business Review* 81 (5), pp. 116–23, especially p. 116.

14. Peter B. Vail (1999) *Managing as a Performing Art: New Ideas for a Chaotic World* (San Francisco: Jossey-Bass), pp. 1–2.

15. Ralph S. Larsen, chairman and CEO of Johnson & Johnson, quoted in Alden M. Hayashi (February 2001) "When to Trust Your Gut," *Harvard Business Review* 79 (2), pp. 59–65, especially p. 61.

16. Agor, op. cit., p. 38.

17. Chester I. Barnard ([1938] 1968) *The Functions of the Executive,* with an introduction by Kenneth R. Andrews (Cambridge, Mass.: Harvard University Press), pp. 301–322, especially p. 303.

18. Agor, op. cit., pp. 29–30.

19. Hoffmann, op. cit., p. 222.

20. Thompson, op. cit., p. 14.

21. Hayashi, op. cit., p. 60.

22. Noel M. Tichy and Stratford Sherman (1993) *Control Your Own Destiny or Someone Else Will: Lessons in Mastering Change from the Principles Jack Welch Is Using to Revolutionize GE* (New York: HarperBusiness), p. 12.

23. Agor, op. cit., p. 55.

24. Barnard, op. cit., p. 302.

25. Eric Bonabeau (May 2003) "Don't Trust Your Gut," *Harvard Business Review*, pp. 116–123, especially p. 118.

26. Ibid., p. 118.

27. Ibid., p. 119.

28. Ibid., p. 120. See also David G. Meyer (2002) *Intuition: Its Powers and Perils* (New Haven, Conn.: Yale University Press) and his briefer treatment, (November/December 2002) "The Powers and Perils of Intuition," *Psychology Today* 35 (6), pp. 42–52.

29. We are indebted to Dorothy Leonard-Barton for the term "wellsprings of knowledge" that triggered the emergence of our phrase "wellsprings of discovery." See her 1995 book, *Wellsprings of Knowledge: Building and Sustaining the Sources of Innovation* (Boston: Harvard Business School Press).

30. Peter M. Senge (1990) *The Fifth Discipline: The Art and Practice of the Learning Organization* (New York: Currency/Doubleday), pp. 238–239.

31. See Arthur S. Reber (1996) *Implicit Learning and Tacit Knowledge: An Essay on the Cognitive Unconscious* (New York: Oxford University Press), pp. 23–24, 140, for what he terms the "polarity fallacy."

32. Michael Polanyi (October 1962) "Tacit Knowing: Its Bearing on Some Problems of Philosophy," *Review of Modern Physics* 34 (4), pp. 601–602, 605. See also Michael Polanyi (January 1966) "The Logic of Tacit Inference," *Philosophy: The Journal of the Royal Institute of Philosophy* XLI (155) pp. 1–4, 8.

33. Polanyi (1962) op. cit., p. 601; Arthur S. Reber (1989) "Implicit Learning and Tacit Knowledge," *Journal of Experimental Psychology* 118 (3), p. 231.

34. Reber (1996) op. cit., pp. 24–25.

35. Polanyi (1966) op. cit., p. 7.

36. Reber (1996) op. cit., pp. 73–88.

37. Nicholas Wade (August 15, 2002) "Language Gene Is Traced to Emergence of Humans," *New York Times*, p. A18; and Nicholas Wade (July 15, 2003) "Early Voices: The Leap to Language," *New York Times*, pp. F1, F4. See also Nature.com's archive entry, John Whitfield (October 4, 2001) "Language Gene Found," www.Nature.com.

38. Schön, op. cit., p. 25.

39. Reber (1996), op. cit., p. 16.

40. Polanyi (1966), op. cit., p. 7.

41. Reber (1989), op. cit., p. 225.

42. Noam Chomsky (1980) *Rules and Representations* (New York: Columbia University Press), p. 188.

43. Polanyi (1962), op. cit., pp. 604–605; Noam Chomsky ([1968] 1972) *Language and Mind*, enlarged edition (New York: Harcourt, Brace Jovanovich), pp. 100–102.

44. Polanyi (1966), op. cit., p. 13.

45. The tacit process of subception was first reported (and the term coined) by Robert A. McCleary and Richard A. Lazarus (1949) "Autonomic Discrimination without Awareness: An Interim Report," *Journal of Personality* 18, pp. 171–179. Richard S. Lazarus and Robert A. McCleary (1951) "A Study of Subception," *Psychological Review* 58, pp. 113–122; and Richard S. Lazarus (1956) "Subception: Fact or Artifact? A Reply to Erickson," *Psychological Review* 63 (5), pp. 343–346. Possible

validation of subception was provided by Harvard psychologists Nalini Ambady and Robert Rosenthal who compared strangers' consensual judgments of "thin slices" of three brief 10-second (and shorter) silent videotapes of professors' non-verbal behavior in classrooms with traditional end-of-semester student evaluations. They found the "thin slices" to be significantly accurate. The three even briefer two-second "slices" also proved to be similar to student evaluations. See Nalini Ambady and Robert Rosenthal (1993) "Half a Minute: Predicting Teacher Evaluations for Thin Slices of Nonverbal Behavior and Physical Attractiveness," *Journal of Personality and Social Psychology* 64 (3), pp. 431–441.

46. Reber (1996), op. cit., pp. 86–87 as well as Keith J. Holyoak and Barbara A. Spellman (1993) "Thinking," *American Review of Psychology*, 44, pp. 265–315, especially pp. 286–290.

47. Neil R. Carlson (1998) *Physiology of Behavior*, 6th ed. (Boston: Allyn and Bacon), pp. 56–85 and 478–508.

48. Reber (1996), op. cit., p. 86.

49. Ibid., p. 87.

50. Ibid., pp. 15–16, 45–50.

51. Reber (1996), op. cit., pp. 80–88.

52. Daniel Goleman, Richard Boyatzis, and Annie McKee (2002) *Primal Leadership: Realizing the Power of Emotional Intelligence* (Boston: Harvard Business School Press), p. 44.

53. Chester I. Barnard ([1938] 1968) addendum "Mind in Everyday Affairs," in *The Functions of the Executive*, with an introduction by Kenneth R. Andrews (Cambridge: Harvard University Press), pp. 309–310, citing Koffka (1935) *Principles of Gestalt Psychology* (New York: Harcourt, Brace & Co.), pp. 626–627.

54. Barnard, op. cit., pp. 301–22; Daniel Cappon (1994) *Intuition and Management: Research and Application* (Westport, Conn.: Quorum Press), pp. 15–28. Examples of what we term "fast" and "slow" tacit knowledge are drawn from these sources.

55. Barnard, op. cit., p. 322.

56. Goleman, op. cit., p. 44.

57. Reber (1989), op. cit., pp. 230–232; Reber (1996), op. cit., pp. 15–17; see also Lynn Hasher and Rose T. Zacks (December 19, 1984). "Automatic Processing of Fundamental Information: The Case of Frequency of Occurrence," *American Psychologist* 39 (12), pp. 1372–1388; as well as Barnard, op. cit., pp. 306–309.

58. Ibid., p. 306.

59. Ibid., p. 306.

60. Ibid., p. 308.

61. Polanyi (1966), op. cit., pp. 1–5.

62. Ibid., pp. 5–7. See also Polanyi (1962), op. cit., pp. 602–605. Polanyi drew on the work of Robert A. McCleary and Richard A. Lazarus cited in footnote 45 above.

63. Reber (1996), op. cit., p. 16.

64. Ralph S. Larsen, chair and CEO of Johnson & Johnson, as quoted in Hayashi, op. cit., p. 61.

65. Polanyi (1966), op. cit., p. 1.

66. George Sand's precise words: "Nulle creature humaine ne peut commander l'amour," are found in George Sand (1842) *Jacques*, presentation de Georges Lubin (Paris: Editions D'Aujourd' Hui), Letter LXXXI from Jacques to Sylvia, p. 339.

67. Charles M. Brower, advertising agency executive and president, Batten, Bar-

ton, Durstine & Osborn, before the Association of National Advertisers in "What They're Saying . . ." *Advertising Age* (August 10, 1959), p. 12.

68. Personal communication from McDaniel to Karl Weick, quoted in Weick's chapter, (2001) "Leadership as the Legitimation of Doubt," in *The Future of Leadership: Today's Top Leadership Thinkers Speak to Tomorrow's Leaders,* edited by Warren Bennis, Gretchen M. Spreitzer, and Thomas G. Cummings (San Francisco: Jossey-Bass), pp. 91–102, especially p. 92.

69. Agor, op. cit., p. 18.

70. Barnard, op. cit., p. 310.

71. Thompson, op. cit., p. 14.

72. Robin Fry (August 2001) "Corporate Knowledge Management: e-learning makes capital out of knowledge," *e-learning magazine* 2 (8), p. 17.

CHAPTER 5

The Pragmatics of Knowledge Creation: Care, Respect, and Trust

We grow in relationship to others and the foundation of relationship is your ability to listen and indicate your caring.

—Allen Ivey[1]

Gathering information, and above all developing trust, have become the key source of sustainable competitive advantage ... the human relationship serves as the platform upon which companies deliver greater value.

—Gary Heil, Warren Bennis, and Deborah C. Stephens[2]

The real challenge to organizations has not yet been taken up. The key challenge to managers in the Information Era is to create an environment in which care, respect, and trust are present, for only then can the inquiry that surfaces each individual's new and tacit knowledge occur. Knowledge creation is a social process in which groups of individuals come together to actively express their ideas. It begins with each individual, and ends with an ecology of ideas.

The Postmodern Era has forced change on organizations. Conventionally, managers have responded by establishing flatter and simplified hierarchies, more flexible roles and procedures, and more open communication. New structures and processes are becoming more common among successful organizations in the new economy. The underlying assumptions of organizations are undergoing re-evaluation and change. However, this conventional sort of change may be insufficient. It is what may be referred to as "first-order change" or what mainstream management literature and practice calls "single-loop learning."[3]

First-order change does not alter the system in which it occurs; rather, it involves endless repetitions of the same behavior without ever solving the problem. Paul Watzlawick and his coauthors call this first-order change a "Game without End." They write: "A system which may run through all its possible internal changes (no matter how many there are) without effecting a systemic change, i.e. second order change, is said to be caught in a *Game without End*. It cannot generate from within itself the conditions for its own change"[4] [emphasis in original]. Thus, it is an "inside-the-box" or single-loop learning managerial response. In too many cases, individuals continue to be treated by organizations much as they always have been—with the anonymity of bloodless, dispensable "cogs" on bureaucratic wheels in organizations structured according to the Modern Management Tradition.[5]

Today's organizations may be trying to solve new problems using old paradigms that yield "more of the same" outcomes. In this new era, there is a need to re-evaluate the basic assumptions and practices regarding what constitutes the building blocks of every organization—its individuals. In times of profound paradigmatic shifts, a "second-order change" may be necessary. Such change requires a shift in assumptions by going outside the paradigm or "outside of the box." Second-order change is one whose occurence changes the system itself. Only by approaching the situation from a different perspective can problems be solved. Managers who focus their attention on changing the structures and processes of organizations and consequently treat individuals as valuable resources to the organization are on their way toward effecting second-order change. Once second-order change or double-loop learning begins to occur, the "Game without End" ceases, and new outcomes can be generated.[6] It is then that the real challenge to organizations can be taken up. Second-order change will occur when organizations practice care and respect for the most valuable resource in their midst—the individual.

It is time to access and harness the greatest of all resources—the tacit knowledge of each worker. As stated previously, tacit knowledge is fragile and personal. It is a new experience for individuals to disclose their innermost and fragmentary thoughts and ideas. The disclosure of one's most tentative ideas—which are untested and yet to be thought out— makes one vulnerable. Knowledge creation is a deep intellectual and emotional experience, for it involves the articulation of one's most tentative and fleeting thoughts. The vulnerability of opening oneself to share one's thoughts, albeit tentatively, requires an enabling environment. Relationships become critically important in such settings.

The basic elements of an enabling environment are care, respect, and trust. It is in this safe context that individuals feel free to voice their initial and tentative ideas. Such an environment sharply contrasts with one in which suspicion, competition, and intimidation sabotage the spontaneity and vulnerability of individuals, and leave them open to criticism and even derision. These settings—which are antithetical to knowledge creation—still prevail in many organizations characterized by the Modern Management Tradition. In such firms, intellectual combat and verbal conflict continue to be mainstream practices. However, such a climate of conflict and disagreement hampers the spontaneous emergence of tentative ideas. In the process of knowledge creation, care provides the security that tacit knowledge craves.

Care has been an important concept to human as well as intellectual development throughout history. It has ancient roots. Socrates and Plato cared about the development of their students. Through their dialogues and inquiry, known as the Socratic approach, their attempt was to help students articulate their spontaneous ideas, and hence participate in what we today term knowledge creation. They also cared that there would be a next generation of philosophers who would carry on their work and ideas about philosophy, politics, and ethics.[7]

Today we continue to recognize the critical role that human relationships and care play in developing the next generation of professionals. Throughout history, older scientists, artists, and teachers have taken promising young protégés under their wings, and provided the care and support to nurture their professional development. Fittingly, the word "protégé" means "being protected," and comes from the French verb "protéger," which means "to protect." More recently, the business world has come to recognize the importance of caring and nurturing human relationships. During the past few decades, the heretofore-informal practice of "mentoring" has become explicitly recognized with the establishment of formal corporate programs in which older, more experienced managers mentor younger ones. In fact, formalizing the mentoring process has real value to organizations that must rapidly develop leadership talent to meet the challenge of tumultuous times.

The practice of mentoring is not new, however. In Greek mythology, "Mentor" was the loyal and caring friend to whom Odysseus entrusted his house and the education of his son during his epochal wanderings that Homer immortalized in *The Odyssey*. The root of the word "mentor" means "wise advisor" or "loyal friend." In the case of both protégés and those who are "mentored," the key appears to be caring and trusting human relationships in which formal and explicit, as well as informal and tacit, knowledge is conveyed.

Today's workers generate and share more knowledge than ever before in history. They do so via human "face-to-face" as well as computer "interface" exchanges. In the vital area of *accessing the knowledge of individuals*, however, too many organizations continue to treat individuals as they always have—according to the assumptions of the old paradigm. The paradox is that, although we are creating more information than ever before, we still do not know the "how to" of accessing the knowledge that each individual possesses. This is particularly true of the most valuable knowledge—tacit knowledge. The key to success for managers and organizations in this Information Era is to understand how to facilitate the continuous surfacing, expression, and sharing of this knowledge. However, few companies look on the key ingredients—care, respect, and trust—as practical components of their social architecture.

THE PRACTICALITY OF CARE, RESPECT, AND TRUST IN ORGANIZATIONS

[F]ew companies to date have made relationships a priority . . . often because the language of caring, relating, and enabling sounds so foreign in a business context. . . . But ironically, a company may need to flip some of that cutthroat attitude on its head in order to remain competitive over the long haul. Knowledge workers cannot be bullied into creativity or information sharing. It is time that managers put care on their agendas. . . . They can do so by fostering care in organizational relationships—the very essence of knowledge enabling.
                —Georg von Krogh, Kazuo Ichijo, and Ikujiro Nonaka[8]

Some managers may find it unusual to read about care, respect, and trust in organizations, yet there are some extraordinarily practical reasons for managers to practice these values toward each and every individual whom they encounter in their work activities. A firm's most valuable workers usually are the hardest to retain. In this Information Era, a firm's chief resource is not just its employees, but more specifically, the knowledge they possess. Money alone is not necessarily the primary way to motivate or retain the best workers; rather, for these talented individuals, it may be the chance to work in a caring and respectful environment in which they feel valued and appreciated for their contributions. Such a climate makes it possible for talent to flourish. Successful firms create the conditions that make this possible.

The structures and processes of organizations are changing under the turbulent onslaught of disruptive technologies. The price for not doing so is to join the growing number of companies, sectors, and industries that are vanishing. Under such circumstances, yesterday's rigid hierarchies can no longer coordinate the shifting activities of today's *ad hoc* teams that appear with organizational needs and disappear with their completion. Once-clear organizational boundaries between departments and divisions have become fuzzy, and relationships among workers are more complex than ever before. The Modern Management paradigm's tight command and control of workers is vanishing in our Postmodern Era in which workers are encouraged to be more autonomous and self-directed in what they do and how they do it. Consequently, the practice of management also is changing. In such an environment, it could be that one "tells" less and supports more, one "orders" less and encourages more, and one becomes as much "people oriented" as "task oriented."[9] Thus, care—for perhaps the most human and practical reasons—enters a manager's lexicon. Finally, nothing is more practical to a firm's bottom line than the process of continuous knowledge creation that care, respect, and trust bring about.

The remainder of this chapter addresses the question: "What might be the basic conditions that foster the surfacing of tacit knowledge and the creation of new knowledge in Information Era organizations?" Our response is that there are three such conditions—care, respect, and trust. We begin with the most necessary of all conditions—care.

Care

> Man cares because it is his nature to care. Man survives because he cares and is cared for . . . the goodness inherent in man is no theory. It cannot be a product of culture because no species constructed as peculiarly as man could have survived to a point of culture without possessing at its core a supremely loving nature. Rather, we must see our culture and institutions themselves as being derived from the caring aspect of our species' nature.
> —Willard Gaylin[10]

> Care is not a word to be found in many organizational textbooks . . . but it should be.
> —Charles Handy[11]

Care is an essential element in human relationships. Caring gives individuals the grounding that makes them feel valued. It strengthens and generates a sense of self-worth. Whenever present, caring enhances self-agency. As the scholar who coined the term put it, self-agency is: "the ability to act, feel, and think in a way that is liberating, that opens up new possibilities or simply allows us to see that new possibilities exist. When I think of self-agency, I think of the *freedom*"[12] [emphasis in original]. The freedom in this context is the courage to be genuine, to be oneself.

Care also creates the hope that invigorates and musters the antidote to despair and cynicism. Caring is an enduring and intense feeling that evokes in others a genuine sense of warmth and connection. "Care alleviates anxiety, and anxiety is the enemy of all creativity and productivity."[13]

In the realm of knowledge creation, care is the *sine qua non* for evoking the personal knowledge that is within. Care encourages. Tacit knowledge emerges via a sensitive, if not delicate, process. It may take just a negative quip or the arching of a brow to suppress it. As Milton Meyerhoff, a scholar of care, wrote: "In caring for another person, I encourage him, I inspire him to have the courage to be himself. My trust in him encourages him to trust himself and to be worthy of the trust."[14] Care gives courage, strength, and hope.

New ideas are delicate; they are susceptible and likely to be repressed not just by a caustic remark, but by the anticipation of one. The relationships that prevail in a group can encourage or discourage the emergence and sharing of new ideas and perspectives. Persistent criticism can stifle the risk taking involved in the willingness to speak up, which is necessary when one is groping for a new thought.[15] On the other hand, a new idea is more likely to find expression in a supportive atmosphere, one that fosters the spontaneous articulation of one's new and incompletely formed thoughts. Care creates the context in which knowledge can be easily and spontaneously shared with others.

Research substantiates that care leads individuals to work collaboratively rather than in isolation, increases interest and support among colleagues, and generates more articulation of knowledge as well as feedback among participants—all crucial to the knowledge creation process.[16] Caring is the very foundation of cooperative inquiry.

MIT's Edgar Schein recognized the importance of feeling safe (and, by implication, being cared for) to learn and change. He proposed that firms create "psychological safety" in training sites, meetings, and other similar situations in which managers could test new ideas in a risk-free environment without the fear connected with criticism, ridicule, or the shame associated with being wrong.[17] Perhaps care serves Schein's purpose of providing "psychological safety."

The care that we suggest in our 21st-century organizations need not necessarily be the affective, emotional care that we feel for our closest friends or family members. Such primary relationships are not necessarily the norm in the secondary and even tertiary relationships that are the stuff of high-velocity Information Era organizations. As a baseline, however, effective managers should seek to care for others in the sense of *understanding them*. As Milton Meyerhoff put it: "To care for another person, I must be able to understand him and his world as if I were inside it. I must be able to see, as it were, with his eyes what his world is like to him and how he sees it himself."[18] For managers, perhaps care begins with seeking to understand colleagues, and moves from there to other horizons.

In addition, it has long been known that caring is a powerful spur to human growth. Researchers who analyzed more than 50 different types of psychotherapy for effectiveness found that the strongest forecaster of success was a strong, caring relationship between therapist and client.[19] The results in corporate offices are likely to be the same as in therapy rooms—individuals respond best to care. It is in such a climate that individuals, regardless of the setting, are likely to express themselves openly and without reservation. This is especially true when one is seeking the personal and new knowledge that is fragile—tacit knowledge.

Perhaps surprising to some, care is of central importance to the military—a profession that more than any other is characterized by strength and confidence. It is curious that the philosophy of leadership taught to West Point cadets is, "The job of the leader is to be absolutely trustworthy and to put the needs of others first, most particularly ahead of personal considerations."[20] Would such concern not be caring in the most profound sense? Alexander the Great knew his soldiers by name, constantly asked about their lot, and often dismounted from his horse to walk with them on long and arduous campaigns. Just before his decisive 1805 victory over Napoleon's fleet in the Battle of Trafalgar, Britain's Admiral Horatio Nelson won the hearts of his sailors by ordering the return of the last mail ship (just before battle) to take on what might have been the final letter to his family by a seaman who had burst late on the deck of Nelson's ship from his quarters below. Word of Nelson's action flashed through the fleet by semaphore, and, officers said, Nelson's men fought harder. "Be hard on others, not on your own crew" might be the motto of this event.[21]

Involving others in the process of generating new ideas and perspectives may be best accomplished by adopting attitudes of care and respect in the workplace. Only in an environment in which individuals feel valued, respected, and safe will it be possible for them to freely share their inner thoughts, experiences, and perspectives. It is in such a context that new ideas surface and create a holding environment for the tacit knowledge that generates new options and new possibilities. To care is eminently practical, for it is the precondition that enables tacit knowledge to emerge and be expressed.

Respect

Respect conveys an individual's nonjudgmental acceptance of the worth and value of others. Being nonjudgmental means assuming a stance of unreserved acceptance that allows individuals to be free to be themselves while, at the same time, respecting them for it. Psychologist Carl Rogers described what he termed "positive regard" as "attitudes of warmth, caring, liking, interest, respect."[22] Such an attitude is conveyed not just verbally, but by being congruent in one's verbal and nonverbal communication. This is an important consideration because between 65 to 90 percent of interpersonal communication occurs at the nonverbal level.[23] It is through this process that warmth, acceptance, and empathy are conveyed, which, in turn, create the conditions for the expression of honest thoughts, ideas, and feelings. Such a respectful and caring stance frees individuals to be themselves, to express their innermost thoughts, and to clearly apprehend their reality and those of others.

Perhaps, in its simplest and most powerful sense, *to respect others* is *to attend* to them. And to *attend* is simply to listen respectfully. Few work experiences are as uncomfortable as the performance appraisal interview, and few managers look forward to this experience, yet, according to one study, the type of interview that workers found most satisfying was surprising. Those who were appraised, reported that the most satisfying performance appraisal interviews were those in which *they were attended to—when they were able to say all that they wanted to say . . . and be heard.*[24]

Another study found a powerful physiological response to respect, warmth, and positive regard. In measuring the psychogalvanic reflex to threat or anxiety, a correlation emerged between galvanic skin responses (GSRs) of clients and the warmth and acceptance expressed by therapists. Even slight reductions in the warmth and acceptance of therapists triggered significantly increased GSR levels in clients. Such minimally threatening behaviors as the "[a]pparent failure by the therapist to understand the patient's words or his interruption of the patient, or some form of scolding, or his apparent determination to force his own interpretations and points of view on the patient" triggered autonomic responses of tenseness and defensiveness in patients at the physiological level.[25] As stated earlier, anxiety, criticism, and stress are counterproductive to task performance, let alone creativity. Research substantiates that anxiety inhibits one's ability to concentrate, due to the intrusion of thoughts that are irrelevant to the performance of tasks. Hence, lower levels of job performance result, and the work of individuals suffers.[26] Anxiety and lack of warmth and acceptance tend to negatively impact individuals' ability to freely express their most personal and tentative ideas and thoughts. Under such circumstances, it is more difficult for individuals to freely and spontaneously express themselves, particularly when it comes to uttering one's tacit knowledge. It is essential for individuals in the workplace to be participants in the knowledge creation endeavor on which organizations in today's environment depend. Care and respect are required for every individual to participate in the knowledge creation process. These conditions create an environment in which barriers to communication become nonexistent, and individuals feel free, comfortable, and confident to express their tacit knowledge.

Trust

In today's disruptive environment, care and respect may be even more necessary in the workplace, for they are the antecedents of trust—they create trust.[27] Care is the precondition to trust, and respect is its companion. Scholars who have studied trust in business and everyday life agree: "*Care* is perhaps the most essential ingredient of authentic trust"[28] [emphasis in original].

Today, trust may be the "number one differentiator" between the most and least successful organizations. In their 1999 *Innovation Survey* of 200 global corporations, PriceWaterhouseCoopers researchers found that trust is the most important element that distinguishes the top 20% of surveyed companies from the bottom 20%. The researchers concluded: "The top performers' trust empowered individuals to communicate and implement change in order to turn strategic aims into reality."[29] Because innovation and discovery are the primary requirements of today's organizations, trust becomes the *sine qua non* of survival and success.

Trust is a highly elusive, but basic, element of cooperative activity. It is one of those essential elements of communal existence that is rarely thought of, and whose meaning is not often put into words. However, "without trust, the everyday social life which we take for granted is simply not possible."[30] English political theorist, Thomas Hobbes's famous 17th-century words and definition of anarchy, a "Warre of everyone against everyone,"[31] may, on reflection, describe human existence in the absence of trust. It also illustrates "the decisive role of the growth of trust . . . for building viable societies" of which Hobbes himself was conscious.[32]

Trust is important to managers and to knowledge creation. Carl Rogers's research found that trust is not only a critical initial factor in establishing relationships, but also indicated that increased trust makes heightened creativity possible by diminishing the physiological need to be defensive against threat. Rogers concluded: "When we are able to free the individual from defensiveness, so that he is open to the wide range of his own needs, as well as the wide range of environmental and social demands, his reactions may be trusted to be positive, forward-moving, constructive."[33] In an applied setting, Andreas Rihs, CEO of Phonak, a Swiss high-tech company, arrived at a similar conclusion: "For your people to be innovative and motivated, you need to consider human needs. If you feel good and appreciated, you are much more open to many things than if you always need to defend yourself."[34]

Other researchers discovered that low levels of trust influence dyads and groups in numerous ways. Low levels of trust can increase misperceptions and misunderstandings of a situation or a problem. Distrust can reduce individuals' willingness to share new ideas about a problem. Finally, low trust may shift a group's focus from solving problems to a concern with defensively protecting themselves from each other. In summary, "trust can significantly alter managerial problem-solving effectiveness."[35] On the other hand, high levels of trust greatly benefit dyads and groups by simplifying the complexity of interactions; diminishing the attention, time, and energy that goes into constant surveillance of colleagues; and deepening the personal relationships that lead to enhanced participation.

Trust also may be crucial to developing and sustaining a competitive advantage. As one study concluded: "To distrust means to become more and more dependent on less information. Strategies of distrust often leave little energy to explore and adapt to the environment in an objective and unprejudiced manner, and hence allow fewer opportunities for learn-ing."[36] Trust is a significant and underestimated element in the facilitation of every type of human interaction that enhances every organization's human resources—most especially knowledge creation. Psychologist Sol-omon Asch found trust, honesty, and self-respect to be the "moral norms for socially achieved knowledge."[37]

Trust is crucial to human relationships and endeavors. It usually re-quires time, experience, and familiarity to develop among individuals. However, trust is equally important for the success of the *ad hoc* teams that increasingly characterize today's Information Era organizations. In such temporary groups, professionals who may not know each other are assembled to achieve specific tasks during a limited time period, and then dissolve, not to be reconstituted again. To achieve their tasks, researchers have discovered that such groups develop a kind of "swift trust" that is based on care. Such professionals care about their reputations, they care about their craft, and they care about a job well done. Therefore, this "swift trust" emerges as a crucial element that makes possible the high-caliber work of even *ad hoc* temporary groups.[38]

Paradoxically, trust may be more essential in the Information Era than ever before. The fast pace of technology mandates an exponential increase in our need to deal with strangers—whether faceless strangers on the World Wide Web with whom we are transacting business or temporary workers in our organization who may be critical to a specific business task.[39] In either case, we are dealing with individuals in interfaced as well as face-to-face relationships; individuals with whom we are bereft of the time and familiarity, the shared experience, and the personal relationships on which trust usually has been built. "Trusting strangers," some scholars have concluded, "becomes the very heart of wisdom and strength rather than foolishness, a promising investment in the future rather than a lia-bility. The cost of trust may on occasion be devastating, but the high cost of distrust is virtually guaranteed."[40]

Trusting is often viewed as depending on others, and thereby becoming vulnerable to them. However, what trust may truly engender is a strength—an even more reliable *interdependency* that opens possibilities. Such trust lays the foundation for collaboration. Even entrepreneurship—the seeming paragon of "individualism"—may, on reflection, epitomize trust and interdependence. In today's business environment, successful entrepreneurship is based on relationships of trust. This endeavor begins with the spark of a new idea that can create a new product or service if not a new industry. After that, trust is critical to the execution of that idea.

One entrepreneur, Sam Walton, founder of Wal-Mart, succeeded in his pioneering endeavor because others trusted him at critical times when every "hard fact" of Wal-Mart's financial situation would dictate other-wise. At one critical juncture, Walton found himself in a desperate cash crunch. His Texas bank would not advance him a nickel on an already-established line of credit; the key decision-making officer was unavailable. Needing the money that day, he frantically called James Jones, his former Dallas banker who had taken a new position as president of a bank in New Orleans. "Wild-eyed" and "almost in tears" in Dallas, Walton explained the situation. Listening intently on the phone, Jones then (to let him tell the story) told Walton, a private pilot, to: "fly on down to New Orleans. I'll wait in my office. Doesn't make any difference what time you get here. . . . It was a little after six o'clock when Sam came into my office. . . . We visited for a while and I calmed him down. He said, 'You going to be able to help me?' I said, 'Yes, Sam.' And I pushed a note across the desk, an unsecured note, and told him to just sign it. He did. I said, 'You've got the money.' " Sam Walton's entrepreneurship founded what would be one of the world's greatest fortunes because he generated the trust that earned the support of others at critical moments in his career.[41]

In the early 21st century, the American financial markets experienced convulsions. Although there were many technical reasons—ranging from changes in accounting standards, pressure on executives to reach sometimes-unreasonable profit goals, and personal venality—the net result was a loss of trust. At no time had the vital role of trust been clearer than in the collapse of many high-technology companies. Many companies lost magnitudes of shareholder value simply due to the irrational exuberance of this new technological era. However, it was the personal venality of some top executives that brought about the massive loss of shareholder value for other corporations. For example, the top four executives of Enron together sold at least $994 million of their company's stock to shareholders between January 1999 through May 2002 before their company's bankruptcy. Even more startling, Gary Winnick, Chairman of Global Crossing alone sold $951 million of his company stock before it became virtually worthless.[42] Such violations of executive trust triggered the Sarbanes-Oxley Act of 2002 that mandated CEO and CFO certification by signature of the accuracy of their company's financial statements. Executives found guilty in courts of law of knowingly signing misleading statements could face lengthy incarceration terms. Another manifestation of the value of trust to a society's economic system was the decision of the New York Stock Exchange to issue public letters of reprimand or delist corporations whose CEOs and CFOs did not sign the required financial statements.

There are internal consequences to low levels of trust. Firms that do not embody trust will find that they move too slowly to compete. Instead of being able to capitalize on opportunities, distrustful "corporate politics" corrodes and diverts energy away from the common purpose, which alone gives meaning to effort. Trust will be the only way to realize the grand visions that will build the great organizations of the Information Era as contemporary history is proving.

In conclusion, care, respect, and trust are essential elements that make it possible for managers to perform a novel yet increasingly crucial task in this tumultuous era: to make sense of their organizations' environment. Today's business environment is unknowable and unpredictable. It is increasingly difficult to rationally make plans according to any preordained steps. Instead, the best that managers can do is to try to "make sense" of it. Sense making, according to the University of Michigan's Karl Weick, is most optimally possible in a context that is caring, respectful, and trustful. When such an approach is taken, managers will be more likely to uncover opportunities, provide direction, detect changes or co-variances in the environment, and encourage updating through heightened awareness to the situation that is actually unfolding.[43] They will best be able to do so in an environment that *"facilitates respectful interaction* in which trust, trustworthiness, and self-respect develop equally and allow people to build a stable rendition of what they face"[44] [emphasis in original]. Weick stresses that dialogues and conversations are the vital medium by which sense making happens:

How can we know what we think until we see what we say? People need to act in order to discover what they face, they need to talk in order to discover what they think, and they need to feel in order to discover what it means . . . the "we" that makes all this happen takes the form of candid dialogue that mixes together trust, trustworthiness, and self-respect.[45]

Indeed, one of today's leading management and leadership theorists, Warren Bennis, concluded: "The key to future competitive advantage will be the organization's capacity to create the social architecture capable of generating intellectual capital."[46] High in this pantheon is the need for managers to develop care, respect, and trust.

CONCLUSION

The sustained creation of knowledge ultimately rests on strong and supportive human relationships. It is in the context of such relationships that individuals are collectively able to think generatively. Trusting relationships enable individuals to more easily voice their tentative new ideas, and to listen attentively to those of others. Such safe havens provide the context that encourages colleagues to explore new domains with one another.

All successful collaborative work rests on the strong relationships that care, respect, and trust engender, and that some of today's leading authors in the field of knowledge management identify as a priority.[47] However, the conventional managerial wisdom continues to hold that competition and conflict generate creativity and new solutions. Even scholars sometimes have urged managers to engage in practices that create anxieties which "provoke unpleasant emotions in others" as the means to bring about change and innovation in organizations.[48] The conventional managerial wisdom and practice has been that conflict causes employees to question their premises and make new meanings of situations. In his groundbreaking 1991 article, "The Knowledge-Creating Company," Ikujiro Nonaka identified the importance of dialogue in knowledge creation. At that time, he reflected the then-conventional wisdom when he stated: "This dialogue can—indeed, should—involve considerable conflict and disagreement. It is precisely such conflict that pushes employees to question existing premises and make sense of their experience in a new way."[49] Since then, however, Nonaka and his colleagues have rethought the conditions for knowledge creation. In a more recent work, they abandoned their past view. Instead, Nonaka and his colleagues came to the conclusion that knowledge creation: "is a network of interactions, determined by the care and trust of participants."[50]

The weight of today's research indicates that earlier conventional managerial wisdom which advocated conflict was precisely antithetical to the creation of knowledge, and to the supportive conditions that the expression of tacit knowledge requires. Views and practices change over time in our pursuit of knowledge, and it may be that the care, respect, and trust with which we accept such new findings (and ask the same for our own weak efforts) that will enable greater advances in the understanding of all.

Conflict and anxiety tend to polarize, minimize, and paralyze the unique and valuable ideas and perspectives that workers can contribute to conversation in the workplace. The negative energy generated by conflictual issues tends to make individuals defensive. It thereby closes rather than opens them to the positive energy that creates new options and possibilities. It is their collective individualities and their shared expression of individual ideas that create the unique context from which nascent ideas are likely to spring forth. It is such a caring, respectful, and trusting environment that purges fear and distrust from the creative process in which inquiry best unfolds. Care, respect, and trust enable participants to co-create together the new knowledge that springs forth from their innermost and tentative thoughts and musings.

NOTES

1. Allen Ivey (1997) *Basic Attending Skills*, 3rd edition (North Amherst, Mass.: Microtraining Associates), p. 5.
2. Gary Heil, Warren Bennis, and Deborah C. Stephens (2000) *Douglas Mc-*

Gregor, Revisited: Managing the Human Side of the Enterprise (New York: Wiley), p. 6.

3. Chris Argyris and Donald Schön introduced managers to the terms single-loop learning and double-loop learning in their path-breaking 1978 study, *Organizational Learning: A Theory of Action Perspective* (Reading, Mass.: Addison-Wesley Publishing Co.). They cite Gregory Bateson as a source for these terms. See Bateson's (1972) *Steps to an Ecology of Mind* (New York: Ballantine Books).

4. Paul Watzlawick, John Weakland, and Richard Fisch (1974) *Change: Principles of Problem Formation and Problem Resolution* (New York: W.W. Norton), p. 22.

5. Max Weber (1946) *Essays in Sociology*, edited and trans. by H. H. Gerth and C. Wright Mills (New York: Oxford University Press), pp. 214–216.

6. For a more extensive treatment of first- and second-order change, please see John F. Kikoski and Catherine Kano Kikoski (2000) *Reflexive Communication in the Culturally Diverse Workplace* (Westport, Conn.: Praeger), pp. 195–200.

7. Although he sometimes utilized irony with them, Socrates cared about educating his students to become the next generation of philosophers. See Georg von Krogh, Kazuo Ichijo, and Ikujiro Nonaka (2000) *Enabling Knowledge Creation: How to Unlock the Mystery of Tacit Knowledge and Release the Power of Innovation* (New York: Oxford University Press), p. 48.

8. Ibid., p. 5.

9. Thomas H. Davenport, "Knowledge Work and the Future of Management," pp. 41–58 and James M. Kouzes and Barry Z. Posner, "Bringing Leadership Lessons from the Past into the Future," pp. 81–90. Both in (2001) *The Future of Leadership: Today's Top Leadership Thinkers Speak to Tomorrow's Leaders*, edited by Warren Bennis, Gretchen M. Spreitzer, and Thomas G. Cummings (San Francisco: Jossey-Bass). See also Ronald A. Heifitz and Donald L. Laurie (January–February 1997) "The Work of Leadership," *Harvard Business Review* 75 (1), pp. 124–134.

10. Willard Gaylin (1976) *Caring* (New York: Alfred Knopf), p. 13.

11. Charles Handy (1990) *The Age of Unreason* (Boston: Harvard Business School Press), p. 232.

12. Harlene D. Anderson (1995) "Collaborative Language Systems: Toward a Postmodern Therapy" in *Integrating Family Therapy: Handbook of Family Psychology and Systems Theory*, edited by Richard H. Mikesell, Don-David Lusterman, and Susan H. McDaniel (Washington, D.C.: American Psychological Association), p. 31.

13. Gaylin, op. cit., p. 86.

14. Milton Meyerhoff (1971) *On Caring* (New York: Harper & Row), p. 32.

15. Morris B. Parloff and Joseph H. Handlon (1966) "The Influence of Criticalness on Creative Problem Solving Dyads," *Psychiatry* 29, pp. 17–27.

16. Georg von Krogh (Spring 1998) "Care in Knowledge Creation," *California Management Review* 40 (3), pp. 133–153, especially pp. 136–142.

17. Edgar Schein (Winter 1993) "How Can Organizations Learn Faster? The Challenge of Entering the Green Room," *Sloan Management Review* 34 (2), pp. 88–92.

18. Meyerhoff, op. cit., p. 30.

19. C. B. Truax and K. M. Mitchell (1971) "Research on Certain Therapists' Interpersonal Skills in Relation to Process and Outcome," in *Handbook on Psycho-*

therapy and Behavior Change, edited by A. E. Bergen and S. L. Garfield (New York: John Wiley & Sons), pp. 299–344.

20. Alan M. Webber (September–October 1994) "Surviving in the New Economy," *Harvard Business Review* 72 (5), p. 78, reviewing Larry R. Donnithorne (1993) *The West Point Way of Leadership* (New York: Currency/Doubleday).

21. Lawrence M. Miller (March 30, 1989) "Lorenzo, You're No Nelson," *New York Times*, p. A25.

22. Carl R. Rogers (1961) *On Becoming a Person: A Therapist's View of Psychotherapy* (Boston: Houghton Mifflin Company), p. 52.

23. John F. Kikoski and Catherine Kano Kikoski (2000) *Reflexive Communication in the Culturally Diverse Workplace* (Westport, Conn.: Praeger), p. 46, citing Ray Birdwhistell (1970) *Kinesics and Context: Essays on Body Motion Communication* (Philadelphia: University of Pennsylvania Press), pp. 57–58; Edward T. Hall and Mildred Reed Hall (1987) *Hidden Differences: Doing Business with the Japanese* (New York: Anchor Books/Doubleday), p. 3.

24. Martin M. Greller (1975) "Subordinate Participation and Reactions to the Appraisal Interview," *Journal of Applied Psychology* 60 (5), pp. 544–549.

25. James E. Ditties (1957) "Galvanic Skin Response as a Measure of Patient's Reaction to Therapist's Permissiveness," *Journal of Social and Abnormal Psychology* 55, pp. 295–303, especially pp. 301–303, as cited by Carl Rogers, op. cit., pp. 44, 54–55.

26. Jacqueline Wood, Andrew Mathews, and Tim Dalgleish (2001) "Anxiety & Cognitive Inhibition," *Emotion* 1 (2), pp. 166–181, especially p. 160. See also Robert A. Baron (1998) "Negative Effects of Destructive Criticism: Impact on Conflict Self-Efficacy and Task Performance," *Journal of Applied Psychology* 73 (2), pp. 199–207.

27. Robert C. Solomon and Fernando Flores (2001) *Building Trust in Business, Politics, Relationships, and Life* (New York: Oxford University Press) is an insightful book on this topic. See also Thomas A. Stewart (2001) "Trust Me on This: Organizational Support for Trust in a World without Hierarchies," in *The Future of Leadership: Today's Top Leadership Thinkers Speak to Tomorrow's Leaders*, edited by Warren Bennis, Gretchen M. Spreitzer, and Thomas G. Cummings (San Francisco: Jossey-Bass), pp. 67–77.

28. Solomon and Flores, op. cit., p. 105.

29. Kouzes and Posner, op. cit., p. 85, citing PriceWaterhouseCoopers (1999) *Innovation Survey* (London: PriceWaterhouseCoopers), p. 3.

30. David Good (1988) "Individuals, Interpersonal Relations, and Trust" in *Trust: Making and Breaking Cooperative Relations*, edited by Diego Gambetta (Oxford: Basil Blackwell), pp. 31–48, especially p. 32.

31. Thomas Hobbes (1914, 1959) *Leviathan*, with an Introduction by A. D. Lindsay (London: J. M. Dent & Sons), p. 67.

32. Diego Gambetta (1988) "Can We Trust Trust?" in *Trust: Making and Breaking Cooperative Relations*, edited by Diego Gambetta (Oxford: Basil Blackwell), pp. 213–237, especially p. 215. See also Francis Fukuyama (1995) *Trust: The Social Virtues and the Creation of Prosperity* (New York: The Free Press) for the crucial role of trust upon nations (more trusting nations tend to be more prosperous).

33. Carl Rogers, op. cit., p. 194.

34. von Krogh, Ichijo, and Nonaka, op. cit., p. 18.

35. Dale E. Zand (March 1972) "Trust and Managerial Problem Solving," *Ad-*

ministrative Science Quarterly 17 (1), pp. 229–239, especially p. 239. See research he cited by Jack R. Gibb (1961) "Defense Level, and Influence Potential in Small Groups" in *Leadership and Interpersonal Behavior,* edited by Luigi Petrullo and Bernard M. Bass (New York: Holt, Rinehart and Winston), pp. 66–81.

36. Lars Huemer, Georg von Krogh, and Johann Roos (1988) "Knowledge and the Concept of Trust," in *Trust: Making and Breaking Cooperative Relationships,* edited by Diego Gambetta (Oxford: Basil Blackwell), pp. 123–145, especially p. 140. This conclusion draws on Niklas Luhmann (1979) *Trust and Power* (Chichester: John Wiley & Sons) to which the reader is referred. See especially chapter 1, "Defining the Problem: Social Complexity," and chapter 4, "Trust as a Reduction of Complexity."

37. Donald T. Campbell (1990) "Asch's Moral Epistemology for Socially Shared Knowledge," in The Legacy of Solomon Asch: Essays in Cognition and Social Psychology, edited by Irvin Rock (Hillsdale, N.J.: Lawrence Erlbaum Associates), pp. 39–55, especially p. 39.

38. Debra Meyerson, Karl E. Weick, and Roderick M. Kramer (1996) "Swift Trust and Temporary Groups" in *Trust in Organizations: Frontiers of Theory and Research,* edited by Roderick M. Kramer and Tom R. Tyler (Thousand Oaks, Calif.: Sage Publications), pp. 166–195.

39. Rosabeth Moss Kanter (2001) *Evolve! Succeeding in the Digital Culture of Tomorrow* (Boston: Harvard Business School Press), pp. 156–157.

40. Robert C. Solomon and Ferando Flores, op. cit., p. 43.

41. Vance H. Trimble (1990) *Sam Walton: The Inside Story of America's Richest Man* (New York: Dutton), pp. 130–131, as cited in Chris Lemley (1995) "Sam Walton and Wal-Mart Stores," in *Tales from Successful Entrepreneurs,* edited by Amar Bhide (Boston: Harvard Business School Publishers), pp. 5–15. See also Robert C. Solomon and Fernando Flores, op. cit., pp. 50–51.

42. Mark Gimein (September 2, 2002) "You Bought. They Sold," *Fortune* 146 (4), pp. 64–68, 72, 74.

43. Karl E. Weick (2001) "Leadership as the Legitimation of Doubt," in *The Future of Leadership: Today's Top Leadership Thinkers Speak to Tomorrow's Leaders,* edited by Warren Bennis, Gretchen M. Spreitzer, and Thomas G. Cummings (San Francisco: Jossey-Bass), pp. 91–102, especially p. 97.

44. Ibid., p. 97.

45. Ibid., pp. 96–97.

46. Warren Bennis (Spring 1999) "The Leadership Advantage," *Leader to Leader* newsletter (12), p. 2.

47. See von Krogh, Ichigo, and Ikujiro Nonaka, op. cit., pp. 45–68.

48. Edgar H. Schein, op. cit., pp. 85–92, especially pp. 88–89; Robert I. Sutton (Winter 2002) "Weird Ideas that Spark Innovation," *Sloan Management Review* 43 (2), pp. 83–87.

49. Ikujiro Nonaka (November–December 1991) "The Knowledge-Creating Company," *Harvard Business Review* 69 (6), p. 104.

50. von Krogh, Ichigo, and Ikujiro Nonaka, op. cit., p. 49. See their chapter, "Care in the Organization: Why an Enabling Context Matters," pp. 45–68 for a treatment of the essential role of care in knowledge creation.

CHAPTER 6

The Microskills for Knowledge Creation

People talk about what other people will listen to. . . . Nothing is more satisfying than being heard.

—Allen Ivey[1]

Truth is not introduced into the individual from without, but was within him all the time.

—Soren Kierkegaard[2]

Today's managers have a new charge—to systematically re-create the organizational context that encourages the surfacing of tacit knowledge. Hence, the creation of new knowledge is made possible by knowing how to tap the natural resource of their colleagues' "collective individualities."

It behooves us to recognize the "soft power" that care, respect, and trust evoke in the surfacing of tacit knowledge. These values are more likely to encourage new thoughts to emerge. Such knowledge is less likely to surface in the context of the "hard power" of agonistic debate, combativeness, and strife.[3] Until recently, agonistic debate was the conventional vehicle of organizational dialogue, and decision making. Perhaps the time is ripe to adopt new axioms for interpersonal communication.

We communicate not just via language. In general, managers tend to place too much emphasis on words. Communication involves more than the verbal transmission of messages. It also incorporates the nonverbal components that comprise an even more significant share of a message. As communication theorist Paul Watzlawick and his colleagues alert us, because "one cannot *not* behave," it is axiomatic that "one cannot *not* communicate"[4] [emphasis in original]. For example, the behavior of an airline passenger seated next to us who immediately buries herself in reading communicates the message that she is not interested in talking at this time. Activity or inactivity, words or silence—all have their message or communication value.

Another communication scholar, Allen Ivey, points out that nonverbal behavior establishes the basic condition of communication; it demonstrates to others that "they are truly heard."[5] Scholars in the field of face-to-face communication estimate that between 65 and 90 percent of face-to-face communication occurs at the nonverbal level.[6] It behooves us to attend as much, if not more, to nonverbal behavior as to verbal behavior.

The earlier discussion of tacit knowledge pointed out that the body is an organic extension of the brain. The messages, then, that we unconsciously send and unconsciously receive via our "body language" may not be just *nonverbal* communication (from the rational or conscious perspective), but also *tacit* or *intuitive* communication (from the arational or nonconscious perspective). To this point, the main focus has been on verbal communication that is explicit. In fact, we conventionally categorize all communication from this perspective. Thus, we not only pay the greatest attention to verbal communication, but we label all communication that is not verbal as "nonverbal communication." However, what is conventionally termed "nonverbal communication" in fact could be tacit or intuitive communication. Although verbal communication tends to be more conscious, volitional, and intentional in the messages sent, nonverbal communication tends to be less conscious, less volitional, and less intentional in the messages sent. Communication—like knowledge or understanding, in their most profound sense—may be tacit, for as some of the most perceptive scholars in this field have concluded: "Understanding . . . is not achieved until all participants in a group truly feel that the expression or concept corresponds with what they know tacitly."[7] Thus, there is no true understanding until there is tacit understanding.

Care and respect, then, may not just be emotions or values, but relevant and profoundly deep behaviors by which we tacitly communicate. Considering our response to just a few questions might illustrate this point. When others are speaking to us:

- Might we better convey our care by looking at or away from them?
- When we speak, do we better show our respect by listening to them until the completion of their thoughts, or by interrupting them?
- Would we better express our care for colleagues by listening and asking clarifying questions about whatever they are addressing in order to better comprehend their thoughts, or by changing the topic to issues we wish to talk about?

We demonstrate respect for our colleagues when we attentively listen to others and confirm our understanding of their ideas. We do so by articulating in our own words the essence of what a colleague has just said. Only when listeners understand the essence of what is said in conversation are they able to take an active and responsive posture *vis-à-vis* the speaker. Every time we suffuse our communication with the care and respect that encourages others to go on, we lower the barriers for the surfacing of tacit knowledge into the conscious domain, and make progress toward establishing the trust that makes human relationships and inquiry possible. As one scholar found: "We are likely not only to think ourselves into action, but also to act ourselves into a way of thinking."[8]

THE MICROSKILLS FOR KNOWLEDGE CREATION

It is astounding that communication has played such a central role in humankind's development through the ages, and that only in the late 20th century did scholar and communication theorist Allen Ivey begin to isolate and identify the skills that made for more effective face-to-face communication. Ivey's "microskills of communication"—which he identified in the early 1970s—provide a vehicle by which individuals can communicate more effectively, and make explicit what had largely been implicit about key aspects of human communication. Hundreds of scholarly studies throughout the world, as well as tens of thousands of executives and civil servants, have been trained in their use.[9] The effective use of these skills can convey the critical dimensions of care, respect, and trust, which are the building blocks that establish the context for creating knowledge.

The microskills are a set of hands-on, one-at-a-time, learnable communication skills. They help individuals transcend their own thoughts, and gain access to the thoughts as well as the feelings, values, and meaning making of others. In short, the microskills can help individuals to access the personal knowledge of others. In the context of knowledge creation, the microskills become critical for surfacing tacit knowledge.

The microskills of communication are comprised of two subsets: nonverbal attending skills and verbal attending skills. The nonverbal attending skills include eye contact, body language, vocal style, and verbal following. The verbal attending skills include open and closed questions, paraphrasing, reflection of feeling, reflection of meaning, and summarization.

Nonverbal Attending Skills

Eye Contact

Patterns of eye contact and gaze are among the most primary, yet underestimated, nonverbal behaviors. Generally, in the mainstream American business culture, listeners tend to look at speakers during face-to-face communication. This behavior conveys interest in, and respect for, what is being said. On the other hand, a break from normal gaze patterns, or looking away, can convey a lack of interest and even a lack of respect for what is being said. Either pattern tacitly encourages or discourages the flow of conversation.

Research indicates that differences exist in gaze patterns between males and females. When speaking, males tend to look away from listeners most of the time, making eye contact usually to emphasize significant points. While listening, males tend to look at speakers most of the time, thus indicating their attention to what is being said.[10] On the other hand, women tend to maintain more eye contact in conversations than do men. In fact, in single-gender as well as mixed-gender interactions, women tend to maintain more eye contact than do men, whether speaking or listening.[11]

Whatever the pattern, eye contact in the mainstream business culture signifies interest in what the speaker is saying. It is a powerful signal of attention and encouragement for more communication. In nonverbal communication, eye contact and gaze may be among the most relevant of behaviors that convey that one is attending and listening to others. It also sends a message of care and respect.

Body Language

There are two relevant aspects of body language—kinesics and proxemics. Kinesics involves messages that are communicated by body movement. Leaning forward or backward can encourage or discourage verbal communication. Research substantiates that leaning forward expresses interest in what is being said, whereas leaning backward generally conveys disinterest or disengagement. There appear to be some gender differentials in this area also. Men tend to recline backward when talking with others, whereas women tend to lean forward. Women's posture, therefore, may tend to encourage communication, whereas men's body posture may tend to inhibit it. Women also tend to mirror more of the body posture of their conversants. This synchronicity of body posture denotes an ultimate attending behavior that tacitly encourages others to speak.

Proxemics involves the sending and receiving of messages through the use of interpersonal space. The proximity or distance of individuals from one another can send a powerful message of comfort or discomfort about speaking. Research points out that males and females tend to stand and sit at different distances: regardless of whether the group is single or mixed gender, males tend to stand and sit farther away from one another, whereas females tend to sit or stand closer. Such nonverbal behaviors convey powerful cues that facilitate or inhibit comfortable communication.[12] A reminder: through body language we send powerful messages of which we are not aware. Congruent behavior (when words and behaviors match) therefore becomes an asset for open, full, and candid conversation. It is interesting to note that in mainstream American business culture, the most attentive body posture is a slight forward lean of the upper body trunk while seated, or a speaking distance of about an arm's length while standing.

Vocal Style

When conversing with others, the tone and pace of speech can encourage or inhibit communication. Thus, a lower tone and slower pace of speech tends to optimize interaction between participants. Such a protective tone is useful in according individuals the freedom to accept or ignore an idea or thought, in addition to the choice of listening to it. Speaking in as naturally a low tone of voice as possible and slowing down one's pace of speech are generally helpful practices that encourage others to share their thoughts and partake in a conversation.

Verbal Following

Simply staying on the topic conveys a powerful message of respect for what another person is saying. Verbal following or verbal tracking gives confidence to speakers that what is being uttered is meaningful and important. Thus, they are encouraged to tell us what they wish to say. An example of verbal tracking is when we unconsciously utter such simple verbal followers as "uh-hmmm" or "ah-ha." These utterances invite speakers to further participate and elaborate on their story or idea. However, interrupting the speaker imparts the message that what is being said is irrelevant and valueless. Thus, participation in the conversation is likely to come to a halt.

It is Monday morning, and Bill has called the three managers who report to him—Joe, Dinah, and Chris—to a special meeting:

Bill: [Seated behind his desk and ruffling through papers] I am glad you are all here. Take a seat. This is a very important meeting. The bigwigs upstairs have instructed me to tell you that they are expecting better results for this quarter. We have been given six weeks to begin meeting the new goals. Time is of the essence; we have to get this done.

Dinah: Would there be enough time to do this?

Bill: [Crossing his arms and staring into space] I see no choice in this matter.

Joe: If there is not time, how about moving resources around to make this possible?

Bill: [Frowning as his voice becomes sharp and brittle] As you know, money is tight. These are hard times. You've got to be creative in meeting these new goals.

Chris: Well Bill, I do not think that we can manage . . .

Bill: [Interrupting] There is only one answer here; you've got to.

Chris: I am not so sure we can manage to do this alone. Everyone is working . . .

Bill: [Interrupting again] Go and figure it out among yourselves and report back to me within the next two days.

Dinah, Joe, and Chris walk out of the meeting discouraged and bewildered about the problem.

It is likely that such scenarios occur all too frequently in offices across America. In many ways, it is the antithesis of effective nonverbal communication. As we witnessed, Bill, in his nonverbal behavior (seated behind his desk and ruffling papers), did not evidence any care or respect in dealing with his workers. Additionally, leaning backward in his chair and breaking eye contact denoted little interest in developing a relationship with them. Furthermore, his sharp, grating voice and interruptions reinforced the rigidity of the hierarchy that stifled collaboration.

In the next scenario, Bill produced a different outcome by using nonverbal attending microskills that generated more enthusiasm and greater participation by his team.

It is Monday morning, and Bill has called the three managers who report to him—Joe, Dinah, and Chris—to a special meeting:

Bill: [Gets up from behind his desk to greet each one of them] I am glad you are all here. Let us all sit down and talk. I've just come back from an important meeting. The managers upstairs are expecting better results for this quarter. We have been given six weeks to begin meeting the new goals that I mentioned in my last memo. Time is of the essence; we have to get this done.

Dinah: Would there be enough time to do this?

Bill: [Leaning forward and making eye contact]. That is why we are all here, to figure this out together.

Joe: [Enthusiastically] One idea I have is to move resources around to make this possible?

Bill: [Smiling, with a comfortable tone of voice] As you know, money is tight. These are hard times. I would like to hear your most creative ideas about how to meet these new goals.

Chris: Well Bill, I do not think that we can manage on our own, given the cutbacks we've had already.

Bill: [Leaning forward and maintaining eye contact] Uh-hum. Uh-hah. Say more. I'd like to hear your ideas.

Chris: I have an idea. Perhaps we can handle this situation by checking with other departments about how they are dealing with it.

Bill: Chris, that is a good idea. I look forward to hearing from you within the next two days for all the other good ideas you three will come up with.

Dinah, Joe, and Chris walk out of the meeting encouraged and confident about the possibilities for generating a solution to their problem.

It is likely that such scenarios occur all too infrequently in offices across America. In many ways, this meeting exemplifies effective nonverbal communication. Bill expressed his care and respect for the team by coming from around his desk to talk with them. By doing so, he nonverbally expressed a collaborative demeanor. Additionally, by leaning forward in his chair and maintaining eye contact, he denoted genuine interest in their ability to successfully address this problem. Furthermore, his use of minimal encouragers conveyed his confidence in their abilities to collaboratively solve this problem. What this conversation reflects is that Bill and his team were able to communicate at a congruently tacit level that furthered the unraveling of the problem.

Verbal Attending Skills

The verbal attending skills involve a process of first listening attentively, and then using the microskills to generate more comprehensive communication with one another. The use of these verbal attending skills helps to establish more comfortable relationships with others. They also encourage individuals to share information more openly. Among the most useful verbal attending skills for knowledge creation are open and closed questions, paraphrasing, reflection of meaning, and summarization.

Open and Closed Questions

It is common knowledge that one asks questions to gather information. However, different questions elicit surprisingly different responses. There are two types of microskill questions—closed questions and open questions.

Closed questions tend to generate a narrow range of responses. They typically begin with words like do, did, are, or is. Closed questions almost always generate yes, no, or brief answers. Such questions are particularly useful to establish specific facts or information. However, closed questions generally do not encourage self-expression or full responses.

Open questions tend to generate a wider range of responses. They are invitations to talk and generate far more information and conversation. Typically, open questions begin with words like what, could, would, or how.

Asking the same question in an open or closed fashion tends to generate very different responses, as the following example indicates:

Closed Question: "Is the research proposal ready?"
Open Question: "How is the research proposal coming along?"

The closed question invariably elicits a brief yes or no answer. The open question has the uncanny power to encourage a response of greater length and depth. In a knowledge creation situation, open questions widen the scope of possibilities. Open questions, by their nature, elicit more complete responses than do one-word answers. These longer responses trigger new insights and unrealized perspectives that are likely to lead to knowledge creation. For example, the use of certain stems invariably provokes different responses.[13]

Open questions that being with:	Generate responses dealing with:	Example:
What	Facts and information	"Jane, what's going on with your research?"
How	Process	"Fred, how is the new project coming along?"
Why	Analysis	"Hank, why was your team late with its proposal?"
Could you and would you	Maximal response	"Lisa, could you tell me more about your new idea?"
		"Jeff, would you tell us about the meeting you attended?"

Paraphrasing

Paraphrasing is another powerful skill that encourages others to say more and speak at greater length. Any indication of understanding what another person has just said encourages him or her to elaborate more fully on thoughts and details. Paraphrasing involves restating in one's own words the essence of what has just been said. There are three components to a paraphrase: The beginning stem; the restatement; and the concluding, checking stem.

A beginning stem may be as simple as:

"What I hear you saying is that . . . "
"It seems that you perceive the situation as . . . "
"You're telling me that . . . "

An example of a restatement in one's own words of the essence of what has just been said is:

Statement: " . . . the office politics is interfering with our productivity."
Restatement: " . . . the infighting among teams has cut productivity."

Examples of concluding, checking stems include:

"... is that about right?"

"... does this make sense?"

"... did I get it right?"

The following dialogue demonstrates the use of all three components of a paraphrase:

Laura: I'm stuck in a situation. I've been trying to market our new line of software. The public relations firm we outsourced to in the past does not seem to understand that this new product operates at a whole new level of technology, or how to position and market it. I am spending a great deal of time with them and getting nowhere.

Larry: What I hear you saying, Laura, is that because this firm doesn't understand this new generation of technology, it cannot market the product effectively, is that so?

Laura: That's it! Maybe we ought to consider new options. I've just realized that there may be other firms that are more up-to-date about this new technology. That's the problem.

In this example, Larry's paraphrasing conveyed to Laura that he understood her dilemma, and thus clarified the problem. His ability to express Laura's thoughts in his own words encouraged her to express her tacit knowing, and thus to find her own solution to the problem. As this example demonstrates, paraphrasing is one of the most powerful microskills that facilitates knowledge creation.

Reflection of Feeling

Communication is more than the objective sharing of information, and effective management involves more than the machine-like achievement of goals. Emotions pervade communication between human beings, and strong currents of feelings often swirl below many workplace issues. This is true not only of individuals but of groups as well. Feelings may be held not just by an individual, but by an entire group. Thus, reflection of feelings can be made of a group as well as an individual. Hence, the microskill of reflection of feeling captures the emotional aspects of human beings. The skill of reflection of feeling seeks to identify and to make explicit the emotions, be they overt or concealed, thus permitting one to tap into a speaker's or a group's emotions. There is a specific structure to elicit the reflection of feeling.

A beginning stem that includes the name of the person:

Peter, you seem to be feeling ...

A label is given to the emotion being expressed:

Peter, you seem to be feeling frustrated . . .

A brief, present-tense paraphrase of the context for the situation follows:

Peter, you appear to be feeling frustrated because of the extensive responsibilities
that have been assigned to you lately.
(Useful words here are: because, about, or when)

A concluding checking stem follows:

Could that be it?
Is that about right?

In the following conversation, Jim attempts to understand and reflect on Joan's feelings:

Joan: It seems that Bill is consistently assigning me people to work on my project,
and then deciding to reassign them to other projects.
Jim: Joan, you seem to be angry about Bill's vacillating management style. Am I
hearing you correctly?
Joan: Absolutely. And what's more yet . . .

Jim's reflection of feeling conveys to Joan his awareness of her feelings. This encourages Joan to go on and provide more information about the situation. A word of caution: the listener needs to be careful about correctly labeling the speaker's emotions. Otherwise, one runs the risk of expressing inattentive listening, misunderstanding, or disinterest in the situation, as well as a lack of empathy for the person.

Reflection of Meaning

Making meaning of one's world is basic to human experience. Every human being possesses a deep structure of beliefs, experiences, and values that are implicit. These meaning structures pattern life experience as well as the environment in which we find ourselves. Individuals make sense of their environment and their experiences through the meaning(s) they draw from them. At this level, fragments of seemingly random thoughts constantly crisscross our minds as we engage in our daily activities. Reflecting on and clarifying these deeply held fragments of thoughts, ideas, and their meanings leads to their clustering into more coherent wholes. Thus, seemingly random thoughts coalesce to form new gestalts. To access them is to clarify or surface meanings that heretofore were ambiguous and of which we may have been unaware. The process of reflecting meanings tends to enable the surfacing of tacit knowledge from the implicit or unconscious level to the explicit or conscious level.

The reflection of meaning may be the microskill that is most relevant to the process of knowledge creation. This microskill helps us access the deep areas of an individual's implicit knowledge. Hence, the avenues toward knowledge creation vary, because each individual possesses a different structure of meaning that impels behaviors.

As is true of other microskills, in using the skill of reflection of meaning, there is a certain structure to follow.

1. Open with a beginning stem, such as: "You mean that . . . " "Sounds like the sense you make of this is . . . " "Could it be that you mean . . . "
2. Use the speaker's very words to describe the essence of the meaning. It is important to avoid any interpretation and instead to remain within the confines of the speaker's frame of reference.
3. Follow with a paraphrase of the speaker's central thoughts that encapsulates his or her essence, always remaining within the speaker's frame of reference.
4. Close with a checking-out stem such as: " . . . is that about right?" or " . . . did I hear you correctly?"

Let's look at a scenario that depicts the microskill of reflection of meaning:

Peter: I have an idea about a research project that I would like to run by you. I have been thinking about asking Tom to join the new project team, yet for some reason, I am reluctant to ask him.

Jane: Sounds like you are hesitant about asking him.

Peter: That's right. I don't know where my reservations come from.

Jane: What sense do you make of your reservations?

Peter: Well, the thought just crossed my mind that he appears to be very knowledgeable in this area, but I am not sure if he can function collaboratively in this group.

Jane: What was your thinking when you first had the idea of asking him?

Peter: My first thought about him was the extent of knowledge he could bring to the effort.

Jane: Am I hearing you correctly, that Tom's knowledge could be critical to this effort and seems to supersede your doubt about his ability to collaborate?

Peter: Yes, that's it exactly! Now, it makes sense to include Tom on the team. I feel comfortable with this decision.

This scenario illustrates the use of the microskill of reflection of meaning. In this dialogue, Jane initially elicited from Peter his perception of the problem. Then, she captured the essence of Peter's own words while, without interpretation, carefully remained within his frame of reference.

Next, Jane paraphrased his central thoughts, again remaining within Peter's perspective of the problem. Through this process, she was able to clarify Peter's thoughts and meanings about this problem. In so doing, Peter was able to make better sense of his dilemma, and thereby act more decisively on it.

Used appropriately, the reflection of meaning can evoke understanding and trust. Used ethically, this microskill can be extraordinarily useful in determining the way an individual perceives a problem, the sense another makes of a dilemma, the values that motivate behavior, or how a colleague arrives at a particular solution to a problem. As such, the reflection of meaning is one of the most valuable microskills in the process of knowledge creation.

Summarization

The microskill of summarization compels listeners to listen closely to what is being said, as well as pay attention to the nonverbal behaviors that are being expressed. Summarization meaningfully integrates the essential elements of what has been said, and can be of value to both speaker and listener. It is a skill that integrates and brings together elements of information that may have surfaced at different points during a conversation, which makes it possible for participants to generate a more global view of the situation at hand. Summarization is a helpful skill that also can bring into a coherent whole a number of dialogues that may have occurred over a period of time. Thus, this skill can denote issues that were immanent in these conversations, and focus attention on them. As a result, a holistic picture emerges that provides everyone with the chance to understand the situation in a new way. Furthermore, summarization provides a check on distortions or misunderstandings of what might have occurred in the conversation. Periodic summarizations encourage the checking of perceptions and more attentive and accurate listening. In short, effective summarization can dispel confusion, organize major issues, clarify thinking, and bring information together as the basis for common action.

When summarization is implemented accurately, it can be of tremendous assistance in moving a conversation forward from exploration to problem-solving and action. Below is a suggested sequence to follow during summarization:

1. Make use of every attending skill to listen fully.
2. Note inconsistencies and dichotomies in conversations.
3. Pay close attention to central threads of information.
4. Summarize all that you have heard as accurately as possible.
5. Use a checking stem at the end to ensure accuracy.

The following vignette between Ray and his supervisor, Amy, demonstrates the microskill of summarization:

Amy: Ray, when we met last week, you were preoccupied with some problems with the team, is that right?

Ray: That's right. As you know I am trying to get some new ideas off the ground, and the team thinks that I should come up with the solutions.

Amy: I hear you saying that you want the whole team to participate in searching for new ideas together rather than you alone, is that so?

Ray: That's right. And furthermore, I want everyone to speak their minds and share their ideas with the group. This is how out-of-the box innovations are generated.

Amy: If I understand you correctly, you want the team to stop relying on you. Rather, you want them to become involved with you in generating creative ideas together. Did I get that right?

Ray: Precisely! What I have not conveyed to them is how much I value their ideas and the process of sharing them together.

In this vignette, Amy used the microskill of summarization to draw together the central threads of Ray's dilemma. In so doing, she clarified his thinking and Ray was then able to proceed more effectively with his team's endeavor.

CONCLUSION

One of the most important axioms of communication is: "one cannot *not* communicate"[14] [emphasis in original]. Whether or not we are aware of our behavior, we are always sending messages to others, not only by our verbal but, even more so, by our nonverbal behaviors. This is true in every human interaction and in every setting. However, it is especially relevant to those who work in Information Era organizations. In such workplaces, not only does the coordinated achievement of goals depend on successful communication, but—today more than ever—on the creation of knowledge. In this new era, a higher level of communication is required, and the microskills of communication provide us with the specific tools to more fully communicate with one another. These skills are a key to externalizing the tacit knowledge we all possess.

NOTES

1. Allen Ivey (1997) *Basic Attending Skills,* 3rd ed. (North Amherst, Mass.: Microtraining Associates), pp. 9, 52.

2. Soren Kierkegaard (1844) "Philosophical Fragments, or a Fragment of Philosophy," trans. by David F. Swenson, in (1947) *A Kierkegaard Anthology,* edited by Robert Bretall (Princeton, N.J.: Princeton University Press), p. 153.

3. "Soft power" and "hard power" are terms adapted from Joseph S. Nye (2002) *The Paradox of American Power: Why the World's Only Superpower Can't Go It Alone.* (New York: Oxford University Press), pp. 8–12. Nye suggests that co-optive power is soft (like American democratic ideals), whereas command power (like American military might) is hard.

4. Paul Watzlawick, Janet Beavin Bavelas, and Don Jackson (1967) *Pragmatics of Human Communication: A Study of Interactional Patterns, Pathologies and Paradoxes* (New York: W.W. Norton), pp. 48, 51.

5. Allen E. Ivey (1994) *Intentional Interviewing and Counseling: Facilitating Client Development in a Multicultural Society,* 3rd ed. (Pacific Grove, Calif.: Brooks/Cole Publishing Company), pp. 23–34.

6. John F. Kikoski and Catherine Kano Kikoski (2000) *Reflexive Communication in the Culturally Diverse Workplace* (Westport, Conn.: Praeger), p. 46, citing Ray Birdwhistell (1970) *Kinesics and Context: Essays on Body Motion Communication* (Philadelphia: University of Pennsylvania Press), pp. 57–58, and Edward T. Hall and Mildred Reed Hall (1987) *Hidden Differences: Doing Business with the Japanese* (New York: Anchor Books/Doubleday), p. 3.

7. Georg von Krogh, Kazuo Ichijo, and Ikujiro Nonaka (2000) *Enabling Knowledge Creation: How to Unlock the Mystery of Tacit Knowledge and Release the Power of Innovation* (New York: Oxford University Press), p. 136.

8. David G. Myers (1987) *Social Psychology* (New York: McGraw-Hill), p. 148. Cited by Dorothy Leonard-Berton (1995) *Wellsprings of Knowledge: Building and Sustaining the Sources of Innovation* (Boston: Harvard Business School Press), p. 259.

9. Ivey (1994), op. cit., p. 4.

10. For chapters delineating the verbal and nonverbal behaviors of white males, as well as women, African Americans, Hispanics, and Asian Americans, see individual chapters in John F. Kokoski and Catherine Kano Kikoski (1999) *Reflexive Communication in the Culturally Diverse Workplace* (Westport, Conn.: Praeger Publishers). Ralph V. Exline (1963) "Explorations in the Process of Person Perception: Visual Interaction in Relation to Competition, Sex, and Need for Affiliation," *Journal of Personality* 31, pp. 1–20; Michael Argyle (1979) "New Developments in the Analysis of Social Skills," in *Nonverbal Behavior: Applications and Cultural Implications,* edited by Aaron Wolfgang (New York: Academic Press), p. 139; and Adam Kendon (1967) "Some Functions of Gaze-Direction in Social Interaction," *Acta Psychologica* 26, pp. 22–63.

11. John F. Dovidio and Steve L. Ellyson (1985) "Patterns of Visual Dominance Behavior in Humans," in *Power, Dominance and Nonverbal Behavior,* edited by Steve L. Ellyson and John F. Dovidio (New York: Springer-Verlag), p. 140; Judee Burgoon (1994) "Nonverbal Signals," in *Handbook of Interpersonal Communication,* 2nd ed., edited by Mark L. Knapp and Gerald R. Miller (Thousand Oaks, Calif.: Sage Publications), p. 244; Barbara W. Eakins and R. Gene Eakins (1978) *Sex Differences in Human Communication* (Boston: Houghton-Mifflin), p. 150; and Judith A. Hall (1985) "Male and Female Nonverbal Behavior," in *Multichannel Integrations of Nonverbal Behavior,* edited by Aron W. Siegman and Stanley Feldstein (Hillside, N.J.: Lawrence Erlbaum Associates), pp. 210–213.

12. Argyle op. cit.; Elizabeth Aries (1982) "Verbal and Nonverbal Behavior in Single-Sex and Mixed-Sex Groups," *Psychological Reports* 51, pp. 127–134; Judee Burgoon (1994) "Nonverbal Signals," *Handbook of Interpersonal Communication,* 2nd

ed., edited by Mark L. Knapp and Gerald R. Miller (Thousand Oaks, Calif.: Sage Publications), p. 244; Dovidio and Ellyson, op. cit.; Alice H. Eagly (1987) *Sex Differences in Social Behavior: A Social Role Interpretation* (Hillsdale N.J.: Lawrence Erlbaum Associates), p. 103; Eakins and Eakins, op. cit.; Exline, op. cit.; Hall, op. cit.; Adam Kendon (1967) "Some Functions of Gaze-Direction in Social Interaction," *Acta Psychologica* 26, pp. 22–63; and Anneke Vrugt and Ada Kerkstra (1984) "Sex Differences in Nonverbal Communication." *Semiotica* 50 (1/2), pp. 2–11.

13. Ivey (1994), op. cit., p. 4.
14. Watzlawicket al., op. cit., p. 49.

CHAPTER 7

Asking Questions: Widening the Lens, Sharpening the Focus

Judge a man by his questions rather than his answers.

—Voltaire[1]

Indeed, the most common source of mistakes in management decisions is the emphasis on finding the right answer rather than the right question.

—Peter Drucker[2]

Questions are not only the wellsprings of inquiry; they are the pathways to intuition. Socrates, the first great philosopher in the Western tradition, was renowned for asking questions. He is remembered less for any particular philosophical doctrine than for a method of arriving at them.[3] As one scholar wrote, Socrates not only asked individuals "to state and defend their moral *intuitions* which underlie their way of life," but also dialogued with them "to facilitate discovery"[4] [italics added for emphasis]. Perhaps Socrates should be remembered more for engaging others in what we today call knowledge creation, rather than for teaching a set of arrived-at truths. Socrates' approach has had an enduring impact for 2,500 years because it did not involve a set of answers, but rather a way of questioning—the Socratic Method of questioning—that involves dialogue.[5] One scholar may have touched on the power and fascination with dialogue when she stated: "The essence of dialogue lies in the interaction of human minds."[6] Socrates bequeathed not a fixed doctrine or body of philosophical knowledge, but rather a dialogical (process of dialogue) or conversational method for realizing our own insights, thoughts, and conclusions—ones that are new and yet to be discovered.[7]

Plato's dialogues provide ample evidence that Socrates was a good listener, and one with whom others could hold a fair, respectful, and steady dialogue. He also was concerned with the everyday—Socrates' earliest dialogues (sadly lost) may have been with Simon, a cobbler.[8] In today's terms, Socrates' position can be compared with that of a consultant, a coach, or a discussion leader, and his fellow conversants can be compared with customers, clients, or partners.[9] Given the complexity and variation among individuals, Socrates used a number of techniques in his dialogues—satire, irony, flattery, myth, paradox, and others—to enable the conceptual breakthroughs in the thinking of others that he sought[10] However, above all, Socrates used and is known for asking questions. In fact, the Socratic Method rests on asking questions. As one scholar noted, Socrates' approach was one "of continual questioning, of continual testing of hypotheses; it is the narrative of a search, an account of the process itself, of thinking, rather than of conclusions arrived at."[11] For Plato, Socrates' student who carried on his teachings, the purpose of the back-and-forth activity that is inherent in dialogue was to be found in its original Greek meanings—not only "to confer with others," but also "to examine" or "to consider." Perhaps more importantly, a *dialectician* (for the ancient Greeks) was an individual who "knows how to ask and answer questions."[12]

Could there be modern-day applications for managers in these ancient formulations and meanings? Socrates used questions extensively to clarify partially formed perceptions or thoughts, as well as to determine new directions. In so doing, Socrates did not use just ordinary questions. Rather, as one scholar put it, he utilized a "deeply reflexive strategy" that used powerful questions in a novel way—he triggered responses that surfaced new awareness, generated new meanings, and created new knowledge.[13] Socrates may have been among the earliest and most ancient of humans who sought, as we do today, to create knowledge. It is possible that in this era, knowing how to ask questions that create knowledge may be more important than ever before.

Managers and leaders during the Industrial Era tended to be "strong" leaders who "knew," who "had a vision," and whose individual charisma as well as personal assuredness almost commanded others to follow in their path. Information Era leadership may be different. Information Era leaders more likely may be individuals with humility who may not "know" completely, but whose admission of this fact, paradoxically, invites the highest level of participation from their colleagues. The old leader "knew," and thus commanded. The new leader—who may not know everything—asks questions.[14]

In Industrial Era organizations, "information went up" and "decisions came down" the unilinear, unbroken, relatively inflexible "chain of command." Communication in meetings often meant agonistic and disputatious "battles." In such situations, discussion may have been less important than was obedience. Today, information flows multilaterally in flexible, "networked" channels in which multiple inputs and rapid responses (given the nonlinear environment) are necessary. In such situations, egalitarian discussion and especially asking questions may be advantageous.

Perhaps surprising to some, the Socratic dialogues and the Socratic Method may provide valuable contemporary guidance, because Socrates—no less than today's manager or executive—was interested in *clarifying partially formed perceptions or thoughts*, in *determining new directions*, and in *creating new knowledge*. He did so through a sort of cooperative inquiry that involved fewer assertions of individual will and more emphasis on a common, respectful search for mutual understanding via conversation. Each character in Plato's dialogues stood for a point of view, and Socrates drew them out by means of a variety of techniques—irony for some, paradox for others, questions for all. As Princeton philosopher Cornel West put it: "Socrates said he wanted to be a midwife of ideas."[15]

Today's modern scholarship provides a more explicit understanding of the use of questions than does the era of Socrates or Plato. Today, we need new knowledge and new types of questions. Such questions may be better suited to help decision makers make sense of their increasingly complex environment. Questions that are embedded in the new paradigm, General Systems Theory (GST), focus on the system as a whole. This paradigm provides a perspective that better explains the web of relationships among the elements that constitute a system, whether it is an organization or its environment. Hence, questions asked from the GST perspective are likely to generate responses that evoke information which, in turn, generate additional information that provides broader understandings of problems or situations. In contrast, linear (or lineal) questions asked from the linear paradigm tend to limit responses, because the focus is on causality.

SYSTEMS THEORY

Through the end of the modern era, the scientific method dominated thinking in the fields of science as well as management. Traditionally, scientists as well as managers were taught to solve problems as Newton did—by breaking them into separate parts and subjecting them to linear cause-and-effect analysis.

The scientific method worked well in explaining the physics of machines or electricity, as well as the geology of rocks. However, it did not adequately describe the operations of the environment in its wholeness or the dynamic complexity generated by the multiple variables of domains such as meteorology or ecology, nor did it begin to explain human behavior—which is not only complex, but operates with a purpose and intentionality that is not true of the inanimate objects that have been the purview of traditional science.

As we entered the 21st century, ecosystemic perspectives gained greater prominence not only in the natural sciences, but also in organizations. Scientists increasingly realized that the world in its natural state was not necessarily broken down into parts or described by linear, cause-and-effect operations; nor was nature relatively static with a limited number of operating variables. The traditional, Newtonian paradigm worked well in explaining the limited number of variables that brought about advances in such fields as physics, mechanics, and energy, which resulted in the Industrial Era machines and the electricity that drove them. However, scientists increasingly realized that the tools made available to them by the traditional scientific method to solve more fluid and complex problems—such as those posed by meteorology and ecology, let alone human behavior—were inadequate.

Scientists came to conclude that both the biological sciences and behavioral fields were better explained and understood from an ecological or systemic perspective. The advantage of the systemic approach is that it embodies the interrelatedness of the many parts of a system that, through their multiple interactions, create a unique and dynamic environment. Scientists studying the natural environment (or ecosystem) realized that working from the separate perspectives—for example, of chemistry, physics, or biology—limited their ability to comprehend the wholeness of nature, its complexity, and the relationships among its component parts.

Given these realizations, the time was ripe for a paradigm shift—a significant departure in the way one perceived and made sense of the world. The shift involved seeking to understand patterns, processes, and ways of behaving from a systemic rather than a linear perspective. The theory that emerged focused on the wholeness of an entity rather than its parts, and thus introduced a new conceptual framework to perceive patterns and make sense of complexity.

GST was developed by Ludwig von Bertalanffy, an Austrian biologist with broad research interests.[16] His far-ranging theory has had an enduring impact on the physical sciences, the social and behavioral sciences, and the study and practice of management. Departing from the prevailing mechanistic and reductionistic approach of science, which focused on linear and continuous sets of cause-and-effect explanations, GST offered a new framework that focused on wholeness, relationships, and interacting variables. The constraints of deductive, scientific analysis that demanded facts were replaced by a holistic systems perspective that enabled gestalts or patterns to be better apprehended.

As one scholar put it, GST can be described as "attention to organization, to the relationship between parts, to the concentration on patterned rather than on linear relationships, to a consideration of events in the context in which they are occurring rather than an isolation of events from their environmental context."[17] Such an approach is far more useful to those who manage organizations in today's nonlinear environment than is any other approach. GST focuses on the dynamic context—which today is continually changing—rather than on linear causality.

Social scientist Gregory Bateson illustrates the operations of the linear approach in contrast to the systemic approach. He found that the linear or "billiard ball" model inadequately explained the natural world of living beings. In the Newtonian-influenced scientific method (much like the billiard ball model) a limited number of "billiard balls" or variables act unidirectionally on each other.[18] However, in the more complex world of ecology (as in the world of organizations), managers (like meteorologists) find themselves contending with many variables that operate in circular or recursive, ways. Furthermore, in the living world, force and energy, as well as relationships and information, are operative.

Gregory Bateson clearly explained the difference between linear and systemic approaches via the illustration of kicking a stone versus kicking a dog. In kicking an inanimate stone, the kick transmits energy that moves the stone a unilinear distance that is predictable, given the limited number of variables—the weight of the stone and the strength of the kick. However, should a man kick an animate dog, the dog's reaction is not contingent on the energy of the man because the dog possesses its own energy and volition, which render the outcome unpredictable. This example conveys information about a relationship between the person and the dog. The dog could react in a variety of ways that depend on the existing relationship and how the dog responds to the kick. The dog could jump and angrily bite the man, cower, or run away. The dog's response then transmits information to the man that may change his own ensuing behavior. In the event that the dog bites the man, he may ponder about his next action.

GST is most fitting for work with organizations as well as any system—whether teams, divisions, departments, or the enterprise as a whole—in relation to its environment. This approach does not focus on the isolated, single elements of a system in its efforts to understand or change it—such as a single action or problem. Rather it focuses on the interrelationships among all the different parts of that system that have created the problem or can dissolve it. As such, GST provides a new framework within which to perceive, interact, and bring about the desired changes in an organization.

GST is built on a recursive or circular paradigm, which focuses on assessing the multiple variables that operate on each other within a system. Such an approach creates an increased awareness and understanding of situations for managers who operate in fluid environments. Hence, one is able to apprehend the relationships among the different parts that create certain dynamics within a system. Once the dynamics of a system become evident, it is then possible to bring about the desired change.

Managers, supervisors, CEOs, or workers who adopt the GST paradigm no longer see themselves as managing others or the system via skill or personality. The concept of the manager as change agent and the worker as recipient may no longer be an effective approach. Managers who adopt a systemic perspective no longer see themselves as the only energizing agents of change, and workers as simply passive recipients. As the earlier example of the man kicking the stone or the dog illustrated, all individuals operate in a larger system in which manager, worker, environment, and other factors interact and influence each other in nonlinear ways. Every interaction and reaction constantly alters the dynamics of the field that the components of the system have created.

Frequently, it is difficult for managers to understand systems thinking. One reason, Peter Senge suggests, may be that our English language, with its subject-verb-object linear structure, leads us to perceive and think in a linear way. Senge further states that, "Reality is made up of circles but we see straight lines. . . . If we want to see systemwide interrelationships, we need a language of interrelationships, a language made up of circles. Without such a language, our habitual ways of seeing the world produce fragmented views and counterproductive actions."[19] A new, systemic language is most fitting to our present-day complex era—one that would enable us to shift our view of organizations from a linear, cause-and-effect perspective to a systemic perspective. Hence, through this lens, new dynamics emerge that create new and differing contexts. Such shifts transcend the linear causality of events and open up new possibilities and options for change.

Three major concepts of GST are relevant to our discussion of communication and the circular use of questions: recursion, feedback, and neutrality.

Recursion/Circularity

> When the phenomena of the universe are seen as linked together by cause-and-effect and energy transfer, the resulting picture is of complexly branching and interconnecting chains of causation.
>
> —Gregory Bateson[20]

Recursion, which also is referred to as reciprocal causality, situates individuals and events in a position of mutual interaction and influence. Elements or individuals are not perceived in isolation; rather the focus is on their relationships and the ways in which they mutually interact and influence each other. Similarly, one cannot control an individual unless the other individual is willing to submit and be controlled. As Bateson states that, "Any person or agency that influences a complex interactive system thereby becomes a part of that system, and no part can ever have control of the whole."[21] The contribution of recursion is that it induces us to take into consideration that we inevitably are part of a larger context and are an inextricable part of that which we seek to change.

GST is built on a recursive epistemology, whereby the manager focuses on the recursiveness of interactions among the parts in order to perceive the holistic pattern. Members of a system can then understand their dilemma of being caught in a circular pattern with significant ramifications. In contrast, a linear approach is limiting because it focuses on only a partial arc of a larger circular whole. Thus, the circular approach provides a more complete and coherent perspective. Via a circular perspective, observers come to see themselves as part of the pattern that they are observing.

It is unfortunate that our conventional language and structures of grammar tend to emphasize linear thinking and description. For example, rather than referring to a team member by saying, "Joe is inefficient" (linear language), one might use more systemic language by saying "Joe's job performance is inefficient." The former statement takes the employee out of his context, whereas the latter places the emphasis on the context and the relationships in the context, rather than on the individual himself. Such systemic language leads one to consider other factors in the context that could play a role in the employee's inefficiency, and cues us to speculate on the elements in that situation that may account for this behavior. This approach inclines one to perceive the problem from a circular, rather than a linear, cause-and-effect perspective. It easily could be the case that Joe is ineffective by virtue of his personal nature, as the linear language suggests. However, by using more systemic language, one opens up the situation to the consideration of many more factors in the context that could account for the problem (like his coworkers or his boss), or to the discovery of new and yet-unrealized factors that could motivate Joe to new and higher levels of efficiency.

Human behavior is complex. It could be misleading to evaluate an individual on a single segment of performance, rather than taking into consideration the existing dynamics of the larger system. Given the complexity of human nature, the systemic approach offers a wider lens by which to understand the contextual factors that lead to this worker's performance.

Understanding circularity is as easy as

understanding the difference between a line and a circle. . . . This circular process was understood as . . . feedback loops. . . . Events that exchange information in a system or context could no longer be viewed as sequential or lineal deterministic chains of events. The feedback loop describes a circular or spiraling information process in which D circles back to A and has an effect on A that, of course, includes the information distributions from B and C. A now has a context (A, B, C, and D) and is a part of a system in which it both acts and is acted upon by the components of its system.[22]

Undergirding circularity is the knowledge that all parts within a system are connected with one another. Thus, no single element of the system ever totally controls another. For example, every individual is seen as influencing and is influenced by every other individual. Hence, one cannot conclude that a single element has caused a problem in a department, but rather that the problem is likely to reside in the relationships among the individuals who constitute that department.

Feedback

Feedback is an important concept in GST. It is the information loop that is fed back into the system in a circular manner. A thermostat that turns a furnace on or off to regulate the temperature in a room provides a simple example of feedback. Feedback signals the system whether change is imminent or the status quo is to be maintained.

There are large numbers of biological phenomena that can be best understood by feedback operations. For example, the maintenance of equilibrium or balance in an organism is a model of feedback. Feedback systems in the human body are responsible for the regulation of our actions. When we try to pick up an object, a report is sent to our central nervous system indicating the distance by which we have failed to pick up the object; this feedback is then sent to the central nervous system so that our movement is altered until the goal is reached.

According to one of its most incisive but comprehensive definitions, feedback occurs when: "part of a system's output is reintroduced into the system as information about the output."[23] In the context of an organization, the "output" is composed of the ideas, thoughts, beliefs, interpretations, actions, and behaviors that have been communicated. To feed that output back into the system as information is to add breadth, depth, and richness to the flow of information. Such enriched dialogues increase the options, possibilities, and chances for the organization not only to survive, but also to thrive, because of this augmented information—the collectively generated feedback. Therefore, communication techniques and practices that enhance feedback promote organizational success, whereas communication techniques and practices that inhibit feedback threaten organizational demise. Thus, feedback processes are mechanisms responsible for self-correction. They are responsible for signaling the changes and fluctuations that make possible the survival of the system.

Neutrality

The third concept, neutrality, promotes the flow of feedback. In an organizational setting, neutrality means that participants need to (1) be curious and (2) listen respectfully to every utterance, every bit of feedback that provides information about the system that constitutes the organization.[24]

Coming from the Latin *neutralis*, or *not either*, neutrality may at first bring to mind thoughts of being noncommittal or not favoring any stance. However, neutrality takes on a more positive posture in that it encourages acceptance of ideas without condition. Assuming a stance of neutrality in a group setting invites multiple perspectives to emerge without any sense of threat, rejection, or dismissal. Rather, an appreciation of differing views is better promoted without any support or coalition with any individual or party.

Neutrality is a multipositional rather than a nonpositional stance. It means that one is available to listen without judgment. Neutrality or *respectful curiosity* enables one to ask additional questions, thus creating even more feedback that further deepens the pool of ideas.[25] In so doing, neutrality increases the possibilities for developing new meanings, as well as providing greater appreciation for, and openness to, multiple points of view. Hence, by at least provisionally relinquishing oneself from attachment to any perception or point of view, neutrality affords more freedom and flexibility. Consequently, in conversations characterized by neutrality, the free flow of information is more likely to encourage the surfacing and expression of tacit knowledge in response to questions.

An outstanding attribute of neutrality is that it confers on individuals the ability to move from one position on an issue to another in difficult settings. In meetings characterized by strife and sticky coalitions, in which everyone is vying for position and escalating, a stance of neutrality enables one to move through these dissenting claims untarnished. Neutrality also enables one to better sense or discern the partial values of differing positions that, in a new synthesis, can bring about new outcomes.

THE FUNCTION OF QUESTIONS

[T]he questions one asks themselves determine what answers one will produce.

—John T. Kirby[26]

There once was a manager who was having a productive meeting with some staff members. They had been coming to him for several weeks about some difficulties they had experienced while working together on a project. They had made much progress in their working relationship and on the project. After laughing and regaling him with positive stories about their recent achievements, the manager asked them: "Now, tell me how you are coming along with your problem." Imperceptibly, the mood between the staff changed such that by the end of the meeting, the two of them were criticizing and sniping at each other as bitterly as before. It was not until he thought about it later that the manager understood what had happened.

As the manager realized, just asking about a problem is to elicit its emergence and to validate its existence. The awareness created is that however a manager responds, whatever she does or does not do, whatever he does or does not say, creates a process that can yield positive, negative, or neutral outcomes for the situation. This opens up a spectrum of possibilities and options that, being unsaid, were not previously available.[27]

It may be surprising to realize how little we know about that verbal construction that we use every day of our lives—asking questions. We are all familiar with the first function of questions—to provide information and to inform ourselves. We ask questions to orient ourselves to a situation that is new to us and because we seek to make sense of the world around us. Such questions change us.

A second function of questions—whether intended or unintended—is to change others. There are times when managers ask "orienting questions"—questions that are not only intended to secure information about a particular situation but which can trigger unintended outcomes in respondents. To ask in an investigative, but conventional, fashion—"Who did what?" "When?" and Where?"—may be to secure the "facts" about a situation. Such questions are "linear questions." These questions seek to determine the specific and overt "causes" of problems so that they can be "solved" according to a "rational," linear, "a leads to b," "cause-and-effect" process. Such linear questions also "tend to convey a judgmental attitude that something within the individual is wrong, and ought not be the way it is."[28] In so doing, what a questioner may be unintentionally accomplishing is to "evoke shame, guilt, and defensiveness" in another.[29] For example, asking "Why did you do that?" "What's your problem?" or "Did you cause or contribute to this problem?" almost invariably leads to a cause-and-effect response—with the respondent as the cause. If reciprocity is one of the most powerful dynamics in life, then such questions could lead listeners to shrink, if not to close themselves off, from such questions.

A third function of questions is to open up listeners and invite them to become participants in a conversation or dialogue. These types of questions *can change the listener.* In fact, it is possible that these questions can not only change the listener, but reflexively change the questioner as well. In such situations, both questioner and questioned can realize a heightened state of awareness of their surroundings and their own role, as well as the role of others upon them. With the acquisition of skills to formulate such questions, managers and leaders are in a better position to monitor the impact of their own behavior on others. Thus, the focus shifts from solving others' problems to monitoring one's own behavior and its impact. This category of questions is termed systemic questions.

SYSTEMIC QUESTIONS

Three types of systemic questions are treated in this section: circular questions, hypothetical questions, and reflexive questions. All three types of questions are based on GST. The concepts of feedback, neutrality, and circularity provide the pragmatic guidelines for asking these questions.

Circular Questions

Circular questions are based on the GST paradigm according to which systems in the natural world operate. The operations by which one apprehends the natural world—for example, determining a hurricane's path—are better described by multiple, interacting circular loops rather than linear cause-and-effect factors. Circular questions are more effective in eliciting information about the context and dynamics of a system. Hence, circular questions widen the scope and deepen perspectives of both questioner and questioned.

Circular questioning is particularly useful in generating feedback. In asking circular questions, one reintroduces previously elicited information—feedback—back into the system as information about the output. Circular questions tend to trigger sets of mutually interactive feedback loops that recursively create additional loops that, in turn, widen and sharpen one's perspectives. Another characteristic of circular questions is their tendency to elicit responses from others in nonchronological and nonlinear sequences. The information elicited via these questions often provides fresh and clear pictures of the existing dynamics within a system.

We ask circular questions according to the same process that the eye uses to scan the natural world—the process of *micronystagmus*. According to this process, the eye rapidly flicks back and forth across objects and detects *differences* in form, texture, color, and so forth. In other words, we "see" by *differentiating* one item from another, and thereby unconsciously assemble patterns.[30] In circular questioning, the intent is to surface differences in relationships and feed them back into the system.

Circular questions are useful in exploring situations and opening up space for a systemic view. They are useful to the manager or researcher who wishes to discover new " 'patterns that connect' persons, objects, actions, perceptions, ideas, feelings, events, beliefs, contexts, and so on, in recurrent or cybernetic circuits."[31] Circular questions tend to liberate members of a system from previously held linear views, and induce them to perceive their world from a systemic perspective.

In the following scenario, Jack, the manager of a large division, has come to consult with his vice president, Carol. Jack has a team member, Tom, who is dissatisfied with Jack's strategy in handling the merger of the group care and health insurance divisions. Tom is obstructing the implementation of the strategy.

Carol: What can I do for you today?

Jack: I have a problem communicating with a member of my team.

Carol: With whom?

Jack: With Tom and myself mainly.

Carol: How is your communication with the rest of the team members?

Jack: O.K. most of the time.

Carol: Can you tell me more about it?

Jack: I think that I communicate better with the team when Tom is not around.

Carol: How do Tom and the team communicate?

Jack: I am not sure.

Carol: Can you tell me who Tom communicates better with on the team?

Jack: My impression is that he gets along pretty well with Jill, my assistant.

Carol: If Jill was a part of this conversation, would she agree with you?

Jack: I do not know.

Carol: How do you think the team responds to Jill and Tom's relationship?

Jack: My guess would be that it confuses them.

Carol: How do you explain this situation?

Jack: Now that you are asking, when I think about it, there might have been a split on the team that I was not aware of.

Carol: Can you describe what happens when you are in a meeting with the team?

Jack: Somehow, the team and I seem to come to a consensus on a matter, but when I try to move forward on it, there is resistance.

Carol: I wonder, who do you think is responsible for causing the resistance?

Jack: Well, it looks like . . . I never stopped to think about the situation from this angle . . . it seems to me, in retrospect, that Jill and Tom create a ripple that blocks any movement forward.

Carol: Can you explain this "ripple?"

Jack: Well, I have to think about it, but there is more to this situation than I realized when I started talking with you about it.

Carol: It seems to me that now you have a different view of the problem, on the relationships among your team members. I wonder what your sense of it is now?

Jack: I think I have a clearer understanding of on the problem now than when I first came in. I am realizing that the problem is not just Tom but the team as a whole. I need to work on the existing dynamics between the team and myself so that we can move forward.

In this scenario, Jack initially saw Tom as the problem. However, Carol's use of circular questioning enabled Jack to take a different perspective from which to view the problem with Tom. It thus shifted his perception of the problem from Tom to the relationships with other components of the system, and, in so doing, widened the context of the problem. Furthermore, through her questions, Carol elicited feedback about the existing relationships among team members. By broadening Jack's view of his problem, Carol triggered in Jack a new awareness of his situation.

Jack came to realize that, in fact, he and Tom are operating in a system wherein sets of elements—such as Jill and the rest of the team—are acting and reacting with one another in ways of which he had been unaware. In this context, each interaction and reaction dynamically altered the nature of the relationships among team members. Jack also came to realize the nature of the relationships among the team members that may have blocked him and the team from moving forward with their strategy.

In this particular example, the use of circular questioning generated feedback in the conversation that enabled Jack to alter his perspective on the problem. Thus, Carol's use of this particular format of questioning opened up alternative views to perceive the situation. Jack was then able to consider new ways to interact with his team and transcend the problem.

Hypothetical Questions

Hypothetical questions are somewhat different from circular questions, although both are steeped in the systemic paradigm. Because these questions are oriented toward the future, their articulation propels listeners almost into another space and time—one that often opens up new options to them. Such questions promote the thinking or rehearsal of new ways of viewing a situation—new solutions that can trigger alternative actions.

Hypothetical questions, or future questions as they are also known, are critical in situations wherein the organization's main focus is on the on-going ideas, thoughts, or problems of the present. They are useful in connecting the present with the future by "asking questions of now and when, now and if, or now and suppose."[32] This is how different and novel information about the future is fed back into the system. In fact, the repetitive introduction of information about an outcome via this style of questioning opens up possibilities to imagine new solutions based on new ideas.

To speak of the future provides new flexibilities in that the system becomes at liberty to draw a new map. In this age when everyone is entering "new territory," we are without a "map" of the future. This not only causes great consternation to managers, but also increases the vulnerabilities of their organizations. Hypothetical or future questions are specifically designed to *pull the future into the present,* and thus may be of inestimable value.

Hypothetical or future questions also are useful in clarifying a present situation that is problem ridden. Whenever one thinks about a future situation, one is likely to situate it in a new context. In wrapping a future context around the present, one opens new pathways among different levels of meaning. This recursive process opens up a system to change by reintroducing its own ideas about its future by creating a new context.

In difficult situations, one implicitly feels "hemmed in," "pressured," or "overrun" by the surrounding problems that—according to systems theory—are part of the context. By forwarding us into the future, hypothetical or future questions, situate us in a new context that is devoid of problems, but replete with possibilities. By wrapping it around our present context—one that is replete with problems, but devoid of possibilities—and allowing them to interact and react with one another, a recursive process opens up the system to change by reintroducing its own ideas about its future, and thereby creating a new context—or a new future.

Lynn, the CEO of the company, is meeting with Bill, a division head. They are discussing an important project that Bill is heading up, which is falling behind schedule.

Lynn: I'm glad to see you, Bill. I understand that there have been some difficulties meeting the project's deadlines. I wonder if you could fill me in on the situation?

Bill: This project is difficult. I don't understand why we can't move forward on it.

Lynn: Right now, you are meeting the deadlines on your other work. I just wonder if there are any ideas you can take from your current projects to improve on the future status of your problem project.

Bill: I know what you mean. I have met my deadlines on all the other projects that I am working on. But this one is different.

Lynn: Could you tell me what is different about this project?

Bill: Right now I am at my wits' end. I just can't see the light at the end of the tunnel.

Lynn: Would you like to talk about what's going on?

Bill: Lynn, there are all kinds of difficulties with this project. The team seems sluggish, I don't see a commitment on their part. In addition, our budgetary and human resources are paper thin.

Lynn: Bill, if you were to infuse this team with energy tomorrow, what would you do?

Bill: All of a sudden, I have an outlandish idea! Are you ready for it? What comes to mind is to take a whole day off from work with the team, and go somewhere where we can just brainstorm ideas. Sort of a retreat with some fun time built in.

Lynn: Sounds great, but just how would you go about it?

Bill: Well, I haven't thought it through, but my gut reaction is to go off someplace and just brainstorm together about how to handle this project. Probably spend the whole day talking to each other about it away from the cues of the office.

Lynn: What possibilities might this open up?

Bill: Maybe instead of assigning jobs to people, as I have been doing, we will open it up to talking about who wants to do what job, who will work with whom, and things like that. I wonder if that's been the logjam. Now, even I am getting excited at the idea that everyone will be doing what they like to do and are best at. In this way, I don't have to assign the jobs.

Lynn: I am curious about what ideas you have to structure the day?

Bill: Only one idea. I am going to ask the team to structure the whole day themselves. That ought to fire them up. In fact, all of a sudden I feel fired up myself. Lynn, I can't believe where these ideas came from. How do you feel about them . . . boss?

Lynn: I feel excited by what I hear you describing. How do I sign up for your team?

In this scenario, using hypothetical questions, Lynn triggered the emergence of fresh, new ideas and viewpoints into the conversation and, more importantly, into this particular situation. Instead of remaining focused on the problems of the present—which tends to be the way most managers respond—Lynn opted to connect the present to the future by introducing the idea of Tom's success in meeting deadlines on his other projects. Lynn chose not to focus on the problems of the present, but instead asked hypothetical questions about the future. This helped Bill to relax and start thinking about a new context that, in turn, triggered fresh possibilities to devise new alternatives. Bill's construction of a new, more positive future context recursively opened up new avenues for change by introducing his new ideas about the future into the present. Through the use of hypothetical questions, Lynn helped Bill "pull the future into the present."

Reflexivity and Reflexive Questions

Reflexivity

It may be relevant to begin by defining and explaining the concept of reflexivity prior to introducing reflexive questions. The concept of reflexivity refers to a "bending back" or "folding back" onto oneself. It may be envisioned as a horizontal "figure eight" communication pattern that reflects and folds back onto itself, thus reintroducing more feedback with each cycle. Reflexivity is a recursive, interactive process that takes place between individuals in which new thoughts, different ideas, or alternative meanings are developed, modified, and/or maintained. Formerly, images of communication resembled straight-line arrows with a single feedback loop. The increase in multiple feedbacks generated by reflexivity better fits today's high-velocity and nonlinear environment by triggering a greater number of perspectives. It is an active process that helps surface more than one meaning or views on a situation. Individuals who come from different hierarchical positions, for this reason alone, may see the same situation differently, and draw different meanings that, in turn, evoke different feedback. Thus, reflexivity is a self-generating process that constantly spawns new perspectives and ideas into the system.

Reflexive Questions

Reflexive questions are a third type of systemic question. They are asked with the intention of facilitating self-discovery by an individual or a group via activating a folding back of perceptions, experiences, and beliefs. This recursive process promotes "meaning making" within individuals. It enables the generation and broadening of self-constructed patterns of cognition and/or action.

To use reflexive questions effectively, it may be important to ask them in a nondirective and soft tone. The intention is to use these questions more like a probe that can cause a gentle ripple within one's thinking. Such mild perturbations are likely to spark some action that enables new connections and alterations in the organization of one's many thoughts and meanings. The success of using these questions comes from respecting the ability of individuals to find their own answers to questions, and their own solutions to problems. More than any other type of question, reflexive questions "call forth" personal or tacit knowledge.

In the following vignette, Mary, the regional vice president of a financial services company, is talking to Bruce, an industry veteran who is a year away from retirement. Mary is Bruce's boss, although she is more than two decades younger than him. Despite their age and rank difference, they have established an extraordinarily warm and mutually supportive relationship. It is the end of a day, and Bruce has just dropped by Mary's office to visit for a few minutes, as he so often does.

Mary: Please come in, Bruce. This has been a particularly trying day, and it is good to see you and just take some time out to talk.

Bruce: What made your day so trying, Mary?

Mary: On top of everything I have to deal with every day, I have a growing prob lem with some managers who report to me. To make a long story short, I sense a great deal of resistance from them to any idea I propose on the issues they bring to me.

Bruce: When you look back on these meetings, what could you have done differently?

Mary: That's a good question. When I am in the midst of these meetings and sense that my ideas are being ignored, I probably become defensive. But to go back to your question, I ought to be able to respond differently.

Bruce: I wonder, Mary, what impact your reaction might have had on your managers.

Mary: By the looks on their faces, I do not think they valued my comments. And in fact, I may have to rethink the position I took, and most likely deal with this situation differently.

Bruce: Mary, if you did change direction, what do you think might happen?

Mary: Maybe, if I didn't push my ideas so hard and listened more, they may become less oppositional.

Bruce: If you became more open to your managers' ideas, do you think it would be more or less likely that they would behave differently?

Mary: Touché! You know, Bruce, that's probably the only way to manage effec- tively today. I wonder if it might be better for me to first listen to others' ideas before jumping the gun. That makes for synergy all around.

In this vignette, Bruce helped Mary to solve her dilemma by asking a series of reflexive questions. In so doing, he facilitated the bending back of Mary's perceptions and experiences of her encounters with her man- agers. This process caused Mary to generate new meanings about her dilemma. It also induced her to widen her own awareness of her own thinking and behaviors. Through the use of the reflexive questions that Bruce raised in his soft and nondirective manner, he was able to gently probe about her dilemma and create gentle perturbations in Mary's think- ing about her behavior. This process allowed Mary to reorganize and re- direct her thinking. Bruce's respectful and caring approach enabled Mary to find her own answers and solutions to her situation.

CONCLUSION

Every question serves a function. Conventional questions fall into the category of linear questions. Although they serve the purpose of gathering information, and establishing relationships that enhance communication, they tend to narrow one's focus in order to solve problems according to the external application of managerial expertise and techniques.

Systemic questions are based on GST. They perform the function of widening one's perspective by triggering interactive feedback loops that mutually and recursively bring forth new perspectives. This recursive process opens the system to change via the process of feedback that reintroduces observations and ideas into the system, and thus creates a new context for change. The purpose of systemic questions is to increase circularity via a neutral stance that augments feedback, and thus induces volitional change in the system. Each of the three types of systemic questions treated in this chapter contributes to this process in a different and unique way. Circular questions tend to be exploratory. Their use opens up space that enables individuals to connect their perceptions with emerging patterns. Their unique power is to induce one to comprehend situations systemically. Such an enhanced awareness tends to free participants from their commitment to narrower linear constructions, and makes it possible to develop new perspectives. Hypothetical or future questions serve to connect the present with the future. Their use enables the emergence of new thoughts that create new possibilities. This recursive process opens up the system to change by introducing new ideas about the future. The outcome leads to creating new contexts for a new future. Reflexive questions are intended to generate new meanings by probing, and thus creating reverberations from within that lead to reorganizing and redirecting one's thinking.

Until recently, organizational change has been viewed as linear and externally induced. These three types of systemic questions hold out a new promise—that change can be systemically and internally generated. Systemic questions help to generate systemic or second-order change—the type of change that alters the system in which it occurs—by generating from within the conditions for change.[33]

NOTES

1. Voltaire, French author–philosopher (1694–1778). Cited in Laurence J. Peter (1977) *Peter's Quotations: Ideas for Our Time* (New York: William Morrow and Company), p. 417. It is more likely that Voltaire said rather than wrote this.

2. Peter Drucker (1954) *The Practice of Management* (New York: Harper & Row), p. 351.

3. Kenneth Seeskin (October 1984) "Socratic Philosophy and the Dialogue Form," *Philosophy and Literature* 8 (2), pp. 181–194, especially p. 181 quoting Gregory Vlastos (1971) "Introduction: The Paradox of Socrates," in *The Philosophy of Socrates: A Collection of Critical Essays*, edited by Gregory Vlastos (Garden City, N.Y.: Doubleday), pp. 3–21, especially p. 12.

4. Seeskin (1984), op. cit., p. 182; Kenneth Seeskin (1987) *Dialogue and Discovery: A Study in Socratic Method* (Albany: State University of New York Press), p. 3.

5. Raphael Demos (1937) "Introduction" in *The Dialogues of Plato*, vol. 1, trans. into English by Benjamin Jowett (New York: Random House), pp. vii–xii.

6. Dorothy Tarrant (1948) "Style and Thought in Plato's Dialogues," *Classical Quarterly* 42, pp. 28–34, especially p. 28.

7. Rosemary Desjardins (1988) "Why Dialogues? Plato's Serious Play," in *Platonic Writings, Platonic Readings,* edited by Charles L. Griswold, Jr. (New York: Routledge, Chapman & Hall), pp. 110–125.

8. Diskin Clay (1994) "The Origins of the Socratic Dialogue," in *The Socratic Moment,* edited by Paul A. Vander Waerdt (Ithaca, N.Y.: Cornell University Press), pp. 23–47, especially p. 42. According to "literary anecdote in antiquity: Simon the cobbler took notes on Socrates' conversations at his shop, not as a stenographer but soon after they had ended."

9. Norbert W. Lotz (1995) "Trying to Coincide the Inner- and Outerworld: The Socratic Dialogue," *Communication & Cognition* 28 (2/3), pp. 165–186, especially pp. 170–171. See Lotz also for Socrates' listening as well as fair and respectful dialogical skills.

10. Seeskin (1987), op. cit., p. 7.

11. Demos, op. cit., p. vii.

12. Jurgen Mittelstrass (1988) "On Socratic Dialogue," in *Platonic Writings, Platonic Readings,* edited by Charles L. Griswold, Jr. (New York: Routledge, Chapman & Hale), pp. 126–143, especially p. 130.

13. Charles L. Griswold, Jr. (1988) "Plato's Metaphilosophy: Why Plato Wrote Dialogues," in *Platonic Writings, Platonic Readings,* edited by Charles L. Griswold, Jr. (New York: Routledge, Chapman & Hale), pp. 143–176, especially pp. 163–164.

14. Ronald A. Heifetz and Donald L. Laurie (January–February 1997) "The Work of Leadership," *Harvard Business Review* 75 (1), pp. 124–134 and Karl E. Weick (2001) "Leadership as a Legitimation of Doubt," in *The Future of Leadership: Today's Top Leadership Thinkers Speak to Tomorrow's Leaders,* edited by Warren Bennis, Gretchen M. Spreitzer, and Thomas G. Cummings (San Francisco: Jossey-Bass), pp. 91–102.

15. Cornel West, interview by Karen W. Arenson (September 25, 2002) "After Storm, Scholar Starts at Princeton with a Whisper," *New York Times,* p. B8.

16. Ludwig von Bertalanffy (1968) *General System Theory: Foundations, Development, Applications* (New York: George Braziller). For concise reviews of his thought, see Ludwig von Bertalanffy (1950) "An Outline of General System Theory," *The British Journal for the Philosophy of Science* 1, pp. 134–165 and Ludwig von Bertalanffy (1968) "General System Theory—A Critical Review," in *Modern Systems Research: A Source Book,* edited by Walter Buckley (Chicago: Aldine Publishing), pp. 11–30. In this article, Bertalanffy uses the concept of "system" and "systems" interchangeably.

17. Peter Steinglass (1978) "The Conceptualization of Marriage from a System Theory Perspective," in *Marriage and Marital Therapy,* edited by T. J. Paolino and B. S. McCrady (New York: Bruner/Mazel), p. 304.

18. Gregory Bateson (1972) *Steps to an Ecology of the Mind* (New York: Ballantine Books), p. 403.

19. Peter Senge (1990) *The Fifth Discipline: The Art and Practice of the Learning Organization* (New York: Currency/Doubleday), pp. 73–74.

20. Bateson (1972), op. cit., p. 403.

21. Gregory Bateson (1970). "An Open Letter to Anatol Rapoport," *Etc.: A Review of General Semantics* XXVII (3), pp. 359–363, especially p. 362.

22. Peggy Penn (September 1982) "Circular Questioning," *Family Process* 21 (3), pp. 267–280, especially p. 270.

23. Paul Watzlawick, Janet Beavin, and Don Jackson (1967) *The Pragmatics of Human Communication* (New York: W.W. Norton), p. 31.

24. David Campbell, Ros Draper, and Clare Huffington (1991) *A Systemic Approach to Consultation* (London: Karnac Books), p. 17.

25. Ibid.

26. John T. Kirby (1997) "A Classicist's Approach to Rhetoric in Plato," *Philosophy and Rhetoric* 30 (2), pp. 190–202, especially p. 190.

27. Adapted from Karl Tomm (March 1987) "Interventive Interviewing: Part I. Strategizing as a Forth Guideline for the Therapist." *Family Process* 26 (1), pp. 3–13, especially pp. 3–4.

28. Karl Tomm (March 1988) "Interventive Interviewing: Part III. Intending to Ask Lineal, Circular, Strategic, or Reflexive Questions?" *Family Process* 27 (1), pp. 1–15, especially p. 7.

29. Ibid., p. 7.

30. Bateson (1972), op cit., pp. 399–468 and Luigi Boscolo, Gianfranco Cecchin, Lynn Hoffman, and Peggy Penn (1987) *Milan Systemic Family Therapy* (New York: Basic Books), p. 11.

31. Tomm, op. cit., p. 7.

32. Peggy Penn (September 1985) "Feed-Forward: Future Questions, Future Maps," *Family Process* 24 (3), pp. 299–310, especially p. 300.

33. Paul Watzlawick, John Weakland, and Richard Fisch (1974) *Change: Principle of Problem Formation and Problem Resolution* (New York: W.W. Norton), p. 22.

CHAPTER 8

Tacit Knowledge and Conversation

> The most essential responsibilities of managers . . . can be characterized as participation in "conversations for possibilities" that open new backgrounds for the conversations for action.
>
> —Terry Winograd and Fernando Flores[1]

Conversation is and continues to be of enduring importance to managers and organizations, and remains critically important to normal business operations—whatever the level of technology or type of economy. In the Industrial Era, conversation was used to transmit information and coordinate activities. Even in this new era, the Internet has been called conversation, and its role remains central in the technology-rich, interfaced information economy. Mutually generative conversation is a kind of conversation that becomes even more important in accelerating the information economy.

Conversation is the most underutilized asset of Information Era organizations. In this knowledge era, corporations have invested billions of dollars in the most cutting-edge hardware, software, Internet, intranet, mainframe, laptop, wired, and wireless tools of information technology. However, it could be that the ultimate wellspring of knowledge literally lies at their feet, unseen and unrealized. This situation is not just true of organizations; our educational institutions and professional training continue to invest more time and resources in teaching students and managers the skills of information technology rather than the cutting-edge skills of conversation that create new possibilities. Similarly, few if any research studies have focused on conversations in organizational settings, although conversation remains the ultimate context for the creation of knowledge.[2]

The role of managers in the command and control organizations of the modern or Industrial Era was mainly to coordinate action. This helps explain why managers then spent so much of their workday engaged in face-to-face communication. There appears to have been minimal change in Postmodern or Information Era organizations. One high-technology company discovered that only one-fifth of information exchange among its employees occurred via information technology, whereas: "up to 80 percent of the information exchange within it takes place through personal dialogue."[3] Whatever the era, face-to-face conversation remains the enduring and vital channel for organizational communication. Thus, conversation continues to be most important for transmitting knowledge and coordinating action. However, in this Postmodern Information Era, conversation assumes an even more critical function: the discovery and creation of new knowledge. Because this has not been a major focus of managerial theorists to date, it will be the intent of this chapter to articulate the "how to" by which managers can create an unfolding process of mutually generative conversation.

MUTUALLY GENERATIVE CONVERSATION FOSTERS KNOWLEDGE CREATION

Conversation is a common activity among humans. Although it may not have occurred to us, the conversations that we engage in share common attributes. The first type, conventional conversation, involves talking to one another about everyday topics such as the weather or shared experiences. These also are conversations for the purpose of exchanging information, such as the events that occur in everyday life. These conversations involve exchanges of casual or professional information, and are not intended to bring about any change in either conversant.

There is a second kind of conversation, however, that is purposefully intended to generate new insights, thoughts, ideas, solutions, and possibilities. This second kind of conversation involves talking with one another in order to inquire. Such a conversation may not only bring about change among the participants, but also transformation through the process of mutually generative conversation. Such conversations are characterized by being free flowing in their "sense making" and intuitive in the direction that they take. This newly recognized kind of conversation fosters creativity and discovery.

A mutually generative conversation occurs when individuals come together to share their views in talking with (rather than to) each other about a situation or a problem.[4] The intent is to search together, to mutually explore and understand a situation or a problem. Such a conversation becomes a vehicle for exchanging views, thoughts, interpretations, and understandings about a situation or a problem, all in an attempt to generate new meanings. This conversation opens up numerous options and possibilities for new sense making, new directions, and multiple solutions about a problem or situation. Mutually generative conversation could be a key to organizational success in the 21st century.

CHARACTERISTICS OF MUTUALLY GENERATIVE CONVERSATION

Mutually generative conversation is *egalitarian and collaborative*. This sort of conversation is not congruent with hierarchical, command-and-control authority. However, top-down conversations remain typical of many organizations today, and tend to discourage involvement. Mutually generative conversation embodies the democratic egalitarianism that characterizes America and its roots—the New England town meeting is an example. Mutually generative conversation triggers involvement because it is nonhierarchical and collaborative. Every participant is assumed to be democratically capable of unique and valuable contributions to the common task.

This new conversation is *open and invites the participation of others*. It is antithetical to the one-down, combative style of debate that is common even today in organizations, for in debate, what one participant wins, the other loses. Such a situation could lead the listener to attitudinally close down, rather than open up, to what the speaker is saying. In addition, knowledge creation is less likely to occur in situations that are win–lose for each individual than in situations that are win–win for all.

Exchanging individual viewpoints encourages participants to begin conversing with each other at new and deeper levels. The process of exchanging perspectives and generating solutions has the peculiar effect of *strengthening relationships* among participants, which is crucial to knowledge creation. Creativity is a fragile process, which is, perhaps, one reason why knowledge-creating conversations are different from normal conversations.

Mutually generative conversation is *free flowing and interactive*. This process fosters crisscrossing conversations whose spontaneity and interactivity reflexively engage participants and draw them into the process. The process of mutually generative conversation helps to surface ideas and generate new notions. It enables us to access the uniqueness of each individual's thinking, as well as each individual's knowledge and life experience—or tacit knowledge. One of the major responsibilities of managers in the Inquiring Organization will be to create workplace environments that possess the characteristics of mutually generative conversation. Such environments could become the wellsprings of knowledge creation. The question, however, is "How do we bring about this new sort of conversation?"

The foundation for this endeavor is a relatively new approach to communication—reflexive communication. Reflexive communication initially was placed in the most difficult of all contexts—cultural diversity. The premises, stances, and skills of reflexive communication helped to surface the tacit knowledge of culture, for culture itself is tacit. As the authors of this approach stated:

> Reflexive communication is a general theory that lends itself to any communication context. Therefore, in any setting or on any topic, the process of reflexive communication will evoke multiple points of view ... Through this approach, individuals can better generate information and co-construct those mutual realities that lead to enhanced problem-solving.[5]

Even when placed in the sometimes-difficult context of cultural diversity, reflexive communication results in outcomes that are congruent with those that the Inquiring Organization seeks to establish today, including helping conversants get beyond the stereotypes of a person or a situation, surfacing the unique thoughts of another individual, generating new information, co-creating new realities, and discovering new solutions. Reflexive communication could be considered the basic foundation for mutually generative conversation. It is a communication process by which one can access the uniqueness of each individual's thinking, as well as each individual's knowledge base and life experience—or tacit knowledge. Such relationships become the basis for generating information and lead to the co-construction of new realities that become the wellsprings of knowledge creation.

THE STANCES AND PRACTICES OF MUTUALLY GENERATIVE CONVERSATION

Three general stances facilitate mutual generative conversation and the exploration and expression of perspectives and thoughts: not knowing, curious, and collaborative. Individually, these stances may not be common in conventional conversation. Used together, they can lift conversations to new and different levels. Used in the context of mutually generative conversation, they become the catalysts that propel the conversation to deeper and broader domains.

The Not-Knowing Stance

In this stance first used by Socrates, one takes the nonexpert position of not knowing. This stance, which invites others to talk, has to do with uncertainty—that is, not being certain about what one thinks or knows. It encourages others to voice their thoughts, and it encourages managers to value them. This stance fosters an exploratory approach to the conversation, with the aim of being a learner and "not-knower." Thus, the not-knowing stance creates the relationship that invites others into an exchange of ideas. It also encourages communication in organizations by leveling the hierarchy of position. Hierarchies exist in all organizations. De-emphasizing them by flattening the hierarchy encourages conversation. Mutually generative conversation emphasizes equal participation and thereby induces a shift from hierarchical to collaborative relationships. The not-knowing stance conveys the message that everyone in the organization is qualified to contribute ideas, thoughts, and perspectives on a situation.

The not-knowing stance encourages listeners to attend to the "outer" conversation of others as well as to their own "inner" conversation. The outer conversation is what others are saying. The inner conversation consists of one's tacit thoughts and ideas that are activated via conversation. Such an egalitarian approach induces participants to contribute to the exploration of ideas. This crisscrossing triggers additional meanings that continue to unfold into additional new meanings.[6] Let us compare the impact of the following statements:

Before I tell you my decision, let me hear what you have to say on this issue.

And the same manager asking in a not-knowing stance:

I wonder what would happen were we to explore the pros and cons of this matter together before making a decision?

The first statement implies a command that emanates from a hierarchical position. Such a message inhibits respondents who may feel the need to tailor their answers to fit with the boss's ideas. Generally, such top-down conversations tend to be strained and limited. However, the second statement has a relaxed and collaborative tone that invites participation and brainstorming where every thought is equally welcomed. Such an egalitarian climate engenders richer and more open conversations from which new ideas are likely to emerge.

The Curious Stance

When assuming a curious stance, one expresses ideas in a tentative manner.[7] Ideas expressed in an assertive or dogmatic fashion are likely to hinder the creative process. However, voicing them in a tentative or non-judgmental manner encourages others to volitionally take, leave, or modify ideas without territoriality or vesting. Such a climate creates free exchanges of thoughts and ideas as the participants see fit. Such a stance also generates differing and new perspectives on a situation, and thereby evokes evolved solutions. The benefit is that new solutions are likely to emerge from the articulated, varied perspectives. Another positive outcome is that the evolved solutions are likely to be the most fitting to the specific situation. Additionally, the paths of action are designed by the individuals who are the ones most likely to implement them.

The questions asked from a curious stance are formulated with an expression that conveys a tentative thought—typical words or phrases here would include: *could it be, perhaps, this is just an idea, I wonder, possibly.* Thus, we express our curious stance by asking questions that call forth, rather than making statements that set forth.

I wonder what the outcome might be if I don't act on this offer immediately and instead take time to think about it?

Perhaps we can review some of the earlier proposals we received and compare the upsides?

It's just an idea, but what if we postpone this project for the time being until we know more about our financial situation?

The curious stance simply means that the manager expresses his or her ideas in a tentative manner as just another member of a conversational circle. This tentative or nonjudgmental mode of expression is nonthreatening and encourages others to share in exploration. A final advantage is that emergent solutions are not only the most thought out and fitting to the situation, but are also codiscovered and codesigned by the individuals or team who will be most likely to implement them.

The Collaborative Stance

This stance is a natural outcome of the two preceding stances. The shared perspectives, contributed to by the conversants, spark additional ideas and meanings that eventually evolve into new knowledge.[8] This process synthesizes many levels of perceptions and meanings that induce deep if not tacit involvement among team members, thus making possible the collaborative construction of new ideas. Jen and Laura's conversation illustrates how the collaborative stance unfolds.

Laura: Jen, could you tell me how this situation has become a problem for you so that I can understand it?

Jen: I need some help determining which direction to take on the new project you assigned to me. I can see so many possibilities but I can't decide which way to go.

Laura: Well, could we talk a little about the ideas you have first? I always thought that your ideas were perceptive.

Jen: Laura, I am so glad to be talking with you. Somehow, I feel more relaxed about discussing my ideas with you, and I hope you can help me find my own sense of direction for the project.

Laura: I am interested in how you plan to proceed with this project.

Jen: I would like to talk about different avenues from which to approach this project and who should be involved in the process. At times, I feel over-whelmed in determining the sequence of steps that need to be taken, as well as staffing the team.

Laura: Well Jen, the reason you were given this project is that you have expertise in this area in addition to managing collaboratively, as you have shown in the past. I will be happy to talk about your ideas so that you can sift out the best direction to follow. How does this sound?

Jen then began to offer all the well thought-out ideas she already had but was unable to express. The longer Laura listened attentively to her and inquired about options and alternatives, the clearer it became to Jen that what she was thinking and saying was sensible and worth listening to. It was evident that Laura's engagement in the conversation denoted her understanding of the problem by being in sync with Jen's thoughts and ideas. In addition, Laura's tentative questions, ideas, and conjectures conveyed her support and provided the space for Jen to find her way. Thus, Laura's collaborative demeanor was crucial to Jen's realization about the way to proceed.

This stance demonstrates to others that you value their participation, and that what they think and say is important and worth hearing. Such a stance, in and of itself, encourages others to go on and discover the value of their own personal or tacit knowledge.

Guidelines for the Use of Stances

To successfully implement these stances in the workplace, the following guidelines may prove to be useful.

Let Your Colleagues Take Center Stage

Create the space for your colleagues to tell their story. Allow them to say what they want to say fully and completely. Interruptions tend to inhibit the natural, free flow of ideas and create competition. Few people are willing to listen until they have said all that they have to say.

Try Not to Assume or Know—Too Quickly, if Ever

It may be best to generate and retrieve as much information on a situation as possible. More information makes for better decisions. Taking the stance that one does not assume or understand too quickly, if ever, tends to prevent narrowing the focus or closing a conversation too quickly. A mutually generative conversation is not an ordinary conversation: one should not assume that one understands the other person, what he or she is saying, or even the basic assumptions underlying the conversation. One way to ensure this is to ask questions.

Listen with Care and Respect

When you listen with care and respect, you demonstrate that what the other person thinks and shares is of value and worth hearing. It is via conversation between individuals that the delicate process of sharing one's unique ideas and perspectives unfolds.

CONCLUSION

The stances and practices discussed in this chapter trigger a mutually generative process that multiplies perspectives. Such a conversation becomes a shared inquiry in which participants co-explore ideas that others bring, and co-develop new ones. This collaborative process opens up, in a natural and mutual way, a multiplicity of possibilities. Such a conversation becomes more of a shared inquiry in which the familiar is co-explored and the new is co-created, than a dominating monologue or a combative debate that "proves" or "disproves" right or wrong. Mutually generative conversations foster knowledge creation.

These free-flowing conversations surface the tacit thoughts and trigger the crisscrossing associations that some might call creativity. Because mutually generative conversations are reflexive, they fold back on the participants, and thus generate additional creative thoughts. This new way of conversing fosters a process of mutual inquiry that continuously creates knowledge—one of the best practices of individuals and organizations that will thrive into the era beyond the information economy.

This new conversation multiplies the creative output of the individuals involved with the process into a vastly more powerful collective whole, just as parallel processing multiplies the power of individual computers. It also creates an entire new field for creativity, because it fuses the single, monochromatic prism of individual perspectives into what becomes a shared, technicolor spectrum.

NOTES

1. Terry Winograd and Fernando Flores (1986) *Understanding Computers and Cognition: A New Foundation for Design* (Norwood, N.J.: Ablex Publishing Corp.), p. 151.

2. Ikujiro Nonaka, Georg Von Krogh, and Ichijo Kazuo (2000) *Enabling Knowledge Creation: How to Unlock the Mystery of Tacit Knowledge and Realize the Power of Innovation* (New York: Oxford University Press), p. 127.

3. Ibid., p. 131.

4. Harlene Anderson (1994) "Mutual Inquiry: Therapy as a Generative Process. Workshop 13 in Therapeutic Conversations 2," in *International Conference on Narrative & Cooperative Approaches to Therapy: Psychotherapy for the 21st Century* (Reston, VA: The Institute for Advanced Clinical Training Inc.), pp. 1–2. See also Harlene Anderson (1997) *Conversation, Language and Possibilities: A Postmodern Approach to Therapy* (New York: Basic Books). We are indebted to Harlene Anderson for her pathbreaking and stimulating work in this area, as in so many others.

5. John F. Kikoski and Catherine Kano Kikoski (1996) *Reflexive Communication in the Culturally Diverse Workplace* (Westport, Conn.: Quorum Books), p. 42.

6. Harlene Anderson and Harry Goolishian (1988) "Human Systems as Linguistic Systems: Evolving Ideas about the Implications for Theory and Practice," *Family Process* 27, pp. 371–393; Harlene Anderson and Harry Goolishian (1992) "The Client Is the Expert: A Not-Knowing Approach to Therapy," in *Therapy as Social Construction,* edited by Sheila McNamee and Kenneth J. Gergen (London: Sage Publications), pp. 25–39; and Harlene Anderson (1990) "Then and Now: From Knowing to Not-Knowing," *Contemporary Family Therapy Journal* 12, pp. 193–198.

7. Harlene Anderson and Susan Swim (1993) "Learning as Collaborative Conversation: Combining the Student's and Teacher's Expertise," *Human Systems: The Journal of Systemic Consultation and Management* 4, pp. 145–160.

8. Kenneth J. Gergen (March 1985). "The Social Constructionist Movement in Modern Psychology," *American Psychologist* 40 (3), pp. 266–275.

CHAPTER 9

Reflecting Conversations

[I]t is not yet more or different theory that we need in management studies, but a better understanding of conversation and conversational realities.

—John Shotter[1]

The Postmodern or Information Era has spawned a number of new core assumptions for organizations. Among the most important is that the act of knowledge creation can no longer be random or obscure. Rather, the process of knowledge creation must be explicitly known so that the conditions for its continuous operation can be established. For this to happen, one may need to appreciate the essence of postmodernism as it applies to the creation of knowledge: that is, that knowledge is socially or communally constructed, and is a creation of the preeminently human networks of language, relationships, and community.

Postmodernism recognizes that there is a physical world "out there" that we inhabit and with which we grapple. However, as soon as we begin to speak about it—to describe, analyze, or seek to understand it—the moment we begin to talk about what or how we "know" that world, we begin to socially construct that world. This means that two new assumptions need to be taken into consideration. The first new assumption is that knowledge is created by groups or teams—as happens in meetings countless times a day. This compels us to move beyond the old assumption that knowledge is created by individuals alone or solitary geniuses—like the popular stereotypes of Edison or Einstein. The second new assumption is that language creates our world and, if this is so, that the use of language can diminish the blind alleys and expand the possibilities. The postmodern context provides a fertile environment for the process of reflecting conversations to unfold.

The work of three 20th-century scholars—Viennese-born philosopher-theologian, Martin Buber; physicist turned philosopher, David Bohm; and Donald Schön, MIT researcher and organizational theorist—foreshadowed the emergence of reflecting conversations. Dialogue was the vital thread in the work of all three scholars. Each was an "outsider" to the formal study of communication, yet each made significant contributions to the field, and especially to one of the most remarkable innovations in communication—the reflecting conversation.

Born in 1878, Martin Buber lectured at universities throughout the world on the centrality of dialogue on the spiritual, personal, and interfaith levels. Part theologian, part philosopher, but always the theologian-philosopher of dialogue, Buber, like Socrates, saw "dialogue as the source of knowing."[2] Two themes of Martin Buber's work are important for our endeavor. The first is the importance of dialogue across the "between." Buber held that over and over in history, man in his spirit became solitary, and that man's alienation had increased during the Modern Era, and that bridging the "distance" or the "between" that separated us from each other, as well as from nature and God, was one of humanity's greatest yearnings.[3] The core of his philosophy and, for Buber, the essence of humanity is found in his belief that, "All real living is meeting."[4] According to Buber, it is not our solitary reason or intellect that marks us as human, but rather our being able to enter into relationships with others.

The phrase that may be most closely associated with Buber is "I–Thou"—the profound relationship we yearn for with God and other humans whom we know in their individual uniqueness. We also can have moving "I–Thou" relationships across the "between" with nature, a work of art, or even a ritual. In this, Buber echoes British novelist E. M. Forster's pithy but profound insight about one of the deepest longings of the human condition: "Only connect."[5] However, most of our lives and relationships are described by "I–It," or what may be termed secondary relationships that are necessary but are less satisfying. Dialogue is vital, for it is only via dialogue that humans can transcend the "distance" that is "between" us.

The second important theme in Buber's work is care, respect, and acceptance of others. He held that it is important to dialogue or talk in a way that respects the dignity of other individuals. Buber exemplified these values in a meeting he had with T. S. Eliot—the poet who once had described himself as a classicist in literature, an Anglo-Catholic in faith, and a monarchist in politics—everything Buber was not. When asked by a student how he could have had such a friendly meeting with a man so opposed to his opinions, Buber responded: "When I meet a person I am not concerned with their opinions; I am concerned with the person."[6]

Respectful dialogue across the "between" was critical to Martin Buber. Buber's guiding principle was that the "essence of man which is special to him can be directly known only in a living relation."[7]

Another eminent scholar, David Bohm, wrote about dialogue as a "way we can talk together coherently and think together."[8] However, Bohm's work addressed dialogue in larger groups. He suggested certain general precepts for fruitful dialogue as he envisioned and practiced it. In so doing, one might say that his approach to dialogue concurred with some postmodern themes. For example, recognizing its limitations, Bohm sought to transform the scientific method that gave birth to the Modern Era via a new sort of dialogue. In so doing, he laid out an alternative and more effective approach for groups to mutually generate knowledge.

As a physicist seeking to understand the implicate order of the universe, David Bohm recognized early on the limitations of the scientific method. He sought to counteract its inherent orientation to fragment and divide the world that scientists studied by advancing a new approach to dialogue that enfolded the wholeness of natural systems. In so doing, he was a pioneer in the application of GST to dialogue. In a major departure from the scientific method that seeks to validate hypotheses, Bohm advocated not only suspending assumptions but also agendas in group dialogues. He had two reasons: emotional and rational. Bohm suggested that we emotionally identify with our assumptions, and thus unconsciously react to defend them against opposing or even differing viewpoints. He further commented that rationally, such emotional reactions and defensiveness make no sense: "If the opinion is right, it doesn't need such a reaction. And if it is wrong, why should you defend it?"[9]

He also advocated opening the process of dialogue by talking about how individuals would dialogue together in a meeting. According to Bohm, when such principles were agreed on and adhered to by participants, "truth emerges unannounced."[10] Developing this notion further, Bohm held that every one of us possesses some personal knowledge that is unique. Bohm expressed this view when he stated: "Truth does not emerge from opinions; it must emerge from something else—perhaps from a more free movement of this tacit mind."[11] In certain ways, David Bohm developed a way of approaching dialogue that is congruent with the nature and operations of the tacit mind.

In dialogue with others, Bohm's central principles were to just follow the natural flow of conversation; to openly share one's ideas; to listen attentively; and, most of all, to free oneself of assumptions. When these principles were abided by in dialogues, Bohm found that *this process itself created change*. One way of explaining this outcome is that ideas—when freely and spontaneously shared with others—are likely to pass through one person to another in a constant flow. It is these shared meanings that enable groups to cohere and move forward with purpose together. Seldom, Bohm cautioned, do individuals get entirely novel ideas on their own, because ideas are in constant flow between individuals. Considerable change occurs as the result of merging ideas together.[12] What Bohm wrote in the 20th century foreshadowed and resonates in the thinking of today's most eminent scholars writing about organizations in the 21st century.

Some of today's most perceptive organizational theorists such as Peter Drucker, Rosabeth Moss Kanter, and Thomas Stewart concur that Information Era organizations depend on their employees' sense of shared purpose and continuing relationships for their existence.[13] They hold that so much will change within and without today's organizations that only a sense of shared purpose and continuing relationships among colleagues will enable organizations to cohere and forge ahead.

Bohm's very notion of dialogue was a departure from that of others. From the time of Socrates, students of dialogue had concerned themselves with groups of two individuals or a small number of participants. Buber, for example, is primarily known for writing about "I–Thou" or "I–It" relationships.[14] However, Bohm was concerned with dialogue in groups. His rationale was that larger groups tended to possess the diversity that is likely to generate new and different ideas. Bohm found that this process triggered change, during and even after the experience itself.

Donald A. Schön, MIT organizational theorist, was the third 20th-century scholar whose work foreshadowed concepts relevant to the reflecting conversation process. Schön was intrigued by the difference between what he termed the "technical rationality" (or the explicit knowledge) based on the scientific method that was taught to professionals in such fields as architecture, medicine, engineering, and management, and the way in which professionals actually practiced their crafts. For example, when he asked architects or engineers in the process of designing buildings or roads how they actually did so, he found the formal or "espoused theory" of technical rationality wanting. He also concluded that this technical rationality helped professionals deal with clearly formed problems like how to construct a building or a road—but not the "messy" but real-world problems of *if and where to do so*. He discovered that technical rational knowledge (or the sort taught in graduate schools) applied well to situations of certainty and generality, but not to those of uncertainty and uniqueness.

After years of studying architects, urban planners, engineers, medical practitioners, and managers in the actual practice of their work, Schön found that technical rationality did not adequately explain the actual process by which these professionals carried out their work—especially their creative work—in the real world. He coined the term "knowing-in-action" to describe the tacit or automatic knowledge on which professionals seamlessly act in the successful performance of their craft. Such performances would include a pitcher in baseball, or a manager seeking to determine which technologies will converge in a market sector to best position her firm. In each case, "the knowing is *in* the action. We reveal it by our spontaneous, skillful execution of the performance; and we are characteristically unable to make it verbally explicit"[15] [emphasis in original].

However, in learning a craft or profession, or in dealing with changing situations, another concept—"reflection-in-action" comes into play. Reflection-in-action is "the 'thinking what they are doing while they are doing it' that practioners sometimes bring to situations of uncertainty . . . (and) . . . uniqueness."[16] Schön discovered that reflection-in-action is how architecture students actually learn to design buildings in studio settings via a "dialogue of coach and student that takes the form of a reciprocal reflection-in-action."[17] Learning a craft involves a back-and-forth inner "dialogue of thinking and doing" or "back talk" that gives new meaning and direction to the development of skillful professionals.[18]

Reflection-in-action also is the process by which professionals deal with unique and changing circumstances. A skillful baseball pitcher exhibits knowing-in-action during an entire game. However, he demonstrates reflection-in-action by adapting his pitching style to each particular batter (hitting strengths or weaknesses), each particular situation (how many outs and players on base), and each particular stage of the game (1st or 9th inning).

According to Schön, each step in such a process informs the next in an unfolding manner, and each step opens up new implications. This involves back-and-forth shifts between the practitioner and the situation, as well as tentative "inner talk" within the practitioner. These shifts trigger reflections within the individual. From these shifts of tentative exploration, Schön finds that a professional: "discovers in the situation's back talk a whole new idea, which generates a system of implications for further moves."[19] It is the ideas triggered by such nonconscious "back talk" that is the phenomenon of knowledge creation via the reflexive process.

Unlike Buber, who was a theologian and mainly concerned with dyads, or Bohm, who was a scientist and concerned with larger groups, Schön's work focused on the pragmatics of the professional's work in the actual work setting. Schön focused on the individual's tacit process of task performance—reflection-in-action. Schön's domain is the individual, yet his concepts are valuable to larger group endeavors—such as reflecting conversations.

REFLECTING CONVERSATIONS IN A TEAM SETTING

Reflecting conversations may be one of the significant advances in communication of recent decades and possibly centuries. Indeed, the innovations of reflecting conversations may measure up to novelist Arthur Koestler's observation about truly creative breakthroughs: "The more original a discovery, the more obvious it seems afterwards."[20]

How this breakthrough happened was that in the 1980s, a Norwegian psychiatrist and his team of therapists were observing a family being interviewed. The family had agreed to this process. At one point during the session, the psychiatrist asked the family if they would like to hear what the ideas that the listening team had about what had transpired in the session to that point. In a reversal of the usual process, the family watched and listened in on the professional conversation that normally was held privately between the "experts." With the family's consent, a process of alternating talking and listening unfolded.[21]

When the process had concluded, everyone present realized that something different had happened. There was a new freedom to the relationships among the family members, as well as among the experts. What in fact had happened is that in their conversations, the reflecting group (the team of therapists) and the family had generated new ideas and perspectives that had not previously emerged. In fact, a new way of creating knowledge had evolved through this reflecting process. Those present may have experienced the meaning of Gregory Bateson's definition of the information that brings about profound changes and transformations, the *"difference which makes a difference"*[22] [emphasis in original].

The remainder of this chapter will introduce the reflecting conversation format for implementation in organizations. This format enhances any team's or group's abilities to articulate innovative perspectives ranging from problem situations in an organization to an experimental research team's discovery efforts. The reflecting conversation approach is an effective and proven practice for the creation of knowledge among groups.

Reflecting conversations are congruent with the structure of the postmodern organization. They nest at the precise locus in the organization where they are needed, whatever the level or task. Structurally, their operations are congruent with the emerging profile of 21st-century organizations. Successful organizations today are more likely to be nonhierarchical, open and transparent, inclusive in recruitment and operation, rapid in response, and purposeful. This new profile enables organizations to match and exceed the demands, and especially the velocity, of information required to survive and thrive in today's environment. This process does not take place behind closed doors, or just at the top echelons of the organization. Rather, it can be implemented whenever and wherever the problem exists between the individuals most directly involved in dealing with it, as well as whoever seeks its resolution.

Reflecting conversations flatten the hierarchy, give everyone a voice, recognize that every person has an idea that counts, and are in keeping with today's fast-moving pace in its give and take. These conversations pull together the *collective intelligences* of the work group to make better sense of the dilemmas that confront them. It is through this novel process that perceptions and ideas trigger new perceptions and ideas that merge together to co-create new possibilities. Through the reflexive process of ideas folding over one another, reflecting conversations generate the deeper knowledge that is sought today within individuals and groups.

REFLECTING CONVERSATIONS: DESCRIPTION, PROCESS, AND RULES

Description

The reflecting conversation is a new communication paradigm whose structure and process dynamically generates new possibilities and outcomes. This approach is steeped in GST, for it focuses on the recursiveness among the parts of a system—whether they are events or people—in the context of reciprocal interaction and influence. Its rules help to create a process wherein unique interchanges make room for creative ideas to emerge. The very format of the reflecting conversation structures sufficient time to shift from talking; to listening; to, most importantly, reflecting. An old New England proverb may apply here. It states: "What you see depends upon where you stand." If this proverb rings true, it is these shifts in the dialogical process itself that induce one to see situations from new positions. Finally, this format structures time for participants to experience one of the most valuable, but least practiced, elements of creativity—the chance to have that inner or tacit conversation with oneself that somehow brings forth new ideas.

The Process

The reflecting conversation process begins with gathering a group of individuals who are connected to the problem or issue to a first meeting. In addition, a team of reflectors are enlisted either from inside or outside of the organization. All of those gathered then are divided into two groups—an interview group and a reflecting group. The size of each group varies with the situation. Generally, a trained individual or consultant takes charge of the interviewing.

The interviewer questions the interview group about the problem that has brought them there. Beforehand, she explains that while the interview group talks, the reflecting group remains silent, and vice versa. The reflecting group is instructed not to interrupt the interview group while they are talking, or to talk within their own group. Also, the interviewer points out that it is important that everyone listen to what is being said. When the interview group has finished talking, the roles are reversed. The reflecting group is now asked to reflect among themselves on what they heard members of the interview group say. It is conveyed to both groups that they can talk or reflect for as long as they need to. At some point, a pause in the conversation occurs, and it becomes evident that it is time to shift positions from talking to listening. One, two, or more such shifts may occur during a meeting. One key to this process is the physical separation of the two groups.

The reflecting conversation process involves a simple yet profound departure from the way we normally "talk." In everyday conversations, individuals speak, listen, and shift positions when appropriate. In such conversations, not everyone has the opportunity to speak. This often denies individual perspectives from emerging and thus being contributed. At such times, this can turn conversation into "monopolization." In contrast, the reflecting conversation format makes it possible for every voice to be heard. Its very structure gives everyone the chance to speak, to listen, and to reflect. This process encourages multiple and creative perspectives to emerge.

Rules for Interviewing

When the interviewer meets with the interview group—that is, the group with the dilemma or problem—he or she begins by asking: "Who had the idea for this meeting first?" "Who was told about it?" "Who was in favor and who was not?" The second series of questions asked are: "Who can speak with whom about these ideas in this meeting?" "What issues do you want to talk about in this meeting?" and "What would you like to see happen in this meeting?" Through such questions, participants "talk about the talk." Thus, they enter into a metaconversation and implicitly agree from the start about how they will go about the very important process of communicating with each other. The agreement of each person is requested at every step of the way. Such talk is rich in ideas.

"Talking about the talk" is all important, because it enables the participants to create their own context for what and how they will speak. Volitionally self-constructing their process liberates participants from the usual constraints of dialogue, and thus allows freer range for their tacit knowledge to emerge.

The interchange of reflections that ensues from the above questions typically contributes to a new and multifaceted picture of the problem situation, and provides a wider scope for addressing it. Thus, by the end of the process, the questions, conversation, and reflections create a new picture of the situation that is sufficiently different from what was originally conceived by the interview group and thus opens up new and differing possibilities for its resolution.

The interviewer then conveys another rule of the process: everyone present has unique ideas to contribute. The interviewer proceeds to ex-plain the general guidelines and rules of the reflecting conversation pro-cess. The primary rule is that no one should do or say anything with which they feel uncomfortable. All individuals are free to express their thoughts openly. This process of openly sharing individual reflections with every-one listening encourages the interchange among participants, and thus the collective generation of a multitude of ideas.

There are some additional rules. The interviewer's questions generally focus on issues addressing the relationship of each individual to the prob-lem, rather than the problem itself. Also, the interviewer's focus needs to be on what is said, rather than on what one thinks is meant. To paraphrase what one influential therapist and theorist was famous for telling his col-leagues: "You should listen to what others really say, not what you think they mean."[23] It is best for the interviewer to try to discover what is in-herent in the problem, rather than trying to justify the hypothesis that one personally has about it.

The interviewer uses questions to raise and explore issues at a natural pace. To push, advise, or explain could endanger the existing relationship. It could also raise barriers and close the system, thus interrupting the conversation or even shutting it down. When the process is stymied and the interview group comes to a standstill, it endangers the possibility of the immanent change that is sought. In this context, new or forced thoughts are likely to be rejected by the group when introduced from the outside.

Rules for Reflecting

The reflecting group listens to the interviewer's conversation with the interview group. While reflecting, they talk only about the issues raised in the interview itself. Engaging in any discussion tends to narrow the focus to a limited number of ideas. On the other hand, just engaging in *reflecting,* as opposed to *discussing,* generates many more ideas that are different and unique with each successive reflection.

While listening to the interview group, the reflecting group's focus is on noting "openings" as they happen. Openings are concerns or themes of greater significance that typically are expressed through cue words or phrases, repetition, or nonverbal expressions. Openings occur sometimes repeatedly. The collected openings provide the material for reflections.

The reflecting group is cautioned to avoid interpreting, suggesting, or analyzing any parts of the interview group's conversation. Rather, com-ments are to be presented in a positive or even appreciative fashion. Re-flecting group members are urged to move away from expressions that limit or narrow responses such as "either . . . or." Instead, they are urged to use expressions such as "both . . . and," "can also be considered," "as well as," or "in addition to." Thus, for instance, one might say: "Both this option can be considered, as well as . . ." Such expressions tend to multiply rather than limit responses.

Reflections also are to be made tentatively. Therefore, one may use expressions such as "Perhaps . . . ," "Could . . . ," or "It's just a thought, but . . ." in opening one's reflections. Reflections that are tentatively expressed distance the interview group from the problem and tend to be heard more as suggestions to be considered, rather than as "must do" directives. Thus, they provide more freedom to respond in new ways.

The reflecting group members are cautioned to avoid giving opinions, advice, or interpreting meanings. To do so may be heard by the interview group as injunctions rather than as options or possibilities. Such statements that are extrinsic to the system may trigger defensiveness and even close it.

In conclusion, the reflecting conversation format provides the opportunity to alternate listening, speaking, and reflecting, and thereby to shift positions on situations. Shifting positions according to this process induces members of the interview group to develop a diverse array of perspectives and new ideas on their own about the dilemma or situation they came to address.

A REFLECTING CONVERSATION SCENARIO

Introduction

A consultant receives a telephone call from the CEO of CalTronics, a fictitious Fortune 500 semiconductor corporation. He is calling to broaden the consultant's initial assignment to include a marketing dilemma with which his company is dealing.

The CEO explains that competitive forces dictate corporate restructuring to improve operating efficiencies and the company's bottom line following a substantial write off associated with CalTronics's 3G and Wi-Fi product lines,[24] yet conflicts between two competing chip divisions are hampering the effort. The consultant asks the CEO about identifying no more than two other executives who are closely connected to the situation. In addition, she asks the CEO to bring together a representative group of five managers from these two divisions—MicroCom and BroadGen—who are directly involved in this dilemma.

The consultant explains that she would like to meet with all of these individuals in an initial meeting to secure a snapshot of the problem, as well as to briefly explain the process of the consultation. The consultant then asks whether the CEO would prefer to give her a history of the dilemma to date privately with her prior to the meeting, or in front of the entire group. "Although the choice is yours," she explains, "experience indicates that it is more beneficial to do so in the presence of the group." After some discussion, the CEO indicates his willingness to do the latter.

The day of the interview arrives, and the CEO introduces the consultant to the group he has gathered—two vice presidents and himself who comprise the executive committee, as well as five managers from the firm's two major divisions. The consultant then explains the process that they will be following.

The consultant first will interview one group, the executive committee (the interview group). Concurrently, the other group—the five executives from the two divisions (the reflecting group)—will listen. Following a period of conversation, a shift will occur. The consultant will then invite the reflecting group to reflect on what they have just heard, while the interview group listens.

Having described the shifts between speaking and reflecting, as well as the rules of the process (described above), the consultant further explains the purpose of the process, which is to elicit and reflect on as many ideas about the existing dilemma as possible. "All of you will have the opportunity to openly voice your thoughts about what you heard discussed," she tells them. "This process of openly talking about ideas in front of all those who are concerned has a strong impact on developing a kind of conversation that creates solutions. The hope is that these ideas will open up new possibilities as well as new options for resolving this dilemma."

At this point, the consultant engages the two groups in a conversation to "talk about the talk." In other words, she checks whether this format is acceptable to everyone, and whether they have any other ideas about the process that could be incorporated. Assurance is given that all comments and ideas presented will be taken seriously and become part of the fabric of this process. It is also pointed out to those present that every step in this process is volitional, and everyone's consent must be given.

The Scenario

The consultant meets with the three executive committee members of CalTronics, a fictitious high-tech company, who comprise the interview group: Dave, the CEO; Michael, the vice president of marketing; and Amy, the vice president of operations.

Consultant: Dave, could you give us an overview as to why we are coming together this morning?

Dave: At this time, the company has a momentous problem. Our two major chip divisions need to figure out where they are heading in the chip market, and are battling for marketing dollars. MicroCom is the oldest and most established division. For almost two decades, the PC industry has known MicroCom for the chips it produced. A few years ago, it produced a chip for the 3G market and took a bath because the 3G market wasn't there. On the other hand, BroadGen is a younger division, and its Wi-Fi chip has been on the market for just two years. We anticipate that BroadGen will become a drag on company earnings because it will require a much larger marketing budget to introduce itself and capture a niche in this fledgling Wi-Fi market. MicroCom produces our core chips for PCs as well as 3G cell phones, and we are not sure that we can afford to keep both products and both divisions, given CalTronics's push to improve its overall earnings.

Consultant: Michael, what are your thoughts on the situation?

Michael: Dave summed up the situation pretty well. However, I wonder if we are selling BroadGen short? Could it be too early in the game? The number of Wi-Fi hotspots worldwide is expected to grow at least 400% in the next couple of years because Wi-Fi is so cost effective and economical to deploy, as opposed to the much higher costs of building 3G networks. That's a lot of growth. The market opportunity is expected to jump from 16 million users today to over 80 million in four years. And that's up from 10 million users last year. People are interested in Wi-Fi because of the convenience of eliminating wires at home, and the chance to go online wherever they are logging on at an Internet café during a break, or while traveling anywhere. And that's why we are here. Wi-Fi equipment revenues went from zero to $1.6 billion in just three years—the fastest 0 to 60 acceleration in history. We shouldn't miss out. It could be that BroadGen is CalTronics's ticket.

Consultant: Amy, it looks like you have the last word. Could you share with us your views on this situation?

Amy: From my perspective of overseeing the daily operations of the two divisions, BroadGen is not likely to generate much net profit in the Wi-Fi market over the next few years, since its new products are very costly and right now have low profit margins. And, I wonder, could we be missing something about MicroCom or 3G?

The conversation proceeded along these lines for about 40 minutes. The interviewer facilitated the conversation among the interview group by drawing out multiple perspectives on this situation. At one point, a lengthy pause occurred in the conversation. The interviewer saw an opening and asked the interview group if, at this point, they had said all they wanted to say. If so, would this be the time for a shift? They all agreed.

At that point, the consultant moved to the other end of the room, and signaled to the reflecting group to start their reflections on what they just had heard. She reminded them to follow the guidelines for reflecting.

May: I wonder if we shouldn't be thinking harder about MicroCom? Could it be that 3G and the cell phone industry have more going for them than we give them credit for? We know that too many global telecoms overbuilt their 3G network capacity that had been underutilized, due to the delay in getting 3G cell phones to market. On the other hand, 3G cell phones finally are coming on the scene, and new marketing dynamics are unfolding fast. Might it be a good idea to give MicroCom more time?

Paul: I wonder, what is really at stake right here and now? Everything suddenly seems to be in motion. What does it all mean, maybe not just for MicroCom or BroadGen, but for CalTronics and everyone who works here?

Ann: What you said just triggered a thought for me. I wonder what is the relative size and spending of the cell phone market of which 3G is just the latest part?

Tom: I'm not entirely certain, but I think there are about 1.2 billion cell phone users worldwide, and that could rise to 2 billion in four years. And about one-third of them upgrade to new cell phones annually. That's a bigger market than Wi-Fi . . . a lot bigger.

Paul: And Wi-Fi is only about laptops in hot spots, like Internet cafés or airport passenger waiting areas, but 3G is about cell phones everywhere.

May: You know, it just occurred to me . . . isn't Wi-Fi only about enabling computers to do without wires what computers already do with wires? But isn't 3G about cell phones that can engage in voice transmission (like any telephone) *plus* digital cameras, access to the Web, e-mails and instant messaging, streaming videos, MP3 music, online video games, and global positioning? And who knows what other software applications we can dream up?

Lynn: I wonder if cell phones and computers might not be morphing and merging toward one another? You know, not just voice but data transmission? If 3G cell phones can stream videos, might not the next generation of cell phones stream Health Insurance Portability and Accountability Act (HIPPA) data about a patient's health condition, or the delivery status of truck deliveries—with tremendous health or productivity gains? What else might there be?

Ann: I am curious if we're not just talking about 3G and Wi-Fi, but another whole new revolution in technology and business models? And where we fit into it? And what the opportunities could be—not just for MicroCom or BroadGen, but how CalTronics can thrive in new, unrealized ways?

This interchange continued for some time. After another long, silent pause, the consultant asked the reflecting group if they were ready for a shift. Then she asked the interview group if they were ready to comment on the reflections they had just heard. The shift occurred with the consent of both teams.

Consultant: Was there anything in these reflections that you find useful?

Michael: I found a whole new vista unfold before me.

Amy: What struck me most are the new innovations that are transforming our environment and the reconfiguration of everything I thought I knew. The whole thing took on a new meaning for me.

Dave: I am most intrigued by the sudden realization that we are in the midst of an entirely new territory—an everywhere, 24/7, seamless *Internet II*—a place we've never been before— that opens up new horizons for CalTronics. I wonder where we would be heading if we hadn't had the reflecting team process? Otherwise, we might have seen only the current popularity of Wi-Fi that everyone else conventionally perceives, and put more resources into BroadGen. And we might have missed the shift to a new wireless world in which 3G and its successors—4G, 5G, Wi-Max, and other yet-to-be invented technologies—will create a new, wireless Internet II "superhighway." Its successive technologies and applications—more powerful chips and higher capacity networks—will create new opportunities for CalTronics's growth and success. Today we've created an awareness of something brand new, a new direction before anyone else in our industry. Everything is in motion, but thankfully, we saw a new gestalt emerge.

After mutual agreement, another shift occurred, in which the reflecting group began to reflect on the comments they just had heard from the interview group.

Paul: The process we have gone through today energizes me. I feel unleashed and liberated by it. I am wondering if we can extend this process to include the production team. They may have a lot of good ideas to contribute. I have a sense of the big picture in the communications market place now and how this can impact CalTronics.

Lynn: Beyond the big picture, I wonder if this process was extended to all the employees of CalTronics, how many more ideas could be generated.

Another pause occurred that indicated that it was time for another shift.

Consultant: As the time is drawing near to close this meeting, I wonder if anyone might have any other thoughts to contribute?

Michael: This has been an unusual experience, unlike any other business meeting I can remember. There are so many ideas for me to bring back to my team.

Amy: My feeling is that we have broken new ground, and I sense that now we are in a much better place to see the opportunities ahead.

Dave: When we started this process today, I had no idea what to expect. In contrast to the stress and confusion I felt this morning, I am energized by what has unfolded. I never expected that so many ideas would be generated, and open up so many possibilities. We will be in touch shortly to talk about how to broaden this process to include more of CalTronics's people.

Commentary

The reflecting conversation scenario presented above is only a brief brush stroke of the typical process. The intent was to provide an illustration of the way it operates. This brief synopsis illustrates the structure, the rules, and the operations that are involved. In usual practice, the process unfolds over a meeting of several hours, and sometimes may require several meetings.

This scenario embodies the assumption that knowledge is socially created within groups. It illustrates what occurs when a group of individuals talk and converse together about a situation in a communal setting. The reflecting conversation process takes the normal benefits of sharing thoughts together to new heights. By abiding by the rules of the reflecting conversation, thoughts and ideas are triggered and knowledge is created that could not have been elicited in any other way.

This scenario also demonstrates how the reflecting conversation process better fits the organization of the Information Era. It is egalitarian rather than hierarchical, and more fluid than static. Contributions are not made on the basis of one's fixed position in a vertical chain of command. Rather, the operation of the reflecting conversation format places everyone on a more horizontal plane. On that plane, participants move from the edge (where they listen), to the center (where they talk), and then back again. Everyone has the chance to talk. More importantly, everyone has the chance to listen and reflect—to engage in the "inner talk" that may be the whisper of one's tacit knowledge—the source of creative ideas.

The scenario also makes it evident that language creates our world. Presenting ideas tentatively in openers such as "perhaps," "it's only an idea," or "I was wondering" makes it easier for the listeners to select the "preferred" idea that fits their particular "sense making" of the situation. The objective of the reflecting conversation is to present as many different ideas—a potpourri—as possible. Rather than seek the perfect solution in their reflections, the reflecting group provides new ideas and multiple perspectives that may not have been previously available to the interviewing group.

As they continue to listen, the interviewing team finds more relevance and implications in the ideas presented by the reflecting group. Listening has the potential to exceed one's understanding with the utterance of every additional new idea. In fact, the listener tries to integrate what has just been uttered with what has been said before. It is this experience that opens up new options for the listeners that previously were unavailable and unknown. Once the mind is expanded by an idea, it cannot return to its original shape. Such listening triggers new understandings, new possibilities, and new options for consideration. In the scenario above, this came about because the interview group respectfully listened to the reflections of the reflecting team with the intent being to find possibilities in what they heard. The listeners, then, found themselves in a new position—one in which they could freely select from among the many ideas those that brought strengths rather than deficits to their particular problem. They focused on ideas that were different and yet applicable, ones that directly addressed and fit the resolution of their dilemma in novel ways.

Perhaps the most powerful explanation for the effectiveness of the reflecting conversation process is its structure. On one level, the format structures time to talk, time to listen, and—most importantly—time to reflect. On another level, the process provides space to engage in the "inner conversation" that may be the conduit to tacit knowledge or intuition.

The utterance of a participant generates a description of an idea. The description that the next reflector states is likely to be different. It is the generation of these two descriptions that creates a "double description." The "double description" is a term coined by anthropologist Gregory Bateson that describes the richness of ideas that emanate from the contrast, comparison, and synthesis of two different perspectives.[25] Each idea consists of information that is somewhat different from the previous idea that was just uttered. Such differences intrigue the tacit mind and set in motion a process of comparison and contrast of these two differences during the process of "inner talk." This explains how nascent ideas are reflexively triggered. According to Bateson, "the elementary unit of information—is a *difference which makes a difference*"[26] [emphasis in original].

CONCLUSION

Many of the roots of the reflecting conversation process are found in the work of Martin Buber, David Bohm, and Donald Schön. All three scholars valued dialogue and conversation. Buber's special contribution is in the care, respect, and trust that he thinks is imperative to be accorded to each individual as a prerequisite for full dialogue. The essence of Schön's contribution is found in the notion that reflection-in-action occurs in a "moment-to-moment" reflexive manner. Bohm's contribution, however, merits special attention. His three basic conditions for a true dialogue to occur—to be free of assumptions; to listen attentively to each other; and to freely share thoughts, thereby developing a stream of ideas that flow and build on each other—are keys to the reflecting conversation process.

Reflecting conversations provide a new venue for organizations to address the challenges that confront them in this new era. Its rules and process provide an approach that is fitting with the fast pace and fragmented knowledge of this millennium. The structure of the reflecting conversation creates a context for addressing a dilemma from diverse perspectives. In these reflections, new ideas surface and the process of additional reflections brings forth additional new and different ideas that are triggered by what has been previously expressed. When members of the group have the chance to articulate their own ideas that have been triggered by other ideas including their own inner talk, an ecology of possibilities emerges. When this process is repeated several times, the outcome of reflecting conversations becomes a wellspring of ideas that generate many options and possibilities for the resolution of the dilemma. Despite the many innovations in the power of computing, it is the human mind in conversation that is the ultimate source of innovation and creativity.

NOTES

1. John Shotter (1993) *Conversational Realities: Constructing Life through Language* (London: Sage Publications), p. 148.

2. Maurice Friedman (1996) "Martin Buber's 'Narrow Ridge' and the Human Sciences," in *Martin Buber and the Human Sciences,* edited by Maurice Friedman (Albany: State University of New York Press), pp. 3–26, especially p. 18.

3. Martin Buber (1965) "What Is Man?" in *Between Man and Man,* with an introduction by Maurice Friedman (New York: Macmillan Co.), pp. 118–205, especially p. 167.

4. Martin Buber (1958) *I and Thou,* 2nd ed. (New York: Charles Scribner's Sons), p. 11.

5. E. M. Forster ([1910] 1998) *Howards End* (New York: Penguin Putnam/Signet), p. 148.

6. Friedman (1996), op. cit., p. 17. See also Seymour Cain (1966) "Dialogue and Difference: 'I and Thou' and 'We and They'?" in Ibid. pp. 135–145, especially p. 137.

7. Buber (1965), op. cit., p. 205.

8. Scientists' Dialogue Initiative (September 9. 1999). "Bohm-Style Dialogue: From David Bohm on Dialogue." Available at: http://isis.hampshire.edu/dialogue, html, p. 1.

9. David Bohm (1990) *On Dialogue* (Cambridge, Mass.: Pegasus Communications), p. 4.

10. Ibid., p. 14.

11. Ibid., p. 22.

12. David Bohm (1985) "The Implicate Order: A New Approach to Reality," in *Unfolding Meaning: A Weekend Dialogue with David Bohm,* edited by Donald Factor (Mickleton: England Foundation House Publications), p. 40.

13. Peter F. Drucker (1999) *Management Challenges for the 21st Century* (New York: HarperBusiness), pp. 90–91; Rosabeth Moss Kanter (2001) *Evolve! Succeeding in the Digital Culture of Tomorrow* (Boston: Harvard Business School Press), pp. 192–196; and Thomas A. Stewart (2001) *The Wealth of Knowledge: Intellectual Capital and the 21st Century Organization* (New York: Currency/Doubleday), pp. 29–30.

14. Buber (1958), op. cit. While he is known primarily for writing about the I–Thou and I–It relationships, Buber also addressed dialogue in and between larger groups including communities and nations.

15. Donald A. Schön (1987) *Educating the Reflective Practitioner* (San Francisco: Jossey-Bass Publishers), p. 25.

16. Ibid., p. xi.

17. Ibid., p. xii.

18. Ibid., p. 31.

19. Ibid., p. 64.

20. Arthur Koestler (1964) *The Act of Creation* (New York: Macmillan Co.), p. 120.

21. Tom Andersen (1991) "The Context and History of the Reflecting Team," in

The Reflecting Team: Dialogues and Dialogues about the Dialogues, edited by Tom Andersen (New York: W.W. Norton), pp. 3–14, especially pp. 10–14. The concept of reflecting conversations is drawn from Tom Anderson's innovation of the Reflecting Team that first was presented in Tom Andersen (1987) "The Reflecting Team: Dialogue and Meta-Dialogue in Clinical Work," *Family Process* 26 (4), pp. 415–428.

22. Gregory Bateson (1972) *Steps to Ecology of the Mind* (New York: Ballantine Books), p. 453.

23. This is a paraphrase of Harry Goolishian's statement: "You should listen to what they really say, and not what they really mean," found in Andersen, op. cit., p. 32.

24. 3G (Third Generation) integrated, cell phone networks offer an ultrawide-band wireless capability that connects users via a worldwide network of terrestrial and satellite coverage. It was preceded by the evolution of the first (1G, analog) and second (2G, digital) generations of cellular coverage. 3G enables over a billion cell phone users to roam almost anywhere on the planet and browse the World Wide Web, play interactive games, download music, take photos, stream videos, and access other capabilities in addition to its use as a telephone. Wi-Fi has a more geographically limited capability that provides users the chance to do everything that a broadband, networked computer can do, but without wires—surf the Web, send and receive e-mails, access work files, transfer video and voice, and the like. With a range of about 300 feet, Wi-Fi is currently limited to certain "hot spot" connections in offices, homes, cafés, airport waiting lounges, and the like. Nevertheless, Wi-Fi hot spots are growing exponentially. Even newer wireless communication networks with enhanced capabilities—such as fourth generation (4G) and Wi-Max (with a range of about 30 miles)—are on the commercial horizon. See Michael V. Copeland, Om Malik, and Rafe Needleman (July 2003) "The Next Big Thing" *Business 2.0* 4 (6), pp. 62–69.

25. Gregory Bateson (1979) *Mind and Nature* (New York: E. P. Dutton), pp. 132–135.

26. Bateson, op. cit., p. 453.

CHAPTER 10

New Territory for the 21st Century: The Compass and the Map

A map *is not* the territory it represents.

—Count Alfred Korzybski[1]

It is conceivable that the image of maps and territories itself is dated, and the lowly compass may be the better image.

—Karl E. Weick[2]

What is it in the territory that gets onto the map?

—Gregory Bateson[3]

Today, in this era, CEOs who run the planet's largest corporations no longer feel like "masters of the universe." Instead, they are experiencing something new—a sense of loss of control as they try to guide their organizations through today's postmodern turbulence. When the CEO of Goldman Sachs—one of the world's top investment banks—was asked, "What has changed?" in the quarter century that he had been at the company, he replied: "What hasn't?" When asked to describe the business climate he operated in, and how it was changing, the chairman and CEO of Barnes & Noble said: "Everything is in play."[4]

This is a departure from the way in which leaders have led and have perceived their jobs and their organizations in the past. During the Modern or Industrial Era, CEOs depicted themselves as self-assured captains of vessels who confidently gave orders to a crew who worked to carry out the personal vision of their leader. Leaders then were not aware of the collaborative powers they could unleash by adopting a more egalitarian stance. Further, they never would convey a sense of "not-knowing," because leaders "knew"—that was why they were leaders. They knew the territory, and they had the map. Senior managers were "experienced"; they could "backward reference" to past experiences they had successfully navigated that validated their individual "command and control" of their crew with maximal obedience and minimal input from underlings. The map was known and the territory was familiar, for the leader had traversed it many times before.

However, in the Postmodern or Information Era, leaders have no map and are not familiar with the territory, for no one has traversed it before. However, the need remains to skillfully coordinate the limited resources and complex activities of those who lead and manage today's organizations in an environment that is more tentative and less knowable with each passing day. The need remains in this new era to guide organizations, but how should this be accomplished? Because we have no clear directions to guide us, perhaps the metaphor of the map and the territory that have been surfacing in the words of theorists and managers alike can be guideposts.

During the 20th and 21st centuries, three eminent thinkers addressed the metaphor of the map and the territory in ways that are relevant to us—linguist Count Alfred Korzybski, in the 1930s; management theorist Karl Weick, in the first years of the 21st century; and anthropologist Gregory Bateson, in the 1960s. Perhaps the work of these three thinkers can provide guidance to us in the new territory.

COUNT ALFRED KORZYBSKI: NOT THE MAP BUT THE TERRITORY

Polish Count Alfred Korzybski, founder of General Semantics Theory, was the originator of the famous phrase, "A map *is not* the territory it represents." He used this metaphor to convey two points. The first point was that a map cannot be the territory, because—as a human simplification and representation of the territory—a map cannot include every unit of information about the territory. Second, maps are useful to the extent that they have a *"similar structure* to the territory"[5] [emphasis in original]. Thus, map makers who misperceive the territory and erroneously locate cities out of their proper order on a map—for example, locating Los Angeles between New York and Chicago—misinform travelers and make it uncertain that they will ever reach their destinations. Korzybski wrote at the height of the Modern Era, at a time of printed, static maps when relatively little change occurred. Today, one wonders about the usefulness of maps when so much of the territory is changing.

Like a map, a Modern Management Tradition prevailed during the 20th century and guided executives in their practice of management. Like the familiar territory of a map, this tradition emerged from the relatively stable, continuous, predictable, and knowable environment in which business flourished during the Modern Era. Change was sufficiently linear during this period so that major industry leaders in the early 20th century—Siemens, AT&T, and GE, for example—continued to be industry leaders into the late 20th century. Thus, managers continued to manage according to such principles as rigid hierarchy, command and control, sharply delineated formal roles, and an internal focus on making the business incrementally "run better" like a machine. Maps were useful, because the territory—the reality of management—had not substantially changed in decades, and thus was knowable. However, just as a map must sufficiently approximate the territory or actual terrain so that it can lead one in the right direction, so the Modern Management Tradition sufficiently "fit" the realities with which managers dealt, and was useful as a guide until the last decades of the 20th century.

However, as the new Postmodern Era unfolded, the territory changed, and maps became increasingly inaccurate. This Information Era is characterized by new basic assumptions—instability, discontinuity, unpredictability, and unknowability—in the environment within which managers operate and the reality with which they contend. Driven by the greater complexity of globalization, as well as the higher velocity of new technology—especially communication technology—today's territory has become even more unpredictable. In addition, the threat of terrorism makes our world even less knowable.

KARL WEICK: THE COMPASS FOR DIRECTION

Management theorist Karl Weick provides a different interpretation of Korzybski's statement. As Weick writes: "It is conceivable that the image of maps and territories itself is dated, and the lowly compass may be the better image . . . [because] . . . a compass is a more reliable instrument of navigation if locations on the map are changing."[6] Weick's statement may have been more insightful than he initially imagined, for this is a time when not only locations on our maps are changing, but the very territory itself. For this reason, could maps have become obsolete?

Now, as was true for others in the past, managers all are explorers on a quest, and the compass is their guide. This was the case for seafarers in the 1400s and 1500s who sailed beyond known horizons into what was, for them, unknowable territory during the Age of Exploration. This also was true for American pioneers who went beyond the frontier's edge into unknown territory from the 1600s through the 1800s. Today, it remains true of Information Era entrepreneurs and managers of the 21st century— explorers and pioneers all—for, as is commonly said in the high-technology industry: "Where we are going, no one has been." Today, the only choice is to continue the journey in search of new territory. In the

21st century, the compass has become a more useful instrument than in the Modern Era, for its defining feature of providing direction is exactly what we need today.

The compass points to a new direction—a Postmodern Management Tradition for a Postmodern Era. There are dramatic new challenges in this new environment and new territory. It may not be sufficient for managers to merely manage differently in this new environment, according to first-order change (i.e., more of the same) whereby old maps are adapted or new maps are drawn. Rather, the degree of change that may be required is of a transformative, second-order change—whereby static maps have become obsolete in this Postmodern Era. Unlike the Modern Era, what is necessary today in the Postmodern Era is not the finished product (the map itself), but rather it is the process—the very act of creation, the unending act of sensing, updating, and developing the map—that has become vital.[7] It may be that the unfinished work of collaboratively updating the ever-changing map will become the central task for managers in this Postmodern Era.

Having studied organizations in this era of complexity and chaos, British Management theorist Ralph D. Stacey concluded: "The key to success lies in the creative activity of making new maps, not in the imitative following and refining of existing ones. . . . If managers cannot know where the organization is going or what the right business philosophy for the future is . . . they must develop their navigational principles, draw their maps as they go along."[8]

What are these navigational principles that need to be developed? These principles need to be congruent with and embody the basic management shift of this new era: "the emergence of knowledge as the economy's chief resource."[9] Perhaps it is time for managers to begin by establishing and practicing the core activities of the Postmodern Management Tradition— ones that revolve around the establishment of a process of dynamic inquiry that leads to the surfacing of the "ore" of the Information Era—not coal or iron from deep within the Earth, but the tacit knowledge that needs to be drawn from deep within the inner recesses of every individual.

Managers may find it not just helpful, but incumbent, to develop a new set of management skills, because they bring about competitive advantages, and because organizational survival mandates them. What are these skills? The core skills of the new Postmodern Management Tradition center on knowledge creation.

Managers might begin by treating the skilled employees of knowledge organizations with the care, respect, and trust they deserve. In so doing, they establish the preconditions for knowledge creation. Enacting these values and ethics as organizational practices, however, does much more. Genuinely valuing human dignity—by bringing everyone into the circle and giving them a voice to participate—pays short- and long-term divi-

dends. On a more long-term basis, care and respect deepen the relationships that anchor and connect individuals to one another in an era when
everything else is changing. Successful organizations today, such as
Hewlett-Packard (HP), constantly shift tasks and roles. More than half of
customers' orders are for products that are less than two years old. As a
veteran of 14 different jobs in 24 years with HP put it: "We have to know
each other, know how we work together, so that when a crisis comes we
don't have to spend a lot of time coordinating. . . . The cast doesn't change
nearly as quickly as the show." In addition, because employees' compen-
sation packages are fairly traditional: "HP's magic lies in the primacy of
relationships over tasks."[10] Adopting these values as organizational practices also mutually reinforces the sense of common purpose that guides
organizations in the larger sense. Because the velocity and unpredictability of the era causes so much change, all that organizations may have left
is purpose. As one shrewd observer of Information Era organizations put
it: "In place of planning, we have purposing."[11]

The question that begs an answer is: "How do we draw maps as we
move forward?" The response is: "We will do so collaboratively with others." Accurate map making always has been a group process. In a new
territory, it is difficult, if not impossible, for one individual to construct
an accurate map from a single geographical point. The simplest and most
accurate method to create a map is via the process of geographical
triangulation—where individuals send and receive information from
three or more coordinates within the territory. Otherwise, the map will
lack a "similar structure to the territory," and thus be inaccurate. Map
making literally is a group process that depends on the collective knowing
of a group of individuals who share knowledge across the "between."

In this turbulent, unknowable era, it is not just the creation of the map
that is vital, but, more specifically, the constant process of updating and
recreating it. However, in today's world, the critical information may not
be readily apparent. Once they have accepted the compass's direction,
managers may then begin to develop tentative—only tentative—sketches
of the map. When explorers traverse new territories, they often are unsure
not only of where they are, but frequently of their precise destination.

Thus, managers and organizations that are willing to blaze paths
through uncharted territories are the ones best equipped to take on the
challenge of creating new maps. Given the uncertainty of the era, sensing
and improvising could provide the clues to the alternative courses of action that could lead to viable outcomes. The challenge then becomes to
create new maps from new information. However, all new territory con-
tains an infinity of bewildering new information. From this infinity, it is
important for map makers to select only the most important and most
relevant information. It is this information that will make the most differ-

ence to them. Only information that makes a difference should be placed on the map.

GREGORY BATESON: THE DIFFERENCE WHICH MAKES A DIFFERENCE

Anthropologist Gregory Bateson asks the critical question: "What is it in the territory that gets onto the map?"[12] Bateson's response is that only information that makes a difference is placed on the map. The map is not the territory, because the map is different from the territory, and can only be a simplified representation of the territory. If the territory were uniform, nothing would be on the map except the boundaries that frame it. What is found on maps, however, are differences. Maps are composed of differences—differences in the location of mountains and plains, cities and towns, and roads and highways. The differences that are found on maps are what make them useful; they provide information about change. In the social world as well, change results from differences. According to Bateson, information is difference, and "the elementary unit of information—is a difference which makes a difference."[13] Hence, what Bateson implies is that every bit of information is a valuable commodity, for it can bring about relevant changes to be included on the map. Could such information be the key that explorers need to delineate a useful map as they traverse new territory?

Gregory Bateson lends a second dimension to the role of information when he writes: "The technical term 'information' may be succinctly defined as *any difference which makes a difference in some later event.* This definition is fundamental for all analysis of . . . systems and organizations."[14] Bateson calls our attention to the fact that the impact of change need not be linear and immediate. He further cautions us that the timing of change is unpredictable, and could occur at a later time and in a different place— a valuable insight for managers contending with an indeterminate environment.

Such a systemic approach focuses on the whole rather than the sum of the parts, and leads one to ask "what alternative possibilities could conceivably have occurred and then ask why many of the alternatives were not followed, so that the particular event was one of those few which could, in fact, occur."[15] Such an orientation leads one away from narrowly focusing on explaining events from a linear perspective in which cause and effect occur at that time and in that place. Instead, one is led to assume more of a nonlinear or recursive perspective in which an event could trigger a response not only in the here and now, but at a later time and in a different place. Such a systemic approach enables one to more broadly explore and apprehend the multiple factors that are involved in the unfolding of any system's problems, solutions, or outcomes.

In their unfolding, events are conditioned by limiting factors or "restraints." In the absence of restraints, change occurs according to random chance or "equality of probability." However, when restraints are present, outcomes occur according to "inequality of probability," or possibility. For example, in fitting the parts of a jigsaw puzzle of a map together, many differences in shape, color, and pattern present restraints in the selection of a single piece to fit a specific place in the puzzle. These bits of information or "restraints" all provide clues to select the particular piece that fits a particular space in that puzzle at that precise sequence. These clues—or information about differences—enable us to "put the pieces of the puzzle together." Similarly, it behooves map makers to check for restraints—as well as possibilities—in order to create maps that provide useful information.

In new territory, a universe of information surrounds us. The question is: "Which differences (or information) move from the territory onto the map, from our tacit knowledge to our explicit knowledge?" Our limited consciousness must select elements from this infinitude of information, or risk being overwhelmed. Perhaps, as Bateson suggests, we are surrounded not by an infinitude of facts and information, but rather by distinctions and differences. Humans perceive or tacitly subceive differences—such as differences between one face and another, one fact and another, one idea and another, or one trend and another. Of the multitude of differences, each human mind tacitly chooses a limited number that ineffably become conscious information, and thus contribute to the personal creation of that individual's map. Pragmatically, this explains how any two individuals exposed to the same information are likely to make different distinctions that produce different editings of the same situation. In other words, *they are likely to draw different maps of the same territory.*

Differences in another individual's perspectives on a situation intrigue listeners, because what they are hearing is different from their own view of this situation. These new views are then likely to trigger additional new perceptions that, once uttered, reflexively continue around the circuit. Thus, the utterance of differences multiplies the positions from which a situation is seen, and enriches the flow of conversation about it.

Differences are not just the source of information; they also are the source of change. This change is triggered by the units of information themselves, as well as by the process and type of channels by which information is accessed. Among those channels are questions, dialogues, reflections, and conversations. One intentionally uses these channels to elicit information that becomes transformed via conversation with others in new and different ways, and, in the process, becomes the information that makes a difference.

QUESTIONS FOR KNOWLEDGE CREATION

Questions are the first channel for the retrieval of information. "As inquirers and researchers, we create worlds through the questions that we ask coupled with what we and others regard as reasonable responses to our questions."[16] The microskills of communication provide us with a set of tools to elicit information. Closed or open questions evoke different types of information. Closed questions elicit minimal information because they tend to trigger yes or no responses. Although they are of value in some circumstances—such as in establishing a specific fact—closed questions generally tend to narrow the dimensions of inquiry.

Open questions cast a wider net for the retrieval of information. Open questions provide necessary and useful information. Although these linear questions are limited in the information they elicit, they tend to orient us to situations and provide us with investigative impetus—who did what to whom and why? Generally, the conceptual posture of linear questions tends to assign problems to others, and thus limit information. Consequently, such questions do not tend to open space or foster possibilities, but rather limit information because their focus is on the linear causality that explains the cause of specific situations.

Systemic questions, in contrast, are steeped in GST. The focus of systemic questions is on the ways in which parts relate to one another within a system. The three major types of systemic questions—circular questions, future oriented questions, and reflexive questions—all aim to generate information about the interactional dynamics within a system. These questions seek to bring forth the differences around a described problem that enable one to perceive a problem or one's world differently. Typically, an individual who is made to believe that he is accountable for a problem, when asked questions from a systemic perspective, gradually begins to develop an awareness of the different variables operating within that system that could account for the emergence or existence of that problem. Thus, asking systemic questions allows individuals to develop an awareness of differences in information about the relationships of the variables within that system. When systemic questions are asked, the individual's perspectives on a situation gradually begin to change, because the responses elicited by this mode of inquiry provide information about differences. In this process, an individual begins to make distinctions and differentiations via his responses to these questions. The information that surfaces is the "difference which makes a difference,"[17] and hence is likely to trigger changes in perspectives. It is such information that opens up new possibilities and solutions, not only for problems or situations, but within oneself.

It is the questions that search for these differences that are likely to bring forth change. As discussed earlier, there are two meanings of the concept of difference. First, there are differences in the ways in which we sense and see a situation. Second, there are differences that trigger change over time. Difference as change may occur spontaneously, but it is also likely to take place at a later time. It is only when relevant information (that makes a difference about the new territory) is placed on the map, that the map acquires its usefulness; and it is only when individuals become aware of and, more importantly, accept the differences of which they have been unaware, that they open themselves up to new ideas. These new ideas, in turn, stimulate differences in evolving new and different images. Questions can widen the scope and deepen the understanding of a situation or a problem by adding new information.

CONVERSATION FOR KNOWLEDGE CREATION

Reflecting conversations generate a multitude of ideas and possibilities to view a situation or a problem from multiple perspectives. The very format of this process structures time to talk, time to listen, and, most critically, time to reflect. These shifts in positions evoke new perspectives, as well as create the space for "inner talk," wherein one carries on an inner or tacit conversation about what has just been stated. Thus, there emerge new thoughts that reflect the personal and unique perspective of the individual. Each participant's contribution varies from another's. The process of each individual expressing a different description creates "double descriptions."[18] Double descriptions denote the plethora of ideas that emanate from comparing and assimilating two different and unique perspectives. Hence, the process of reflecting conversation augments and multiplies the richness of ideas generated by double descriptions. The information created by this conversational process is the information that "makes a difference."

Because knowledge is at the core of the Information Era, knowledge creation becomes the leading edge of the Postmodern Management Tradition. The process of conversation then becomes the sine qua non of this era. Business schools to date have not adequately taught the topic of conversation nor are conversational skills widely enough known and practiced by managers, yet leading knowledge management scholars have pointed out that "conversations can unleash the creative powers of individual participants and fuel knowledge creation beyond the capacities of a single mind."[19]

In this new era, what managers may need most are new ways to converse with one another across the "between." If change is the necessary goal that we are seeking to bring about in today's organizational settings, then the most accessible and requisite medium for this change is in communicating with one another. Change can only evolve through interactions, and conversations are the most likely medium to accomplish this goal. Conversation is not only the preferred avenue to originate change, but to coordinate change among the many employees of today's complex organizations. In fact, conversation is the critical, but overlooked, way that managers spontaneously coordinate their everyday mutual activities.

Mutually generative conversation describes a process by which people can come together to freely talk with, rather than to, one another. Thus, talk becomes a continuous and mutual interchange of ideas, experiences, insights, and observations. The co-developed mutuality that emerges can become the pathway to making a different sense of a situation that eventually may lead to co-generating multiple possibilities for new solutions. The primary resource of the Information Era—personal or tacit knowledge—can only be released through communication and, most particularly, through the interactive flow of conversation across the "between." This resource within each individual is what makes possible the co-creation and co-development of new realities.

The elemental vehicle for change is communication and conversation. The source for change is not the rarefied possession of experts or high executives, but rather is found deep within every individual. The source of change is to be found in philosopher Hans Lipps's expression, the "circle of the unexpressed," or in Hans-Georg Gadamer's "infinity of the unsaid."[20] The vehicle for change is conversation. Lipps and Gadamer recognized that every communication—verbal and nonverbal—embodies unexpressed meanings and unsaid knowledge that seeks expression. The most natural and effective way to release the "unexpressed" as well as the "unsaid" is through conversation. Perhaps in releasing this precious commodity, we also are freeing the forces of creativity, originality, and change whose source is the tacit knowledge that lies within each one of us.

TACIT KNOWLEDGE: THE WELLSPRING OF KNOWLEDGE CREATION

Perhaps what is unexpressed and unsaid is that deep, personal knowledge that every person possesses and knows, but cannot say—tacit knowledge. This is the core of each individual's unique knowledge. The critical new task for managers today may be to create a context in which everyone's unexpressed and unsaid tacit knowledge surfaces. This tacit knowledge represents the planet's largest reservoir of energy for the Information Era. The task is to ascertain how to facilitate its expression.

Tacit knowledge in its nascent form is delicate and fragile. It requires a safe and supportive environment in which to take form and emerge. Care, respect, and trust provide an inviting context for the "circle of the unexpressed" and the "infinity of the unsaid"[21] to be uttered. It is only within such a caring and respectful milieu that the unexpressed and unsaid can come forth. There is no limit to this resource, for tacit knowledge is boundless and limitless.

When we utter a thought, it is as if we are placing brackets around a finite portion of our tacit knowledge that cannot be complete or clear to the listener. All the remaining meanings and implications around this utterance remain latent and unsaid in our tacit mind, for we know more than we can say. These unspoken meanings and possibilities need to surface, for their meanings will bring forth additional new perspectives on what was just uttered. Knowledge is amplified and created by wondering about what remains unsaid in an utterance. In this sense, knowledge creation may best be realized by expressing one's own ideas triggered by what was just said.

Tacit knowledge anticipates or "senses" threats and opportunities in the environment. It is congruent with the challenges of the nonlinear era that confronts managers today. Accessing their tacit knowledge might help managers to anticipate what could come next.

CONCLUSION

Management today may be less about making decisions based on "facts" according to an explicit scientific process in a stable world we know and can predict. Rather, it may be much more about "sensing" or "subceiving" changes in the environment according to a tacit process in an unstable world that we cannot know and can no longer predict. Therefore, we are entering new territory in which individuals find themselves making sense on the basis of their hunches or gut feelings that are rooted in tacit knowledge. Perhaps these are the territories that need to be—but by the same token, cannot be—on the map.

Polish Count Alfred Korzybski's famous dictum, "A map *is not* the territory it represents,"[22] applies here and is relevant today. Korzybski's insight is that there are situations in which we no longer can rely on the known certainties of a map to guide us. Instead, managers need to constantly update and even create anew the maps that guide them. One wonders if managers are better served by relying on their intuitive compasses to find their directions in this new era's territory.

Goal setting for an organization may be less relevant today than it was in the past. What may be more relevant now is the capability of managers to understand the indeterminate nature of our unfolding environment. It may be incumbent on leaders to establish processes throughout their organizations for tacitly sensing direction with the understanding that, in the long run, management is a collective endeavor. In this new era, generating knowledge collaboratively provides a clearer sense of the compass's direction, as well as the information that will create the new maps for the new territory.

Today's world needs the Inquiring Organization. In this turbulent and unknowable world of ours, learning what is already known is necessary, but not sufficient. Explicit knowledge does not provide a competitive advantage, nor is explicit knowledge the "oil" of the 21st century. It is only tacit knowledge that provides a competitive advantage. It is tacit knowledge that is the "oil" of the 21st century. Those managers who know how to continuously inquire and create tacit knowledge will benefit not only their organizations, but the higher aspirations of humankind.

NOTES

1. Alfred Korzybski ([1933] 1958) *Science and Sanity: An Introduction to Non-Aristotelian Systems and General Semantics*, 4th ed. (Lakeville, Conn.: The International Non-Aristotelian Library Publishing Co.), p. 58

2. Karl E. Weick (2001) "Leadership as the Legitimation of Doubt" in *The Future of Leadership: Today's Top Leadership Thinkers Speak to Tomorrow's Leaders*, edited by Warren Bennis, Gretchen M. Spreitzer, and Thomas G. Cummings (San Francisco: Jossey-Bass), p. 94.

3. Gregory Bateson (1972) *Steps to an Ecology of the Mind* (New York: Ballantine Books), p. 451.

4. Jeffrey E. Garten (2001) *The Mind of the CEO* (New York: Basic Books), pp. 13, 28.

5. Korzybski, op. cit., p. 58.

6. Weick, op. cit., p. 94.

7. Karl Weick has sensed and studied the significance of managers' sensing in their jobs for some time. For a sample, see Karl E. Weick (1993) "The Collapse of Sensemaking in Organizations: The Mann Gulch Disaster," *Administrative Science Quarterly* 38, pp. 628–652; Karl E. Weick (June 1996) "Drop Your Tools: An Allegory for Organizational Studies," *Administrative Science Quarterly* 41 (2), pp. 301–314; Karl E. Weick (1998) *Sensemaking in Organizations* (Thousand Oaks, Calif.: Sage); Karl E. Weick and Kathleen M. Sutcliffe (2001) *Managing the Unexpected: Assuring High Performance in an Age of Complexity* (San Francisco: Jossey-Bass); and Diane L. Coutu (April 2003) "Sense and Reliability: A Conversation with Celebrated Psychologist Karl Weick," *Harvard Business Review* 81 (4), pp. 84–90.

8. Ralph D. Stacey (1992) *Managing the Unknowable: Strategic Boundaries between Order and Chaos* (San Francisco: Jossey-Bass), pp. 1, 4.

9. Peter Drucker (1999) *Management Challenges for the 21st Century* (New York: HarperBusiness), p. x.

10. Thomas A. Stewart (2001) *The Wealth of Knowledge: Intellectual Capital and the Twenty-First Century Organization* (New York: Currency/Doubleday), p. 29.

11. Ibid., p. 30.

12. Gregory Bateson (1972) *Steps to an Ecology of the Mind* (New York: Ballantine Books), p. 451.

13. Ibid., p. 453.

14. Ibid., p. 381.

15. Ibid., p. 399.

16. Frederick Steir (1991) "Introduction: Research as Self-Reflexivity, Self-Reflexivity as Social Process," in *Research and Reflexivity,* edited by Frederick Steir (London: Sage Publications), p. 1.

17. Bateson (1972), op. cit., p. 381

18. Gregory Bateson (1979) *Mind and Nature: A Necessary Unity* (New York: E.P. Dutton), pp. 132–135. For an illuminating discussion of double description, see Bradford P. Keeney (1983) *Aesthetics of Change* (New York: Guilford Press), pp. 37–40. Also see Peggy Penn (September 1982) "Circular Questioning," *Family Process* 21 (3), pp. 267–268.

19. Georg von Krogh, Kazuo Ichijo, and Ikujiro Nonaka (2000) *Enabling Knowledge Creation: How to Unlock the Mystery of Tacit Knowledge and Release the Power of Innovation* (New York: Oxford University Press), p. 126.

20. Brice R. Wachterhauser (1986) "Introduction: History and Language in Understanding," in *Hermeneutics and Modern Philosophy,* edited by Brice R. Wachterhauser (Albany: State University of New York Press), pp. 33–34.

21. Ibid., pp. 33–34.

22. Korzybski, op. cit., p. 58.

Index

About the Authors

CATHERINE KANO KIKOSKI is Professor and Chair of the Graduate Department of Marriage and Family Therapy at Saint Joseph College in West Hartford, Connecticut. A licensed psychologist and family therapist, she has almost 25 years of experience in researching, publishing, teaching, and training professionals in the field of interpersonal communication as well as organizational behavior.

JOHN F. KIKOSKI is Professor of Political Science and Public Administration at Sacred Heart University in Fairfield, Connecticut. He is a past president of the Section on Professional Organization and Development of the American Society for Public Administration.